CHRISTIAN WOMEN'S RESPONSIBILITY IN SHARING GOD'S WORD

Copyright April 2017

By Sarah Lee Brown

Table of Contents

Introduction		1-7
Chapter 1	The Responsibility to Learn and Teach Others	9-31
Chapter 2	God's Creation and Mankind's Fall	33-49
Chapter 3	God's Chosen People and Promised Seed	51-98
Chapter 4	God's People United under Judges and Kings	99-141
Chapter 5	God's People Divided	143-212
Chapter 6	The Prophecies and their Fulfilment	213-226
Chapter 7	The Miracles of Jesus	227-241
Chapter 8	Jesus' Teachings	243-284
Chapter 9	Events in the Early Church	285-307
Chapter 10	Salvation in the Letters	309-331
Chapter 11	The Church's Organization, Worship, and Work	333-353
Chapter 12	Christian Living	355-368
Chapter 13	There Will Be a Judgment	369-373
References		375-377
About the Author and Special Thanks		378

Introduction

The privilege of being a female Christian is so rewarding and exciting. Along with the privilege comes the responsibility to learn God's will for us and to share it with others. Men are often reminded of their duty to spread the gospel, but we women are not excluded from the responsibility. There are many verses in the Bible showing us the need for each generation to teach the next generation. When this plan for learning and teaching is followed, we have strong families and strong churches. What happens when this plan for learning and teaching as given by God is not followed is we have generations who do not know God. When people do not know God and do not follow His commands, then we have people who are like those in Noah's day and like Sodom and Gomorrah and like the people in the days of the kings. Looking around today at the world in which we live, it seems we may almost be at the point where we are living in the same circumstances as those who forgot God in the olden days before Christ. Christians must do something about this problem.

So what is the role of the Christian woman in this all important duty to share God's word? Before we can properly share God's word and His will for mankind, we must know it ourselves. In reading many online comments concerning how little knowledge people have about the Bible, I realized one of the reasons may be not only have the churches failed to stress the importance of understanding how all of the pieces of the Old Testament fit together and how they are connected to the New Testament, but individuals have also not seen the need to teach these important concepts to their children and families.

Is there anything we women can do today to help improve this lack of knowledge among the people? Is it too late to teach the next generations? What about the present generation? What about those who either do not know God or who have not been taught the whole truth concerning God? Is it too late for them? Can we as women of God, use our talents and knowledge from the Book to bring the lost to Christ? Can we help the saved to learn even more about God's word? Many women do a wonderful job of sharing God's word but the need is still great and I think more of us can use our talents to learn and share.

God said in Isaiah 55:11 (KJV in the public domain) "So shall my word be that goeth forth out of my mouth: it shall not return unto me void, but it shall accomplish that which I please, and it shall prosper in the thing whereto I sent it." But for God's word to accomplish the purpose for which He gave it, the word must be spread. We have examples in the Old Testament of people who forgot God for years and then someone appeared who showed them the right way again. As long as the people walked on the right path, God's blessings were with them, but when they again strayed and allowed sin to enter the camp is when God again forsook them. Can we women of today engage in a sharing of God's word so our homes, families, communities, and even this nation can be blessed?

In writing this book, I had two goals. First was the aim to provoke each reader to look at her responsibility to learn and teach others. I wanted to encourage all women of God to take a more active role in this teaching. Once the flame to spread the word was lit or rekindled, my second goal was to provide in one place a summary review of the Bible by noting accounts one must know in order to share the word with others.

In the Old Testament review, I have placed special emphasis on the accounts of mankind's fall and deliverance while noting how God gave His commands and how man either accepted and was blessed or rejected and was cursed. Many times there are great lessons in these Old Testament books to help us better understand the New Testament, but all too often, readers of the Old Testament find the books very hard to understand and they give up on reading. From these Old Testament accounts, I then wanted to make application to our own learning and teaching others. According to 1st Corinthians 10:11, what happened to the people of old was recorded for our examples and they were written for our admonition.

Finally, in the New Testament I have recounted the life and teachings of Christ and the beginning of His church, becoming a Christian, worshipping God according to His commands, and remaining faithful in anticipation of the coming judgment. With this working knowledge of God's word,

Christian women in all stages of their Christianity will be able to fulfill our responsibility in teaching others. My hope is this book will contribute to the knowledge part and each reader will nurture her own desire to share the knowledge with others.

While the acconts in this book can help one know where to start in teaching others, I wish to stress there is no substitute for reading your Bible. I realize how some passages can be difficult to understand and sometimes when a person can read the same information explained in today's language and have some commentary and thought questions included, the meaning becomes clearer. In addition, asking yourself though questions can help clarify the meaning. Many times, in the book, I have asked questions for that purpose. As you read those questions and think about the answers, it may be helpful to truly consider how you can make application to your own life today. Throughout the book, most scripture quotation was taken from the King James Version which is in the public domain, but often I provided an explanation in terms that may be better understood.

To teach the word, one has to know the word. To know the word, one has to study the word. The Old Testament is filled with accounts of events that are so helpful in explaining New Testament teachings, but in a lot of cases, people will read the Old Testament and get lost in the genealogies or the long descriptions of battles or in the often non-conformance to a timeline. So in this book, while I have tried to cover many of the Old Testament accounts, I have tried to share them in today's language in paraphrased format and in the chronological order in which they appear to have happened. Some of the information shared I have learned from so many wonderful gospel preachers who have preached where I attend service, in gospel meetings nearby, and online. Some of the information comes from my years of teaching Bible class to children and ladies. Some of the information has come from online sources for which I have provided citations. But, much of what I have included comes from reading and hearing the many false teachings in the religious world which show the lack of true Biblical knowledge and a great misunderstanding of the scriptures. It is for these erroneous teachings we must be able to provide a Biblical response.

      The contents of this book may be a review for many readers, but for others, hopefully the study will contain information you have not thought too much about in the past. In all cases, I hope as you read the book and study the Bible verses, you come to share my concern about our responsibility and our power as Christian women to learn God's word first and then to share the word with our children, families, friends, neighbors, and even strangers in an effort to not only make this world a better place for us and future generations but more importantly so we can all go to heaven. So pick up your Bible and use it as you read this book. Look up all of the passages and diligently study them. If we want the world to be converted, then we have to do our part.

Chapter 1 of this book supports the great need for Christian women to share God's word with others. Included are many verses from the Old Testament where the people were commanded to diligently teach God's word. The limitations upon women concerning their teaching is discussed and how authority must be established for all we do in religion is covered. The need to know the word before we can teach it to others is also stressed.

In support of the idea that one must know the word before she can teach it, Chapters 2-5 provide the reader with a brief summary of many Old Testament accounts beginning in Genesis with the creation and going through Malachi, the last book of the Old Testament which contains the promise of the forerunner for Christ. The seed promise is tracked from Genesis 3 throughout the Old Testament. The Israelites are followed from their beginning in Abraham to their captivity in Egypt, on to the Promised Land. The period of the judges, the kings in the united kingdom, and kings in the divided kingdom are included. Job, Esther, and the books of prophecy are included in their chronological place in the narrative to help the reader have a clearer picture of where these books fit and of what was going on with the Israelites when these prophets prophesied.

Chapter 6 covers many of the Old Testament prophecies concerning the Christ who was to come. Found in Chapter 7 is the Christ with His many miracles done to convince the people He was the One for whom they were looking. In Chapter 8, the teachings of this Christ are considered.

The establishment of Christ's church in which we have a promise of salvation and the record of Luke in the book of Acts concerning the early years of the church are the topic of Chapter 9. The theme of salvation in the church is continued in Chapter 10. Then the organization, work, and worship of the church are covered in Chapter 11.

In Chapter 12 are several topics regarding living the Christian life including individual responsibilities contrasted with congregational responsibilities. Special duties of women are included in the chapter. Then in Chapter 13, the final chapter, are references to show there will be a final judgment and our goal is to be ready for the Judgment Day and to teach others what they must do to have their names written in the Book of Life. Hopefully the information contained in this book will be of value to all women who read it as you diligently work toward the goal of eternal life.

Chapter 1
The Responsibility to Learn and to Teach Others

It was God's plan for mankind to learn of Him and teach others. God gave many direct commands in the Old Testament concerning how He wanted His people to behave and conduct their daily lives and how He wanted those commands shared with the family and even with strangers. In the Old Testament, God spoke to the fathers of the families and it was their job to lead the people. In Chapter 1 of this book are covered some of the directives from God concerning learning His will and teaching others and each reader is asked to make some application to her own life.

In Exodus 18:17-20, Moses' father-in-law, Jethro, showed much wisdom in telling Moses he needed to come up with a teaching plan so others might learn God's commands. At this point in time, Moses, who we will read more about later, was trying to hear every case of the children of Israel and it was an all day job according to Exodus 18:13. He was listening to their issues and making decisions according to the laws of God. Jethro told Moses he would wear himself out doing this and he needed to teach the laws to the people and show them what God expected and then they would be able to learn the laws and judge many of the cases being brought to Moses and Moses would be available for the greater matters.

Moses heeded his father-in-law's suggestion to teach others and share the responsibility and it was not long afterwards God called Moses to come up into the mountain and receive the law and commands to be obeyed by the people. In Exodus 24:12 it is recorded that God told Moses to come up to Him in the mount and God would give Moses on the tables of stone, a law, and commandments for Moses to teach.

In Deuteronomy Chapters 4-7, the Nation of Israel was preparing to take possession of the Land of Canaan. In these chapters the author stressed the great importance of obeying the laws of the Lord and of teaching them to the children. It is just as important today we obey the laws of the Lord and teach them to the children. Let's look at a few of the verses in detail.

Beginning in the first verse of Deuteronomy 4, Moses was telling the people to hearken to the statutes and the judgments which he was teaching them so they could live and go in and possess the land which God was giving them. Then in verse 2 God gave one of the most important rules for being led by the word of God. "Ye shall not add unto the word which I command you, neither shall ye diminish aught from it, that ye may keep the commandments of the Lord your God which I command you." Teaching others is such a great responsibility and if we teach someone error, we can expect to be held accountable. According to Matthew 5:19, when one breaks one of the least commandments and teaches others, that person will be called the least in the kingdom of heaven. James warned in James 3:1 that teachers would receive a stricter judgment than those who are not teachers. If we will use

Deuteronomy 4:2 as our basis for teaching others and we do not add to or take from God's word, we will be on the safe side.

Continuing in Deuteronomy 4, Moses reminded the people how they had been able to survive by obeying God's commands. In verse 9, Moses warned the people not to forget what they had seen and not to let them depart from their hearts but instead they were to teach them to their sons and their sons' sons. Throughout the rest of Deuteronomy Chapters 4-6, Moses warned the people not to forget the commands. In 4:10, Moses again reminded them of the need to teach their children. In 4:40, Moses told the people to keep the statutes and commandments so it would go well with them and their children after them. Then in 5:1, Moses stressed the need to learn, keep, and do the commands Moses taught them. In Deuteronomy 6:5, Moses told the people to love God with all their heart and soul and might and then in verse 7 he said for them to teach these words diligently to their children. How were they to teach them? Diligently.

What does it mean to diligently teach God's commands? Does it mean send the children to "church" once a week where they can participate in a 45 minute class? Does it mean leave it to the "Bible class teachers" to do the job? Not according to the way Moses explained it. In the rest of Deuteronomy 6, Moses explained how they were to teach the commands. In verse 7, Moses said the people needed to talk about the commands when they were sitting in their house and when they were walking by the way and when they laid down and when they got up. In verses 8-9, Moses said to bind the commands upon their hands, have them as frontlets between their eyes, and to write them upon the posts of the house and upon their gates. In verse 20, Moses told the people when their children asked them the meaning of the testimonies and statutes and judgments, they were to tell the account of being bondmen or slaves in Egypt and how God had brought them out to their own land and how God had commanded them to do all of the commands and to fear God for their own good so He would preserve them alive.

How many parents diligently teach their children as Moses described in Deuteronomy 6? Compare the time most children spend in sports, school activities, playing games, or other non-religious activities to the amount of time they spend studying God's word, and I think it will be evident in many cases, parents are not diligently (as defined by Moses) teaching their children about God. We want the world to know God and to know Christ. What better place than to start with our own children using the ways Moses described as our starting point. Why not set up a routine or schedule and follow it as strictly as some follow their favorite TV show? Why not put as much effort into learning the scriptures as some put into practicing the sport of choice? Why not become as knowledgeable in the Bible as some are concerning hunting or fishing or gaming? Making up our minds to put in the time and effort is one of the first steps in diligently learning and teaching God's word.

Years ago, I can remember how every night my mother would sit with me and we would read the Bible. In those very early years, she read to me but as soon as I could read a few words, she would stop and let me fill in the words I knew and then before long, she had me reading to her. This continued into my high school years. The grandchildren that lived near my widowed grandmother took turns spending the nights with her. She too, made sure every night before bed, we read the Bible to her. I wonder if these women got this idea of reading scripture daily from these Old Testament examples.

The Psalmist who wrote Psalm 78 reminded the people of the need to teach their children. He told the people he was going to speak to them sayings from the past which they already knew and had been told by their fathers. He said beginning in verse 4, "We will not hide them from their children, shewing to the generation to come the praises of the LORD, and his strength, and his wonderful works that he hath done. 5. For he established a testimony in Jacob, and appointed a law in Israel, which he commanded our fathers, that they should make them known to their children." The writer here reminded the people God had previously told the fathers to make known His laws to the children. The writer went on in verses 6-8 to say: "That the generation to come might know them, even the children which should be born; who should arise and declare them to their children 7. That they might set their hope in God, and not forget the works of God, but keep his commandments: 8. And might not be as their fathers, a stubborn and rebellious generation; a generation that set not their heart aright, and whose spirit was not steadfast with God." Again the writer reminded the reader of how rebellious the previous generations had been. We can look at our own generation and the current generation and say the same things about them. Why?

Every Sunday and during midweek Bible study, it is customary today for God's people to have the opportunity to assemble to hear the law of the Lord. There are many well studied teachers who share the Bible in well planned studies. The problem we face is in all too many cases, we have a lack of diligence in learning so we can teach others. Worldly affairs have taken over and many families no longer take the time to assemble with others and study the word. Not only are some failing to diligently teach their children, but they are not diligently studying the word for themselves both privately and in the assembling of the saints. Why are so many failing in this responsibility to learn and teach?

In addition to the parents teaching their children the law of God, every seven years all of Israel was to engage in hearing the commands of the Lord again. In Deuteronomy 31:9-13, Moses gave the command for this special reading. "9. And Moses wrote this law, and delivered it unto the priests the sons of Levi, which bare the Ark of the Covenant of the Lord, and unto all the elders of Israel. 10. And Moses commanded them, saying, At the end of every seven years, in the solemnity of the year of release, in the feast of tabernacles, 11. When all Israel is come to appear before the Lord thy God in the place which he shall choose, thou shalt read this law before all Israel in their hearing. 12. Gather the people together, men and women, and children, and thy stranger that is within thy gates, that they may hear, and that they may learn, and fear the Lord your God, and observe to do all the words of this law: 13. And that their children, which have not known anything, may hear, and learn to fear the Lord your God, as long as ye live in the land whither ye go over Jordan to possess it."

How many Christians read their Bible through at least once every seven years? How many Christians have never read their Bible through? I once attended services with a congregation where the weekly Bible study was simply reading the Bible through and studying each chapter. It was a very good study and one way the preacher could be sure everyone had actually read the complete Bible. During the class, the preacher brought out how even writings of the Old Testament can have a place in our lives today. He showed us how knowing the Old Testament scriptures can help us better understand the New Testament.

Sometimes a congregation will bring in a preacher from somewhere else who provides the church with a great chance to spend several evenings dwelling upon the word. Again, in so many cases, these gospel meetings are not attended even by the members of the congregation where they are held. Are we being responsible when we fail to use every opportunity we can to learn the word? In the Old Testament, we have an account of one time when the king sent out people to spread the word. In 2nd Chronicles 17 King Jehoshaphat, who walked in the ways of the Lord, took away the worship places the people had made to false gods and according to verses 7-9, he sent out his princes and the priests to teach in the cities the law of the Lord. During Jehoshaphat's reign, while the people were heeding this law of the Lord, they were prosperous. But their prosperity did not last as they soon forgot God and again went back to serving their own false gods. When we do not diligently study God's word and keep it in our minds, it is so easy to go back to serving "our own gods."

  As mentioned in the introduction, God's people of old were so guilty of this idea of following God for a while and then forgetting Him or falling away. For many years, each time they fell away, God sent someone to bring them back. One of these times when the people had fallen away is recorded in 1st Samuel 12 when the people had asked for a king. Samuel, a prophet from God and one of the last judges, spoke unto the people and told them of the evil they were doing. He shared a brief piece of their history with them. In verses 8-12 Samuel told the people how they had forgotten God and then how they had cried unto Him and promised to serve Him again if He would deliver them. God had listened and delivered them and now they were again rebelling and asking for a king rather than submitting themselves to God, the King. In verse 19, the people admitted sinning and asked Samuel to pray for them. He told them in verse 23 he would pray for them and he would teach them the good and right way. Had they so soon forgotten and needed to be taught again? As we will see later, God's people, the Israelites, continued on their path of forgetting God and finally, God chose to forget them.

In too many cases, God's people today may be like some of those people of the past as recorded in 2nd Kings 17:27 who learned about God and learned to fear the Lord, but at the same time continued in their old ways. At the point in time recorded in 2nd Kings, the children of Israel had left the Lord so many times He had allowed them to be captured. The king of Assyria had taken people from other parts of the land and placed them in Samaria. These new people did not know God and when God sent lions among them which killed some of the people, the people asked the king to send in one of the priests from Israel to teach the newcomers the "manner of the God of the land." According to 2nd Kings 17:28, the king allowed this to happen and the priest came and taught the people how they should fear the Lord. The result as recorded in verses 33 and 41 was "they feared the Lord." But did this fear lead to serving God? A careful reading of verses 33 and 41 shows while they "feared the Lord," they continued to serve their own gods, their graven images. How is this any different from people today who claim to love the Lord and claim to serve Him, but on Sunday and midweek service time, they are sleeping in, going to a school function, or working overtime by choice for extra pay? Are they not just as guilty as those foreigners the king placed in Samaria?

After God allowed His people to be taken into captivity and deported to other lands, He once more allowed them an opportunity to return to their land and to rebuild their city, Jerusalem. One of those who chose to return and take up the task of teaching the people was Ezra. Recorded in Ezra 7:10, "For Ezra had prepared his heart to seek the law of the Lord, and to do it, and to teach in Israel statutes and judgments." In verse 25 King Artaxerxes commanded Ezra to teach the law of God to those people who did not know the law of God. What does it mean that Ezra had prepared his heart to seek the law of the Lord? Do you think it might go back to that diligent preparation we looked at earlier where Moses commanded the people to diligently teach their children? How can we prepare our heart to seek the law of the Lord and to teach the word? Hopefully, reading and pondering the passages in this book is one way to do so. But there is a better way.

The best way to prepare our heart to seek the law of the Lord and to be ready to teach it, is to study the word itself diligently. Psalm 119 has the popularity of being the longest chapter in the Bible, but it is more than that. This chapter is actually divided into twenty-two stanzas with one stanza for each letter of the Hebrew alphabet. Each stanza has eight verses. In every verse, except possibly verses 122 and 132, God's word is in some way noted. Words used as synonyms for God's word in these verses include: law, testimonies, ways, precepts, statutes, commandments, judgments, word, faithfulness, and ordinances. The writer loved the law of God and prayed for understanding. He noted in verse 165 "Great peace have they which love thy law." In verse 127, he said he loved God's commandments above gold, yea, above fine gold. Do we truly love God's commands above gold? Do we have the great peace which comes from knowing and abiding in God's word?

God spoke to His people of the Old Testament first through the fathers in the Patriarchal Dispensation, and then through Moses and the prophets in the Jewish or Mosaic Dispensation, and He did so whenever He wanted them to have a message. In the Christian Dispensation, He changed His method of spreading His word. According to Isaiah, this was part of God's plan for the new dispensation. In Isaiah 2:2-3, the prophet said in the last days (those days that began when the first recorded gospel sermon was preached in Acts 2), people would say, "Come ye, and let us go up to the mountain of the Lord, to the house of the God of Jacob; and he will teach us of his ways, and we will walk in his paths: for out of Zion shall go forth the law, and the word of the Lord from

Jerusalem." The writer of Hebrews noted in Hebrews 1:1-2 while God had in the past spoken through the prophets, in the last days He had spoken to the people by His Son. After fully describing this Jesus and showing how He is now sitting on God's right hand, beginning in Chapter 2 of Hebrews, the writer warned the readers of the need to give heed to what had been heard so it would not slip away. This reminds me of what Moses told the people concerning diligently teaching God's laws to their children. Studying a subject one time is not enough. We must be diligent in our study.

In Hebrews 2:3 the writer warned the readers not to neglect this great salvation which had been spoken by Jesus and then confirmed to the people by those who had heard Jesus (His apostles) through the miracles and signs which they did. In Hebrews 5, the writer stated this same Jesus became the author of eternal salvation unto all who obey Him. Then the words of the writer beginning in verse 12 should speak to all of us who have known the word for any length of time. He said: "For when for the time ye ought to be teachers, ye have need that one teach you again which be the first principles of the oracles of God; and are become such as have need of milk, and not of strong meat. 13. For every one that useth milk is unskillful in the word of righteousness; for he is a babe. 14. But strong meat belongeth to them that are of full age, even those who by reason of use have their senses exercised to discern both good and evil." Was the writer here condemning those who are babes in Christ? No, he was only providing them with encouragement and even a command to grow. How do we grow physically? By eating physical food. How do we grow spiritually? By eating spiritual food. First the milk (easier to digest parts) and then the meat (those scriptures that take some digging in order to understand what they mean). But note the writer was not just concerned with which physical food we partake; he was stressing something the readers needed to be doing. He said they ought to be teachers. That is one of our main goals in this book: that we may all be able to teach others.

Proverbs 9:9 says if you give instruction to a wise man, he will be even wiser and if you teach a just man, he will increase in learning. In Jesus' day, there were many who desired to hear what He had to say. In Mark 4:1, when He began to teach by the seaside, a great multitude came to hear. On this particular occasion, He taught them about the sower who sowed some seeds on four types of ground. The first seed was sown but it fell by the wayside and birds got it. The second seed fell among the rocks where it started to grow immediately but then it had no dirt, so when the sun came up it died. The third seed fell among thorns and while it did grow, the thorns choked it out and it did not have any fruit. The final seed fell on good ground and it grew and it produced fruit. The ground where the final seed fell is comparable to the wise and just men noted in Proverbs 9:9. These people are the ones who will hear the word and will bring forth fruit by teaching others the same word. This is where we all should strive to be.

Jesus gave His apostles what is known as the great commission in Matthew 28:18-20 where He told them to go and teach all nations. They were then to baptize the believers and teach them to observe all things that Christ had commanded. This was Jesus' own way of spreading the gospel. You may have heard a preacher say "each one teach one." Think what would happen in this county and in the world if each true Christian taught just one other person to become a faithful child of God and that person taught another and on and on. But we can do more than teaching only one. We can teach many. Peter and the apostles did just what Jesus commanded. They went everywhere preaching Jesus. They were often in trouble for this preaching. In Acts 5:28 is one account where the high priest called them in. In this passage it seems the accusation was they had filled Jerusalem with this doctrine. Wouldn't it be wonderful for someone to accuse us of filling a city with Jesus' doctrine?

But this brings us to a fact we cannot overlook. We are women. So just what is our responsibility when it comes to spreading the word? Two verses we must always keep in mind are 1st Timothy 2:12 "But I suffer not a woman to teach, nor to usurp authority over the man, but to be in silence," and 1st Corinthians 14:34 "Let your women keep silence in the churches: for it is not permitted unto them to speak; but they are commanded to be under obedience as also saith the law." Looking at the verse in 1st Corinthians 14, as one must always do when studying the scripture, we must consider the context. Paul was discussing speaking in tongues and prophesying in the church. Keep in mind, in the early church there was a time period where there were miracles performed to establish the word and speaking in tongues and prophesying were both miraculous spiritual gifts given as confirmation that the word was from God. Paul here told the women they were not to speak out in the assembly and if they had any questions, they could ask their husbands at home. We no longer have the miraculous gifts in the church; thus, we women will not be speaking in tongues or prophesying. The verse in 1st Timothy 2 is a much clearer verse for us and it plainly says women are not to usurp authority over the men. When putting this verse together with the principle found in 1st Corinthians 14:34, it is obvious, we are not responsible for teaching in the assembly of the church nor are we even permitted to do so.

But we have plenty of other opportunities for teaching. Before looking at those opportunities, we need to realize there are three ways of establishing authority for what we do. Generally we divide these ways of establishing authority into commands, examples, and inferences. Sometimes the categories will overlap with our using two or even all three of the methods in order to understand what we are to do today in service to God.

First, we have direct commands from God, Christ, and the writers of the New Testament who were inspired by God and led by the Holy Spirit. An example of this way of establishing authority for what we do is found in Hebrews 10:27 where the writer penned: "Not forsaking the assembling of ourselves together, as the manner of some is; but exhorting one another: and so much the more, as ye see the day approaching." This is a direct command to not forsake the assembling. This is the only verse in the New Testament specifically teaching not to forsake the assembling of ourselves together, but God only needs to say it once for it to be a command.

Then we have accounts of events or examples we can follow. An example of this way of establishing authority is found in Acts 20:7 where we have the account of Paul assembling with the disciples upon the first day of the week to partake of the Lord's Supper. While assembling, Paul also preached to the people. Using this account along with the command in Hebrews to not forsake the assembling, we now have the authority to assemble on the first day of the week and in that assembly to partake of the Lord's Supper and to hear preaching or teaching.

Finally, we have what is called inference. Using the two above ways of establishing authority, command and example, along with the account of Jesus' giving the disciples bread and the fruit of the vine in Luke 22:19 and Paul's record of that sharing in 1st Corinthians 11:18-29, we can infer it is our duty to partake of the Lord's Supper in remembrance of Christ's death every first day of the week. Why do we partake every first day of the week? Go back to the verse in Acts 20:7 where the disciples met on the first day of the week to break bread. How many weeks have a first day? By using our knowledge of the Old Testament, we can establish since every week has a first day, we partake every first day. Let me explain. In the Old Testament, there was a command to "remember the sabbath day to keep it holy," found in Exodus 20:8. Nowhere in the Old Testament was the command given to remember *every* Sabbath Day but to remember the Sabbath Day. Yet, if the people even picked up sticks on any Sabbath, they were punished. So, when we know the disciples met on the first day of the week to break bread, that every week has a first day, that Christ said by partaking we remember Him, and that we are not to forsake the assembling of ourselves together, then we can infer our partaking of the Lord's Supper is to be on the first day of every week.

So how can we use these three ways of establishing authority, command, example, and inference, in helping us to discover how we can fulfil the responsibility to teach others? In the great commission of Matthew 28:18-20 which we have already noted, the apostles were told to teach, baptize, and then teach those they had baptized to observe all of the things Christ had commanded which of course, included the need to teach. So we have a command from Christ to teach. As another example, Paul told the young preacher Timothy in 2nd Timothy 2:2 he was to commit what he had heard from Paul to faithful men who would be able to teach others. Keeping in mind the previous passages we looked at concerning the woman's place in the church, we can now infer from combining the passages that we as women have a responsibility to teach but not to usurp the authority of the man.

As women, we have a specific command to teach found in Titus 2:3-5. Here Paul said, "The aged women likewise, that they be in behaviour as becometh holiness, not false accusers, not given to much wine, teachers of good things; 4. That they may teach the young women to be sober, to love their husbands, to love their children, 5. To be discreet, chaste, keepers at home, good, obedient to their own husbands, that the word of God be not blasphemed." As women, we have an example of Priscilla helping her husband teach in Acts 18:26. This husband and wife team took Apollos into their home and taught him the word of God. Finally, by looking at 2nd Timothy 1:5 where Paul said he was persuaded the faith in Timothy was the same faith as his mother and his grandmother, along with 2nd Timothy 3:15 where Paul said Timothy had known the holy scriptures from a child, we can infer his mother and grandmother were involved in teaching him about God since we know from Acts 16:1 his father was not a believer.

So from a close look at all of the above scriptures, it seems we women do have a responsibility to teach others. Our limitation is we do not encroach or infringe upon the authority of the male in the church. It is the responsibility of the males to be the deacons, elders, teachers, and preachers for the church. We find no command or example of women taking any of those leadership positions in the New Testament writings. There are actually passages showing these duties are to be performed by men, but as long as we women are not taking away the authority of the men, we too can and must teach others.

Before one can teach someone else, it is understood the one teaching must have at some point learned what she is teaching. Earlier in this chapter, we looked at many scriptures in the Old Testament that commanded the people to learn the will of God. The wise man of old, Solomon, had a lot to say about willingness to learn. In Proverbs 1:5 he said, "A wise man will hear, and will increase learning…" In Proverbs 2:3-6, he said, "Yea, if thou criest after knowledge, and liftest up thy voice for understanding; 4. If thou seekest her as silver, and searchest for her as for hid treasures; 5. Then shalt thou understand the fear of the Lord, and find the knowledge of God. 6. For the Lord giveth wisdom: out of his mouth cometh knowledge and understanding." "Get wisdom, get understanding: forget it not…" was Solomon's statement in Proverbs 4:5. On the other hand, if we refuse to accept the words of God as our instruction, not only will we not be able to teach the truth to others, but according to Proverbs 15:32, we despise our own soul.

It seems there were women in the New Testament who knew of their need to learn of God. In the New Testament in Acts 16:13-15, we can read about a group of women who had assembled on Saturday for prayer. Paul went and preached to them and one of the women, Lydia, a seller of purple and a worshipper of the God of the Old Covenant, heard his preaching. She gave heed to what she heard and according to verse 15 she was baptized and then offered Paul and his companions the use of her home while they were in the area. Wouldn't it be wonderful today if women would realize their need to learn of God's will and upon hearing one gospel sermon, would give heed and be baptized?

From the above passages we can see while books such as this one you are reading now may help us in our studies, the best way to learn of God's will for us is to study His word both from the New and Old Testaments. We have seen we have a responsibility to learn for ourselves and then to teach others, so now we must look at some of the ways we teach others. Obviously, we can teach others in children's and women's classes. We can teach others in our homes or their homes. But we can teach in ways other than the typical "Bible study" methods. We can teach others by what we say and what we do in our daily lives. Peter gave us a description of the type of person we need to be in 1st Peter 3:1-4 when he noted how by our actions we might be able to win a husband to the Lord. He said for us to be in subjection to our husbands so they might without the word be won by our manner of life. In verse 2 he explained the life we should be living as one that is chaste or virtuous or faithful and in verse 4 he went on to say we should show a meek and quiet spirit. We have already looked at the passage in 1st Timothy concerning how older women need to teach the younger women, but there is also a passage in 1st Timothy 2:9 indicating we need to adorn ourselves with shamefacedness and sobriety. By showing the world this type of woman, we are teaching others what it looks like to be a servant of God.

One of the best examples of this type of woman is found in Proverbs 31 beginning at verse 10. According to verse 1, this chapter is a prophecy of King Lemuel that his mother taught him. He said a virtuous woman was hard to find but once found by a man, she would do him good. She would be one who got up early in the morning and worked with her hands. She would use money wisely. She would help the poor. She would make sure her household was fed and clothed. Even her husband would be known by others because of her. She would be called blessed by her children and her husband would praise her. This example reminds me of the type of person the Tabitha or Dorcas of Acts 9:36 must have been. According to the account provided, she was full of good works and alms deeds which she did. When she died, according to verse 39, there was much weeping. The widows were showing the coats and garments she had made while she was alive with them. We too can be this type of woman and we too can teach others by how we live.

In applying what we have read from the passages above, we should first of all realize it is God's will for us to teach others, but we must also remember we cannot go beyond God's word when we teach others. We must be in subjection to the men and not take away their authority. We are the one God made as a helper, meet or suitable for man, according to Genesis 2:20-24. As that helper, we will go about living a life that shows others how to live according to God's will and we will use our talents and knowledge to teach God's will within our scripturally imposed bounds.

Having established the need to learn and teach others, we will now look at some of what we need to teach others including the beginning of God's creation and the fall of man. In the next chapter, we will cover some essential points that will help us as we go about teaching others the history of man and how we ended up in the sinful condition in which we seem to continue. We will look at some of the Old Testament concepts that are part of the "schoolmaster" to bring us to Christ. In order to teach others, I believe we must have a good grasp on the history from the Old Testament. There are certain people and specific accounts with which we must be familiar in order to be better able to explain the New Testament to our friends and family. Note, I refer to these Old Testament writings as accounts rather than stories simply because the meaning generally attached to "stories" may imply these accounts are fiction rather than words inspired or breathed by God.

So many times, we can use Old Testament principles in order to explain New Testament writings even though we are under a new law and no longer bound to the commands of the Old Testament. We can use our knowledge of Old Testament prophecies to help show how Christ was the fulfillment of the Old Testament. We can use our knowledge of this "schoolmaster" to help us in bringing others to Christ.

Chapter 2
God's Creation and Man's Fall

Genesis 1:1 "In the beginning God created the heaven and the earth." In my mind, this is the key verse to the whole of God's word. If one does not believe this one concept, then she will not see the need to even learn what God has said much less to obey what God has said. What we believe about this one verse of scripture will frame how we treat all scripture. If we believe God is the Creator and we accept His words from beginning to end as the authority, then we will do our best to diligently study His word and to bring our lives into agreement with what He has given us as our guide while upon this earth. How we apply the scriptures to our lives will also be a direct result of how we accept the fact God is the Creator of all.

As the Creator, God has all power. He knows everything. He is present everywhere. We have some fancy words for these three concepts. The word for having all power is omnipotent (om nip' o tent). God's omnipotence is seen in His creation of the world. This power is also seen throughout the Old Testament when God saved His people from so many destructive forces. We will be looking at some of those later. Our God is all powerful and does what He says He will do. Our job is to obey Him.

The word for all knowing is omniscient (om nish' i ent). The omniscience of God is shown in Psalm 147 verses 4-5 where the psalmist said, "He telleth the number of the stars; he calleth them all by their names. 5. Great is our Lord, and of great power: his understanding is infinite." Our God knows everything about us. There is coming a day when we will give an account for whatever we have done in this life. While we may have kept our secret sins hidden from the world, God knows. According to 2nd Corinthians 5:10, "For we must all appear before the judgment seat of Christ; that every one may receive the things done in his body, according to that he hath done, whether it be good or bad." Then in Matthew 12:35-37, we have even more evidence God knows even our words and we will be judged by them: "A good man out of the good treasure of the heart bringeth forth good things: and an evil man out of the evil treasure bringeth forth evil things. 36. But I say unto you, that every idle word that men shall speak, they shall give account thereof in the Day of Judgment. 37. For by thy words thou shalt be justified, and by thy words thou shalt be condemned." I am sure our hope is to be justified and not condemned.

  Finally, the God we serve is present everywhere. He is omnipresent (om ni pres' ent). His omnipresence means He can be everywhere at the same time. Isaiah wrote concerning God in Isaiah 66:1 "Thus saith the LORD, The heaven is my throne, and the earth is my footstool…" David said of God in Psalm 139:7-10 "Whither shall I go from thy spirit? or whither shall I flee from thy presence? 8. If I ascend up into heaven, thou art there: if I make my bed in hell, behold, thou art there. 9.

If I take the wings of the morning, and dwell in the uttermost parts of the sea; 10. Even there shall thy hand lead me, and thy right hand shall hold me." In being present everywhere, God knows all. He sees what is happening in this world. He has a plan. It is our job to do our part in His plan. To know our part, we must be willing to study and learn.

So in the beginning, this all powerful, all knowing, and ever present God created everything. In His creation on day six, He included humans in the form of Adam and Eve. According to Genesis 2:20, after creating Adam and looking for a companion for Adam among all the creatures He had created, God found none suitable for Adam. From Adam's own body, God created Eve and gave mankind a principle to follow. Genesis 2:24 "Therefore shall a man leave his father and his mother, and shall cleave unto his wife: and they shall be one flesh." God made man and woman for each other and the woman was to be the wife. What more needs to be said on the subject? This principle is one that needs to be stressed to our children very early in life. If everyone diligently taught this one scripture and gave heed to it, we would not have the confusion we now have concerning marriage.

When we get into Genesis 3, we find sin already at work. When God created man and woman, He placed them in the Garden of Eden and they were to dress and keep it (Genesis 2:15). From the description given of the garden in Genesis 2, it must have been a beautiful place. The only command we have recorded for man was he could not eat of the tree of knowledge of good and evil for in the day he ate of it, he would surely die (Genesis 2:16-17). Chapter 3 begins with: "Now the serpent was more subtle than any beast of the field which the Lord God had made. And he said unto the woman, Yea, hath God said, Ye shall not eat of every tree of the garden?" Eve fell right into the trap very much like we sometimes do today. She let the serpent convince her through the three types of lust, lust of the flesh, lust of the eyes, and pride of life (Genesis 3:6), that it would be alright to take of the tree and eat. She ate of the tree and gave to Adam who also ate of the tree. Thus we have the beginning of mankind disobeying God and it has continued throughout the ages.

When we get into the New Testament, we will find these three lusts, the lust of the eyes and of the flesh, and the pride of life, still at work even as the devil tried to tempt our Lord. When we yield to these temptations no matter through whom or what they come, we are allowing sin to control us instead of us taking control of our own lives. I often tell students in my Bible class when they allow themselves to be influenced by their friends to do evil, they are allowing the devil to work through others in causing them to sin. When they do this, they are not in control. Most of the time, my students want to feel they are in control of themselves and when they can see how by letting others influence them to do wrong, they are no longer in control, they begin to see sin in a different light.

When God came to Adam and Eve in the garden and questioned them about their behavior, they were afraid and hid themselves but the all-knowing omniscient God knew where they were. God had told Adam and Eve the day they ate of the fruit, they would die. Since Adam and Eve did not die physically on that day as evidenced by the fact they continued to live and produce offspring, then God had something other than their immediate physical death in mind. According to 1st Corinthians 15:22, "For as in Adam all die, even so in Christ shall all be made alive." So while on the very day they ate of the tree, it was assured mankind would die physically, and since according to Romans 3:23, "All have sinned and come short of the glory of God," mankind died spiritually. Some would have us believe all mankind has inherited Adam's sin, but not according to what the scriptures teach. The verse here in Romans says we have all sinned. It does not say because Adam and Eve sinned, we have inherited their sin.

In the Old Testament, there are passages clearly showing each person is responsible for his or her own sin. In Ezekiel 18, the word of the Lord was reported by Ezekiel. He said in verse 20 the soul that sins will die. The son shall not bear the iniquity of the father nor the father the son. He continued by saying the righteousness of the righteous would be upon the righteous and the wickedness of the wicked upon the wicked. There is hope given in verse 21 for the wicked because he can turn from his sins and do right and live but in verse 24, there is condemnation to the righteous who turns away from his righteousness and does evil. He shall die in his sins.

From this one chapter in the Old Testament, we can see under the old law, people were responsible for their own sins and not for the sins of others. In the New Testament, that same principle is carried forth. In Romans 2:6-9, Paul made it very clear we are responsible for our own sins. In verse 6 he said, "Who (God) will render to every man according to his deeds." In 2nd Corinthians 5:10-11 Paul said we would all appear before the judgement seat of Christ, and our reward or punishment will be based upon what we have done.

So Adam and Eve sinned shortly after they were placed in the garden. Their sinning could have been the end of it for mankind, but God in His infinite wisdom had already made a plan for what He would do when man sinned. We know His plan was already made because in 1st Peter 1:18-23 we can read how before the foundation of the world, Jesus was foreordained to be our redeemer. In Ephesians 1:5, Paul told the Ephesian Christians they had been chosen to be blessed before the foundation of the world and the blessings were to be in Christ. God began to reveal His plan to Adam and Eve in Genesis 3:15 when He mentioned the discord which would come about between the seed of the serpent and the seed of the woman. The seed of woman, we will later discover, is the Christ.

God removed Adam and Eve from the garden. But He also placed some other burdens upon them. In addition to telling the woman her sorrows would be multiplied in conception and her husband would rule over her, He told Adam because he had listened to Eve and eaten of the tree, thus breaking God's command, the ground would be cursed for his sake. The ground would bring forth thistles and Adam would eat his bread by the sweat of his face. Have you ever thought about how man went from living in a garden where everything was beautiful and there was no sorrow to living with thorns and weeds and having to work constantly just to get by all because of one sin? If you are a gardener, when removing those worrisome weeds, do you ever think about why we have them?

After their removal from the garden, sin continued. Adam and Eve had two sons as recorded in Genesis 4. Cain and Abel both brought an offering to God. Cain brought of the fruit of the ground and Abel brought of the firstlings of his flock. God had respect to Abel's offering but not to Cain's. Cain got mad at his brother because God respected Abel's offering and not Cain's and the next thing you know, we have the first murder. We do not know how the brothers knew what to offer, but we know they knew because in Hebrews 11:4 it is written, "By faith Abel offered unto God a more excellent sacrifice than Cain, by which he obtained witness that he was righteous, God testifying of his gifts: and by it he being dead yet speaketh." In Romans 10:17, we have been told faith comes by hearing the word of God. So if Abel offered by faith, he knew what God wanted. Why Cain chose to offer what God did not want, we do not know. The same happens today when we offer worship God does not want or has not authorized. This principle of giving God what He wants in worship is so important and needs to be diligently shared with our children so when they are out on their own and choosing how to worship God, they will make sure their worship is by faith meaning it has been authorized by God's word and not according to feelings or human desires.

    We are not given much history concerning the next few generations other than the names of some Bible characters most children learn about in their classes. Something very interesting about the genealogy of Cain and Seth is both sons had several children by the same or very similar names. We are told in Genesis 4 Cain went to the land of Nod where he and his wife had a son Enoch who had a son Irad, who had a son Mehujael, who had a son Methushael, who had a son Lamech. Seth, the younger son of Adam and Eve had a son Enos, who had a son Cainan, who had a son Mahalaleel, who had a son Jared, who had a son Enoch, who had a son Methuselah, who had a son Lamech, who had a son Noah. It is easy to confuse the two genealogies if you do not read them carefully.

    Since it was only Noah and his family saved in the flood, we can see the blood line of Cain perished from the earth as did the blood line of any other sons Adam may have had except for Seth. It was through Seth's progeny when the world was so sinful, God found a man, Noah, He could call righteous and gave him the task of building the ark.

In the account of Noah, which begins in Genesis 6, we read how God was rather unhappy with the ways of man. In verse 6, the writer said "And it repented the Lord that he had made man on the earth, and it grieved him at his heart." According to verse 7, God said He would destroy man and beast and the creeping things, and the fowls of the air, but in verse 8 we see Noah found grace in the eyes of the Lord.

God told Noah what He was going to do and He told Noah to build an ark. God was very specific in the design of the ark. He told Noah to use gopher wood. He specified the dimensions the ark was to have. He said to put a window and door in the ark. Once the ark was completed Noah was to take of every clean beast seven pairs and of every unclean beast two pairs and place them in the ark to keep the seed alive after the flood. In Genesis 7:5, the writer said Noah did according unto all the Lord commanded him. We do not find any indication Noah added to God's instructions or diminished ought from those instructions.

Many times this example of following God's commands is useful as we teach others about New Testament principles. When people want to add elements such as mechanical instruments to the worship, it is good to refer back to the account of Noah and the ark. God told Noah what to use in building the ark. We have no record of Him telling Noah not to use locust or walnut or some other kind of wood in the ark, but we have a record of God saying to use gopher wood. When questioning about the use of mechanical instruments of music in praise to God, some will say, "Nowhere did God say not to use mechanical instruments." Using this account of Noah and the ark, we can infer it is not necessary for God to specify everything He does not want. It is sufficient for Him to tell us what He wants. In all New Testament scripture concerning musical praise, the only authority we have is to sing and make melody in our hearts. We will look at those scriptures authorizing us to sing in a later chapter.

One of the sad parts of this account of Noah and the ark is the fact only eight souls were saved in this ark. Of all the people in the world at the time of the flood, can you imagine only eight being saved? Many people have provided estimates concerning the population at the time of the flood. Those estimates run from ten million (Creation Concepts) to several billion (Pelletier, 2014), but even if the population was only one million, to think there were only eight people saved is very discouraging to me and very sad. What had happened in less than 1500 years from Adam to Noah? Why were the people not serving God? The same thing happens today in one generation when the parents do not teach their children God's word.

After Noah and the others went into the ark and the animals were inside, according to Genesis 7:16, the Lord shut them in. Then God sent the rains. There is nothing in Genesis to indicate there had been rain before the flood and the fact God set the rainbow in the sky after the flood is another possible indication it had not rained previously. But rain it did. It rained for forty days and nights and the water remained on the land for 150 days. We can only imagine what the people who were left on the outside of the ark were thinking as they saw what was happening, but God had shut the door and it was too late.

God destroyed everything upon the face of the earth, both man and beast. According to Genesis 7:23, only Noah and his family were left alive. It depends upon how one calculates the number of days spent on the ark, but after about one year, Noah and his family were able to leave the ark. Upon their leaving, God blessed Noah and his sons and told them to go and replenish the earth. At this point in time is when God first gave man animals for food. Previous to this, according to Genesis 1:24-31, God had given man plants to eat, but with the end of the flood, until the Mosaic Law went into effect for the Jews, man was free to eat any of the animals desired (Genesis 9:3). It is important to realize God gave man the right to eat of animal flesh for there are some who deny this right. We have to teach them the truth on this matter.

We have another lesson in Noah. How quickly a righteous person can fall. We see Noah, a preacher of righteousness in Genesis 9:21, drunk. There is nothing in the account concerning any punishment for Noah, but due to his drunkenness, Canaan, the son of Noah's son Ham, was cursed by Noah. Again, we can look back to how the sin of Adam and Eve affected many others (all mankind) and compare to how Noah's sin affected others too. There is no indication Noah's children inherited his sin, but there is an indication the grandchild was cursed because of his father's sin.

The same principle applies today. We have those who get drunk and cause an accident. Maybe the drunk is not even hurt in the accident, but others have to pay the cost through loss of limb or even loss of life. While the guilty party may go free in this life, the all-knowing God will settle the score for unrepentant persons in the judgment. We must teach this principle concerning how one's sins can affect so many others to our children and to the world. What if everyone considered others before acting in a certain way? Would we not have a much better world?

Remember God gave a specific command to Noah. He told Noah and his sons to go and replenish the earth, but we see in Genesis 11 instead of going to replenish the whole earth, the people settled in Shinar. They decided to build a tower to heaven to make themselves a name so they were not scattered upon the face of the whole earth (Genesis 11:1-4). God was not pleased with what the people had decided to do and it was in direct opposition to what He had commanded them to do. So we see in Genesis 11:6-9 how God scattered the people upon the face of the earth and confounded their speech so they would not understand each other. Thus we have the beginning of many languages. The place where God confounded the language was named Babel and today we teach our children about the Tower of Babel. In addition to teaching our children about this tower and how God mixed up the languages, we should make sure they understand why this happened. They need to know God chose to scatter the people because the people had chosen not to obey God's command to scatter themselves upon the face of the earth.

We are not given any history in the Old Testament after Babel, other than the record of births in Genesis 11, until we come to Abraham, but many Bible scholars believe the book of Job falls between the flood and Abraham because of several factors. Lyons (2008) quoting from Jackson noted the book was probably written after the flood because of the reference by Eliphaz in Job 22:16 to those who were cut down before their time, whose foundations were swept away by a flood. Lyons' reasoning for the book to have been written before Moses included the lack of mentioning of any of the elements associated with the Levitical priesthood; instead of family inheritance being passed only to the sons, Job's daughters were included; and the length of Job's life was more in line with those who lived long before Moses. Because of this compelling evidence indicating the book of Job was most likely after the flood and before Abraham, here is a good place to look at the account of Job.

Job's home was in Uz where he had a reputation of being a most righteous man. He was a very rich man who had a great faith in God. He even offered burnt offerings for his children just in case his sons had sinned and cursed God in their hearts. According to Job 1:6-12 God and Satan had a conversation about Job. Satan had been going to and fro in the earth and God asked him if he had considered Job of whom there was none like him in the earth. According to God, Job was a perfect and upright man who feared God and shunned evil. Satan told God it was because God had made a hedge around him and his house, but if God would harm Job's possessions, Job would curse Him to His face. God told Satan Job was in Satan's hands and he could do whatever he wanted to, but not to harm Job.

Satan went away from God's presence and then the trouble began for Job. He lost his animals, his servants, and his children all in what appeared to be a matter of a few hours. Job tore his clothes, shaved his head, and fell down in worship to God. What he said in verse 21 is amazing: "…the Lord gave, and the Lord hath taken away; blessed be the name of the Lord." Oh, if we could only be like Job when misfortune falls instead of wringing our hands and asking God "Why me?" According to verse 22, Job did not sin nor charge God foolishly. Having failed in his first attempt to turn Job against God, Satan tried again on another day. According to Chapter 2 of Job, Satan told God if He would touch Job's bone and flesh, he would curse God, again indicating the only reason Job trusted in God was because of God's protection. God told Satan to go ahead and hurt his flesh but to save his life. Satan smote Job with boils from head to toe. Job hurt so bad he scraped himself and sat among the ashes. Even his wife suggested he curse God and die. According to verse 10, Job told his wife she spoke as one of the foolish women. He said, "… shall we receive good at the hand of God, and shall we not receive evil?"

Job had three friends, Eliphaz, Bildad, and Zophar who set a date to come together to mourn with Job and to comfort him. They sat with him seven days and nights and no one spoke a word because of Job's grief. As Chapter 3 of Job opens, Job began to speak. He cursed his day. He wished for death. He wondered why he had not died in birth. From Job 4-31, Job's three friends and Job continued a discussion in which the friends tried to show Job he had sinned and his sin was why all of the troubles had befallen him with Job responding he had not sinned, but he wanted an opportunity to bring his complaint before God instead of listening to the three friends who were telling him he needed to repent.

After the three friends finished reprimanding Job, a fourth man, Elihu was introduced into the text. It seems from Job 33:1-7, Elihu was a prophet. He rebuked the older men for having not answered the issues Job raised and he rebuked Job for his claim of innocence. Elihu contended God had the right to discipline and God does not act unjustly. Elihu stressed God's power. Then beginning in Chapter 38 and going through the end of the book, God spoke to all of the men. He told them it was by His power the universe was created and He had set the limits and provided for His creation. God gave the men plenty of reasons for mankind to fear and respect Him even if God did not bless mankind.

God then told Eliphaz His wrath was against him and his two friends because they had not spoken of Him what was right as had Job. Most of their conversation was centered on what God does to those who do not obey Him and they insisted Job was getting a deserved reward for his sins. God told them to offer up for themselves burnt offerings and Job, God's servant, would pray for them. God then blessed Job with more in the end than he had in the beginning.

While the account of Job is one to definitely help us to understand just because we suffer does not mean we are being punished for our sins and no matter what happens, we should still praise God, it should also help us to better understand the God we serve. We can see how our God is all powerful, all knowing, and ever present. The Lord gives and the Lord takes away, but blessed is the name of our Lord.

We will not find Job in any of the genealogies recorded in the Bible. The genealogy recorded in Genesis 11 goes like this: Noah, Shem, Arphaxad, Salah, Eber, Peleg, Reu, Serug,

Nahor, Terah, and Abram. Historians (Hodge, 2010) tell us there was a period of about 200 years between the tower and Abram's birth. The birth of Abram is one of the major events from the Old Testament that has great importance for understanding the New Testament because the birth of Abram marks the beginning of God's chosen people of the Old Testament period. In the next chapter, we will see how God's chosen people became a nation and we will continue the theme of how mankind remained on the path to destruction by their frequent falling from God's grace.

Chapter 3
God's Chosen People and Promised Seed

In Chapter 2, we looked briefly at the genealogy taking us to Abram in Genesis 11. In Genesis 12, is the account of God telling Abram (before his name was changed by God to Abraham) to leave his country and his kin people and go to a land God would show him. God promised him in verse 2 to make of him a great nation, and in verse 3 God told Abram in him all families of the earth would be blessed. Abram did what God told him to do. He left his country taking with him his wife and his nephew, Lot, whose father had died. He took everything he owned and went to the land of Canaan. According to Genesis 12:7, God appeared to Abram and told him He would give the land of Canaan to Abram's seed. At this point, Abram and Sarai (God later changed her name to Sarah) had no children.

Abram continued on his journey and ended up in Egypt where he asked Sarai to say she was his sister, so the men of the place would not kill Abram in order to have Sarai as she was a very fair woman to look upon. She agreed to say she was Abram's sister. Sure enough, the men of Egypt saw her and recommended her to Pharaoh. She was taken into his house and Abram was treated well for her sake. God plagued Pharaoh because of Sarai and Pharaoh realized there was a problem. Pharaoh called Abram in and reprimanded him and sent him away with Sarai as recorded in Genesis 12.

Abram took Sarai and Lot and the flocks and herds and went back to Bethel where he had previously made an altar to the Lord. Strife was reported in Genesis 13, between the herdsmen of Abram and Lot because the land was not able to provide for all of them. Abram let Lot choose which way he and his men would travel and Lot chose all the plain of Jordan and pitched his tent toward Sodom where there were very wicked people living. After Lot left, God again promised Abram all the land he could see would be given to him and to his seed. God also promised to make Abram's seed as the dust of the earth as far as number was concerned. This makes three promises made to Abram. Earlier God had told him all nations would be blessed through his seed and He would give his seed all the land in view. Now He has promised to multiply his children.

Things did not go so well for Lot as revealed in Genesis Chapter 14. After a while, the kings of Sodom and Gomorrah and three other kings fought with four kings. The four kings prevailed and took away all the goods of Sodom and Gomorrah including Lot and his possessions. Someone escaped and told Abram and he went after the kings. Abram and his men overtook the four kings freeing Lot and recovering all of the possessions. The king of Sodom wanted Abram to keep the goods, but he refused. In addition, a special king, Melchizedek, King of Salem and priest of God, blessed Abram and Abram in turn gave Melchizedek tithes of all he had taken.

Keep in mind God had promised Abram to make him a great nation but up to this point, Abram had no children. Abram told God his servant would be his heir in Genesis 15, but God said he would not be the heir. So in Genesis 16, Sarai decided to take matters into her own hands and she told Abram to have a child by her maid, Hagar. Abram agreed and once Hagar became pregnant, Sarai was mad. She was mean to Hagar and Hagar fled, but the angel of the Lord sent her back to Sarai (Genesis 16:9). The angel told Hagar her seed would be multiplied exceedingly and this son would be a wild man with his hand against every man and every man's hand against him. Abram was 86 years old when Hagar had this son, Ishmael.

Have you ever prayed diligently for something and it did not happen so you decided to take matters into your own hands and make it happen? Chances are, once you got what you thought you wanted, you realized God knew best and you should have left it up to Him to decide what needed to be done. This was what happened to Sarai when she decided it was her responsibility to do God's job.

God did not need Sarai's help in the matter of finding an heir for Abraham. Ishmael was not to be the seed promised to Abraham. In a few years, when Abram was 99 years old, God again appeared to him and promised to multiply him exceedingly. It was on this occasion God changed Abram's name to Abraham and Sarai's name to Sarah. In Genesis 17, God's promise to Abraham to give his seed all the land of

Canaan and to make Abraham a father of many nations was repeated. Here is where God first established the covenant of circumcision. When Ishmael was 13 years old, he was circumcised along with Abraham and all the men of Abraham's house.

Think back to when Abram had told Lot to choose the land he wanted and Abram would take the other land. At that time in Genesis 13:10, Lot looked over the land and decided the plain of Jordan was well watered and was the land he wanted. Sometimes we find ourselves looking up and deciding we want the best in life without considering what may lie behind that desire. You see, the people of Sodom and Gomorrah, where Lot had chosen to live, were so very evil. By putting himself and his family into this situation where evil abounded, Lot was in a sense separating himself from God.

When we choose a job where we know evil abounds, or when we choose friends we know are engaged in evil activities, or when we choose to live in an area where sin is always present in the streets, might we be making the same mistake as Lot made? When we choose to let the TV or Internet broadcast evil programs into our homes or choose to put any number of activities before serving God, are we not separating ourselves from God and putting our children in jeopardy? How can we diligently teach our children the truth with so much evil going on around them? We must teach the children that there is a better way to live.

The evil of Sodom and Gomorrah was so great God decided He would destroy their cities, but He chose to let Abraham know of the plan before He did it. First, in Genesis Chapter 18, the Lord and two other men appeared to Abraham and Sarah and told them they were going to have a son. Sarah laughed because she was so old and did not think it was possible for her to now have a son. When the Lord asked why she laughed, she said she had not, but the Lord told her she had laughed. Two of the men left to go on and take care of the Lord's business in Sodom, but the Lord stayed back to talk with Abraham.

The Lord told Abraham of the plan to destroy Sodom. Abraham began pleading with God to save the city. He started out by asking if there were fifty righteous in the city would God spare it. God agreed, so Abraham went down to forty-five, then forty, then thirty, then twenty, and finally to ten. Each time God agreed if there could be that number of righteous in the city, He would not destroy it. With Lot living in the city one would think if he had done his job in teaching at least his own children and household about God, there should be ten righteous in the city, but that was not the case.

In Genesis 19, two angels came to Sodom and Lot met them. He finally persuaded them to spend the night in his house, but the evil men of Sodom, both young and old, came to Lot's house and demanded he send the men out so they could know them sexually. Lot offered instead his two daughters, but the men insisted on having the male guests sent out. The angels smote the evil men with blindness so they could not find the door of the house. Then the angels told Lot and his family to get out of the place because they were going to destroy it. Lot tried to get his sons-in-law to leave the city, but they just made fun of him. Lot was only able to take his wife and two daughters. What a sad commentary on the family of Lot.

So now there have been two occasions where God was unhappy with the sins of man and chose to destroy them. On the first occasion, only Noah and seven family members escaped out of the whole population of the earth. This time, only Lot and his two daughters escaped since his wife looked back in direct opposition to God's command, and turned to a pillar of salt (Genesis 19:26). The estimated population of Sodom at the time of destruction was between 600 and 1200 people (Wood, 2008). Once Lot and his daughters got out of Sodom, wine again entered the picture. In this case, the daughters made Lot drunk with wine and both daughters became pregnant by their father.

It seems from the accounts of Noah and Lot and from Adam and Eve's first disobedience, mankind has had a hard time obeying God and has often fallen. Thankfully, God's grace has continued to allow mankind time to repent and try again. How long will God allow this to go on? We do not know, but now is the time to teach these accounts to others and help them to realize we have a God to whom we must all answer.

As the Old Testament history continued, Sarah was with child in Genesis Chapter 21. This son, Isaac, was the promised son. In a test of Abraham's faith, God told him to offer this son Isaac as a sacrifice on an altar. Historians are not in agreement as to the age Isaac had reached when God told Abraham to offer him. Miller (2003) referred to several references indicating he was most likely in his 20s or 30s. He was old enough and strong enough to carry the wood for the offering. Abraham's faith was evident in the account provided in Genesis 22 for when Isaac asked him where was the lamb, Abraham said God would provide it. God did provide the offering but only after Abraham had bound Isaac on the altar. God again repeated His promises to Abraham in Genesis 22:17-18 where the author recorded, "That in blessing I will bless thee, and in multiplying I will multiply thy seed as the stars of the heaven, and as the sand which is upon the sea shore; and thy seed shall possess the gate of his enemies; 18. And in thy seed shall all the nations of the earth be blessed; because thou hast obeyed my voice." Before Abraham died, according to Genesis 25:5, he gave all he had to Isaac.

When it was time for Isaac to marry, Abraham had his own servant go back to Abraham's country and find a wife for Isaac. This trip is recorded in Genesis 24. The servant was quickly successful and found Rebekah for Isaac. The servant brought Rebekah back for Isaac and they had twin sons Jacob and Esau. Esau was a very hairy man and Jacob was smooth skinned. As Esau was the first to be born, he was considered the older of the two and would be entitled to the greater inheritance. One day as recorded in Genesis 25, Jacob cooked pottage which we would probably know as some type of stew and when Esau came in very hungry, he agreed to sell this birthright to Jacob for some food. Either Esau was very, very hungry or he put no value in his birthright.

As happens in all too many families, Dad and Mom had favorites. Jacob was his mother's pick and Esau was Isaac's. When Isaac was old, he prepared to bless his son. He called Esau to him and told him to go to the field and get venison and prepare it for Isaac. In Genesis 27, it is recorded Rebekah heard the conversation and since she wanted Jacob to have the blessing of the father, she called Jacob to her and told him to go out and get two kids of the goats and she would cook them for Isaac. Jacob was afraid his dad would discover him because he was not hairy like Esau, but Rebekah took care of the problem by putting animal skins on Jacob's hands and his neck and having him wear Esau's clothes. The trick worked and Jacob ended up getting his father's blessing. So now he had the blessing and the birthright which should have belonged to Esau. Esau was very mad at Jacob and made up his mind when Isaac died, he would kill Jacob (Genesis 27:41).

Rebekah found out about Esau's plan so she talked to Isaac and he sent Jacob to Rebekah's hometown (Genesis 28:5) where he got a little pay back for his tricks. As Jacob was traveling toward Haran, he spent the night in a certain place where God sent him a dream. In the dream, God said, "I am the Lord God of Abraham thy father, and the God of Isaac: the land whereon thou liest, to thee will I give it, and to thy seed; and thy seed shall be as the dust of the earth…and in thy seed shall all the families of the earth be blessed," (Genesis 28:13-14). Here God renewed to Jacob the promises He had previously made to Abraham and Isaac. He had promised them land, a great nation or seed as the dust of the ground, and a blessing through their seed for all the earth to be blessed. Of course, since Jacob was the son of Isaac and Isaac was the son of Abraham, any future progeny of Jacob would be of the seed of Abraham.

Jacob arrived at his destination and there at a well he met Rachel the daughter of his uncle. He fell in love with her and agreed to work for her father for seven years so he could have her as a wife. After the seven years of work, instead of giving Rachel to Jacob, Laban gave him her sister, Leah, for he said it was not after their custom for the younger sister to marry before the older one. Jacob agreed to work another seven years so he could marry Rachel and after being married to Leah for a week, he also married Rachel (Genesis 29:28).

It turned out Rachel was barren but Leah became pregnant. Rachel gave her maid to Jacob so she too could claim children by him. When Leah stopped having children, she gave her maid to Jacob so she could have more children by him. Finally, God opened Rachel's womb and she bore Jacob two sons, Joseph and Benjamin. She died while giving birth to Benjamin. Genesis 29-30 provides the account of the births of Jacob's children by his wives and their maids.

Jacob agreed to work for Laban another seven years in order to build up his own flocks and in everything he did, he seemed to prosper. In Genesis 31:3, God told Jacob to go back to his father's land and God would be with him. Jacob took all he had and headed back to his homeland. While living with Laban, Jacob whose name was later changed to Israel, fathered eleven of his twelve sons. The descendants of Israel became known as the nation of Israel or the Jews. The eleven sons born while Jacob was with Laban were Rueben, Simeon, Levi, Judah, Dan, Naphtali, Gad, Asher, Issachar, Zebulun, and Joseph. The twelfth son, Benjamin, was born on the way back home.

To begin the journey home, Jacob had to sneak out with his family because Laban did not want him to leave. When Laban found out they were gone, he went after Jacob, but after God warned Laban to leave Jacob alone in Genesis 31, they parted in peace. In leaving home, Rachel stole her father's gods and took them with her. She sat upon the chest where she had hidden them and when Laban looked for them and did not find them, he left. But Jacob had someone else to be concerned about. Esau who had planned to kill him several years earlier was still in the homeland.

Jacob sent messengers to tell Esau he was coming home and asked to find grace in Esau's sight. Jacob made a gift of animals for Esau and sent them on ahead. When Esau and Jacob met, they kissed and wept. Would it not be wonderful if families today, both physical and spiritual familes, would resolve anger issues with a kiss and crying instead of speaking evil of each other or going for a gun or knife? Esau told Jacob he did not need the gift but Jacob insisted he take the animals. Esau went back home and Jacob continued traveling. This account of the travels of Jacob and the meeting between him and Esau are found in Genesis 32-33. In Genesis 35, God appeared to Jacob again and told him to go on to Bethel and dwell there.

Before Jacob and his family continued their journey to the homeland, in Genesis 34, Jacob told his family to put away the strange gods that were among them. The family gave Jacob all of their strange gods and their earrings and Jacob hid them along the way. It was during this part of the journey that Rachel died while giving birth to Benjamin. It is interesting she was the one who earlier, when they left Laban, had stolen his gods and hid them and now just before her death, Jacob took all the strange gods and hid them. Why did this family even have strange gods? Did Abraham not teach Isaac and Isaac not teach Jacob and Jacob not teach his family? The same can happen to us today when we allow the gods of this world to overcome our lives and the lives of our children and we fail to teach them the truth.

Isaac died after Jacob returned to the homeland and Jacob and Esau buried him as recorded in Genesis Chapter 35. Before Isaac's death, God changed Jacob's name to Israel in Genesis 35:9-10. Because Jacob and Esau both had so many animals, the land was not able to bear all of them so Esau and his family moved on to Seir. Jacob remained in the land of Canaan (Genesis 36). Of his twelve sons, his favorite was Joseph and he made it very clear by the way he treated him. He made him a coat of many colors. The brothers were very jealous to the point they could not even speak peaceably to Joseph. Jealousy is seen in today's families too. How can we use accounts such as this one about Joseph and his brothers to help remedy the situation?

Joseph was called a dreamer because of the dreams he had which were given to him by God. In one dream he had, he and the brothers were binding sheaves in the field and his brother's sheaves made obeisance to his sheaf. In another dream, the sun, moon, and eleven stars made obeisance to him. Telling these dreams to his family did not help matters (Genesis 37:5-11).

On a certain occasion as recorded in Genesis 37, Israel sent Joseph to check on the brothers who were feeding the flock in Shechem. When the brothers realized Joseph was coming, they planned to kill him. Instead they sold him to some

Midianites who were headed to Egypt. They dipped his coat in the blood of a goat and took it to Israel and asked if it was Joseph's coat. The brothers told Israel they had found the coat. Israel said it was Joseph's coat and an evil beast had devoured Joseph. Israel was so sad and refused to be comforted. In the meantime, the Midianites sold Joseph in Egypt to Potiphar, an officer of Pharaoh who was the captain of the guard.

Potiphar, according to Genesis 39, saw God was with Joseph and all he did prospered, so he made him the overseer of his house. He left everything in Joseph's control. After a while, Potiphar's wife decided she wanted Joseph to engage in sexual activity with her. She tried several times to get him to do so, but Joseph was a good man and he refused. On one particular day, when Joseph again refused, Potiphar's wife caught Joseph by his garment and as he fled from her, he left the garment in her hand. She called the men of the house and accused Joseph falsely of trying to lay with her. Of course, Potiphar had Joseph put into prison, but the keeper of the prison also saw what Joseph did prospered, and he put him in charge.

While Joseph was in prison, Pharaoh became angry with two of his officers, the chief of the butlers and the chief of the bakers. According to Genesis 40, he put them both in prison. Both of them dreamed and Joseph told them that interpretations belonged to God and then he told them both what their dreams meant. He told them the chief butler in three days would have his job back but the chief baker would be hanged in three days. He asked the butler to remember him to Pharaoh when he returned to his position. Both dreams came to pass as interpreted but the butler forgot about Joseph until Genesis Chapter 41 when Pharaoh himself dreamed a dream and no one could interpret it. The butler remembered Joseph and told Pharaoh about him. Pharaoh had Joseph called and told him the dreams. Joseph explained the meaning of the dreams. He said there would be seven good years of harvest in the land and then a severe famine of seven years. Joseph said Pharaoh needed to find a wise man to set over the land of Egypt to take up a fifth of the goods each year for seven years.

Pharaoh set Joseph over the land of Egypt and made him second in command. Joseph gathered of the harvest each year for the seven years and then the famine started. The people of Egypt had food because Joseph had stored it. All the countries around came to Egypt to buy corn and Joseph sold it to them. Early in the famine (Genesis 42), Joseph's father sent ten of Joseph's brothers down to Egypt to buy food. The brothers did not know Joseph, but he knew them. Joseph accused the men of being spies who had come to spy out the country. They denied and told him they were twelve brothers whose father was in Canaan. They said the youngest brother was at home with the father and one brother was not, indicating he was dead. Joseph insisted they go and get the youngest brother and bring him to Egypt to prove their story. He then put them away from him for three days. On the third day, Joseph told them to leave one of the brothers there and for the rest to go on home and take the corn. They were to bring the youngest brother to him to prove their words. They agreed and Simeon was left behind. Joseph commanded his servants to fill the sacks with corn and to put each man's money back in his sack. The brothers loaded up and left.

Upon arriving at an inn, one of the men opened his sack to feed his animal and there was his money. The others checked their sacks and their money was there too. They were afraid. They went on home to Jacob and told him what had happened. They wanted to take Benjamin to Egypt, but Jacob refused to let him go down. Once they had eaten up the corn, Jacob told them to go get more. The men refused to go without Benjamin. Jacob finally agreed to let Benjamin go and he sent a gift with them. In Genesis 43 is the account of this visit. When the brothers arrived in Egypt, they told Joseph's steward what had happened on the previous trip concerning their money. He told them not to be concerned but their God had given them the treasure in their sacks. He brought Simeon out to them. He gave them water and food for their mules. They prepared a present ready for Joseph because they found out they were going to eat with him at noon.

Joseph came in and the brothers gave him the present. They bowed themselves to the earth. He asked how they were, through an interpreter, and how their father was. When he saw

Benjamin, he had to go out and cry. He had them seated from the firstborn to the oldest and the men were amazed. They ate and drank and then when morning came they took their corn and left. They had no idea Joseph once more had their money put back in the sacks and he had his silver cup put into Benjamin's sack. Not long after they had left the city, Joseph sent his steward to overtake them and ask them as recorded in Genesis 44:4, "wherefore have ye rewarded evil for good?"

The brothers did not know what to say when they were overtaken. They told the steward whichever one of them had the cup would die and the rest would be servants. The steward began searching at the oldest and ended at Benjamin's sack where the cup was in the top of the sack. The brothers tore their clothes in anguish. They had promised their father to bring Benjamin home safely. They went back to the city where Joseph was still at his house. They fell on the ground before him. He asked them what they had done. The brothers had now decided this was God's punishment for what they had done to Joseph years ago, but they still had no idea this was Joseph. Judah spoke to Joseph and told him the whole story about how they had first come to Egypt and how Joseph had asked them about their father and brother. Judah told Joseph how Jacob had told them when he allowed Benjamin to go if something happened to Benjamin as had happened to his only other son, Joseph, he would be brought down to his grave with sorrow. Of course, Joseph was not the only other son but the only other son by Rachel, Jacob's chosen wife. Judah then begged Joseph to allow him to stay instead of Benjamin.

Chapter 45 of Genesis is one of the most touching chapters in the Bible. Here Joseph commanded everyone except the brothers to go out from him. Once they left, he wept aloud and told his brothers he was Joseph. He told them not to be grieved or angry with themselves because it was God who had sent him before them to preserve life. He told them there would be another five years of the famine and they needed to go get Israel and all of their possessions and bring them to Egypt. The brothers did so and when the family arrived in Egypt, Pharaoh allowed them to live in the land of Goshen because shepherds were considered to be an abomination to Egyptians (Genesis 47).

In time, Israel died (Genesis 49:33) and Joseph had his body embalmed and then Joseph and the family took the body back to Canaan and buried it. Joseph also died and his body was embalmed and put in a coffin in Egypt to be preserved until God visited the Israelites and brought them out of Egypt (Genesis 50:24-26). Thus ends the book of Genesis with the Israelites having multiplied and become a large group of people.

As Exodus begins, a new king had begun to rule in Egypt. He did not know Joseph and he was not happy the people of Israel were more and mightier than the Egyptians. He set taskmasters over them and made them work for him in building cities. The Israelites continued to grow in number and the Egyptians were harder and harder on them. Finally the king told the midwives of the Hebrew women (also called Israelites), to kill the sons who were born but to let the daughters live. The midwives were afraid and did not kill the male children but told the king the Hebrew women were lively and had delivered before the midwives got there. Then Pharaoh demanded of the Israelites themselves they kill every son who was born.

In Exodus Chapter 2, the author gave the account of the one who would eventually lead the Israelites out of Egypt and back to the land God had promised Abraham, Isaac, and Jacob. This man, Moses, was the son of Amram and Jochebed. When Moses was born, and his mother saw he was a goodly child, she decided to hide him instead of killing him. She did so for three months but when she could not hide him any longer, she made him an ark or a basket out of bulrushes and covered it with pitch. She put him in the container and put it by the river bank. She had his sister stay nearby to watch and see what would happen. Pharaoh's daughter came to the river to bathe. She saw the ark and when she opened it and saw the baby inside, knowing it was one of the Hebrew children, she still had compassion on him and decided to take him for her own son. Moses' sister asked the king's daughter if she would like for her to find a nurse for the baby. The king's daughter said yes, so Moses' sister went and got his mother to do the job.

Moses grew up as the son of a king's daughter. In Exodus 2, is an account where Moses went out and saw an Egyptian smiting one of his Hebrew brothers. He killed the Egyptian and hid him in the sand. He did not think anyone saw him. The next day though, when he saw two Hebrews fighting and tried to stop them, one of the Hebrews asked him if he intended to kill him like he had killed the Egyptian the day before. Moses was scared of what could happen to him, so he fled the county and went to dwell in Midian. There he met and married Zipporah, a daughter of Reuel, the priest of Midian. Moses stayed in Midian until after the Egyptian king died and in Exodus 3, God appeared to Moses and told him to go back to Egypt and bring the children of Israel out of the land.

Moses was not sure he wanted this job God had given him. Moses made several excuses to God and each time, God had an answer back for Moses. I think we often find ourselves in this same situation as Moses. We know there are things God wants us to do, but we make excuses. God is not going to talk to us like He did Moses, but if we have trained our conscience right and diligently studied His word, when we refuse to do what God wants us to do, we will know it.

Moses' first resistance came about when God told him in Exodus 3:10 He was going to send him to Pharaoh to bring forth the people of Israel. Moses immediately asked God, "Who am I, that I should go unto Pharaoh, and that I should bring forth the children of Israel out of Egypt?" God assured Moses

He would be with him. But in verse 13 of Exodus 3, Moses again questioned God. He asked what he should tell the people when they asked God's name. God told him to tell the people "I AM THAT I AM" and "I AM hath sent me unto you." Beginning in Chapter 4 of Exodus, Moses was still finding reasons not to do what God had told him to do. In verse 1, Moses told God the people would not believe him.

God then gave Moses three signs. God asked Moses what was in his hand. Moses had a rod in his hand. God told him to cast it on the ground where it became a serpent. Then God told Moses to pick it up by the tail and when he did, it became a rod again. For the second sign, Moses was to put his hand inside his bosom where it became leprous as snow and then when he put it back in and took it out again, it was clear of the leprosy. For the last sign, God told Moses if the people refused to believe those two signs, then Moses should take water out of the river and pour it upon the dry land where it would become blood. Even with his three signs to show the people, Moses still found an excuse. He told God he was not eloquent, but was slow of speech and of a slow tongue.

God would not hear this excuse either. He asked Moses who had made man's mouth or who made the dumb, the deaf, or the seeing, or the blind. Of course, God had done all of this and could do whatever was needed in order for Moses to speak to the people. Moses was quite persistent in finding excuses and finally he said in Exodus 4:13, "…O my Lord, send, I pray thee, by the hand of him whom thou wilt send." God became angry at this point and told Moses his brother Aaron was coming forth to meet Moses right then and he would be the mouth piece, but Moses was to tell him what to say.

Moses went back to his father-in-law and asked him to let Moses return to his people in Egypt. Jethro told him to go in peace. Moses and Aaron went and gathered the elders of the children of Israel together and told them what God had said. They showed them the signs. The people believed God had visited the children of Israel and they bowed their heads and worshipped.

Chapter 5 of Exodus begins with Moses and Aaron going in to Pharaoh and telling him God said to let the people go. Pharaoh, of course, refused and immediately commanded the taskmasters to increase the work on the children of Israel. Once their work load was increased, these same children who had bowed their heads and worshipped God in Chapter 4, now began to gripe and complain to Moses. This was just the beginning of many years of complaining. As their journey all the way to the Promised Land continued, the Israelites were on a constant roller coaster where they were satisfied for a while and then complained for a while. Does that remind you of our human nature? Do you find yourself happy for a while with what you have and how things are going and then find yourself wanting more or dissatisfied?

Exodus 7-12 provides the account of the plagues God sent against Egypt. There were ten plagues beginning with water turning to blood, continuing with frogs, lice, flies, pestilence upon the livestock, boils on the people, hail, locust, darkness, and finally death of the firstborn of the Egyptians. Only when God took the firstborn of each family of the Egyptians did Pharaoh agree to let the children of Israel leave Egypt. God had instructed the Israelites to borrow from their neighbors jewels of silver and gold and the Egyptians had given freely. So when it was time for the Israelites to leave, they were well supplied.

Before God sent the last plague of death, He gave Moses some instructions concerning what needed to be done. In those instructions given in Exodus 12, God established for the Israelites the Feast of Unleavened Bread to be kept yearly so the Israelites would remember what had happened at this particular time in their history. In keeping with the idea of teaching their children with diligence, in Exodus 12:24-27, God gave them instructions for doing so. Those instructions are continued into Chapter 13 where in several verses (3, 8, and 14-15) God continued to stress how the Israelites needed to teach their children and how they needed to keep the events in their own minds.

In Exodus 12:27 just before the children of Israel left Egypt, they were bowing their heads and worshipping. They had seen all the miracles God had sent. They knew God was delivering them. They began their march toward the Promised Land, but in a very short time, they were again complaining and even wanting to go back to Egypt. Once Pharaoh realized what he had done in letting the people go, he had his army pursue them. The children of Israel cried to God and said to Moses in Exodus 14:11-12, "…Because there were no graves in Egypt, hast thou taken us away to die in the wilderness? Wherefore hast thou dealt thus with us, to carry us forth out of Egypt? 12. Is not this the word that we did tell thee in Egypt, saying, Let us alone, that we may serve the Egyptians? For it had been better for us to serve the Egyptians, than that we should die in the wilderness." Moses told the people to fear not, but to see the salvation of the Lord.

God did provide the salvation for the children of Israel. He opened the waters so they could go upon dry ground and when Pharaoh's army came through, He closed the waters upon them and they drowned. Exodus 14:31 says the Israelites saw the great work the Lord did upon the Egyptians and they feared the Lord and believed the Lord and Moses. This praise did not last long for in Chapter 16, the people were again complaining. This time they were hungry and wishing they were back in Egypt. This reminds me so much of how people will obey the gospel and stay steadfast for a while but when the going gets rough, they begin to think about what it was like before becoming a Christian and they think it was better. They want to go back to a previous lifestyle. All too often, they do. As teachers of God's word, we need to be able to talk to these people, showing them the examples from the past, and helping them to see how they are going against God's will. What better place to take them than here to the Israelites?

God heard the people's complaint and provided them with manna and quail, but even then the people could not obey God. God said for them to gather only enough manna for the day except on the sixth day when they were to gather enough for two days since they were not to work on the seventh day. As recorded in Exodus 16, some people gathered too much during the week and it ended up ruined with worms. Some went out to get the manna on the seventh day, but there was none. How like today's world were these people? God says not to do something and we think we must do it. He says to do something and we choose not to do it. Does it sound like the world is getting any better than it was when Eve refused to obey God? We must make sure our children and those we teach are aware of these accounts and they realize sin has been present since the beginning and if we are not diligently fighting it, sin will win.

In Exodus 17, the Israelites again complained against Moses because they had no water. Instead of asking God for help, they chose to once more remind Moses he had brought them out of Egypt. In verse 3 the people said: "Wherefore is this that thou has brought us up out of Egypt, to kill us and our children and our cattle with thirst?" Where was their faith? After all they had seen God do, where was their faith? God told Moses to take his rod and smite the rock in Horeb and water would come out of it. Moses smote the rock and the water came forth.

How often do we gripe and complain when things are not just what we think they should be? How often do we instead go to God in prayer and wait for His answer? How different are we from these children of Israel?

Next in Exodus is the account of Jethro and Moses which was mentioned earlier. If you remember, Jethro, Moses' father-in-law, watched Moses as he acted as a judge for the people. Chapter 18 of Exodus is where Jethro suggested to Moses he needed to teach the people the ordinances and laws and show them the work they needed to do and how they needed to walk in God's ways. Then he suggested Moses should appoint men to be judges over the groups so Moses only had to hear the harder cases.

In Exodus 19 God told Moses to prepare the people to hear God. He said He would come to Moses in a thick cloud so the people could hear God speak and they would believe Moses. Moses got the people ready and on the third day after God previously spoke with Moses, God appeared. Beginning in Exodus 20, we have the words God spoke. He gave the people what we often refer to as the Ten Commandments. Many people today will tell you God gave the commandments to Moses, and He did, but not until after He had already given them to the Israelites by voice. Read Exodus 19-20 carefully and you will see God spoke directly to the people. Then read Deuteronomy 4:9-15 as further evidence God spoke directly to the people. They heard the voice, but yet they did not continue in obedience. Today, we read the Word, but yet do not continue in obedience.

An interesting aspect of the Ten Commandments given in Exodus 20 is that all of these commands were also found in the New Testament as applicable to Christians except the fourth one recorded in Exodus 20:8 to remember the Sabbath Day to keep it holy. This command for the Israelites was so important. It was so important that in Numbers 15:35 when a man was found picking up sticks on a Sabbath Day, God said he was to be stoned. Back in Exodus 31:14-17, God made it very clear that the Sabbath Day was to be observed, but He did not say every Sabbath Day. He did not have to as the Israelites understood verse 13: "…verily my sabbaths ye shall keep: for it is a sign between me and you throughout your generations…" Note though, the Sabbath was between God and the Jews.

After God spoke His commands to the people and they expressed their fear, God had Moses draw near to Him and in Exodus 20:22 God began to speak with Moses and gave several more commands as recorded in Chapters 22-23. In Exodus 24:4, Moses wrote all of the words of the Lord and according to verse 7, Moses read the book of the covenant to the people. The people said they would do the Lord's will and be obedient in verse 7. In verse 12 God told Moses to come up into the mount and God would give Moses "tables of stone, and a law, and commandments, which I have written; that thou mayest teach them." What was Moses supposed to do when he got God's laws? Teach them. What is our responsibility when we learn the laws of God? Teach them.

    We know from the scripture recorded in Exodus 24-31 God gave Moses much more than Ten Commandments. He gave him instructions for building the tabernacle, instructions for how to make the priestly garments, instructions for sacrifices, and instructions for a very important chest called the Ark of the Covenant or Ark of the Testimony. God gave specific instructions concerning the size of this box, what was to be placed in it, where it was to be placed, and how it was to be moved from place to place. The box was to contain the two stone tablets with the Ten Commandments and later Aaron's rod that budded and a pot of manna. It was to be carried upon the shoulders of the Levites by two poles running through four rings in its top. The ark was to go in front of the Israelites as they traveled to the Promised Land. The lid of the box was called the mercy seat and it was here according to Leviticus 16 where once a year the Israelites were to make an atonement for their sins. The box was to be placed in the Most Holy part of the tabernacle. It represented God's presence among the people.

While Moses was getting this information from God concerning what God wanted the people to do, the people were busy as recorded in Exodus 32 making them gods (verse 1). In verse 9 God told Moses the people were stiff necked. God was ready to destroy them, but Moses begged Him not to. Moses even reminded God of His previous promise to Abraham, Isaac, and Israel to multiply their seed and to give them the land of Canaan. God repented of the evil He thought to do to the Israelites and sent Moses back down to the people with the two tables of stone written on by God.

When Moses arrived at the camp and saw for himself what the people had done, he was so mad, he actually cast the stones out of his hands upon the ground and broke them. Aaron had the people give him their jewelry and he had fashioned them a molten calf according to Exodus 32:4, but when Moses returned, Aaron lied to him in telling him he had cast the gold into the fire and "there came out this calf." Who did Aaron think he was fooling?

Moses stood at the gate of the camp and asked who was on the Lord's side. The sons of Levi came to Moses and Moses had them go throughout the camp and kill about 3,000 men. The next day Moses told the people what a great sin they had committed in making the god of gold. He told them he would return to the Lord to make an atonement for their sin. Moses went to the Lord and asked Him to forgive the people and if God would not forgive them, then Moses asked Him to blot Moses out of the book that God had written. God told Moses in Exodus 32:33, "Whosoever hath sinned against me, him will I blot out of my book." God plagued the people because of the calf Aaron had made and Moses ground the calf into powder and put it into their drinking water.

God had Moses come back to Him the second time for another copy of the commands. The writer in Deuteronomy 10:1-4 recorded God wrote the words again and gave them to Moses. This time while Moses was gone, it appears the people behaved themselves. Beginning in Chapter 35 of Exodus, Moses gathered the people together and they listened to God's words. The rest of the book of Exodus is concerned with the people building the tabernacle and according to Exodus 39:42, they did this work just as God commanded.

In the first chapters of Leviticus, Moses was found telling the people the commands of God concerning how they were to dwell with each other and how they were to worship God. In Leviticus 6 beginning at verse 9, are the commands God gave concerning the fire that was to be burning upon the altar continuously. In verse 13, it is recorded the fire was to be ever burning upon the altar and it was never to go out. This was the fire authorized by God and even commanded by God. This account is so important, as will become evident in Leviticus 10.

In Leviticus 9, is an account of a burnt offering, a sin offering, a meat offering, and peace offerings being made to the Lord. Aaron and his sons followed the many commands the

Lord had given for making these offerings, and in verse 24 the author stated a fire came from before the Lord and consumed the burnt offering and the fat. The people shouted and fell on their faces and then in Leviticus 10:1 is recorded, "And Nadab and Abihu, the sons of Aaron, took either of them his censer, and put fire therein, and put incense thereon, and offered strange fire before the LORD, which he commanded them not."

What does it mean they offered strange fire before the Lord? You can search for yourself and find many possible answers to this question, but I think the passage makes it quite clear for us. The strange fire was fire which the Lord had not commanded. God had not authorized the fire which Nadab and Abihu chose to use. God did authorize a fire, but not the fire Nadab and Abihu chose to use. It is not recorded anywhere that God specifically said to Nadab and Abihu, "This is the only fire you can use. Do not use any other fire." If He did, the information is not recorded for us in the Bible. All we have is the men used a fire which God had not commanded. In other words, this fire was not authorized by God.

What was the consequence of Nadab and Abihu offering strange fire? Did they get a second chance? From Leviticus 10:2, fire went out right then from God and devoured them. They died right then and there. When we go beyond what God has authorized and add to our worship, how are we any better than Nadab and Abihu? While we may not die immediately, our actions will lead to our spiritual death and if we are guilty of adding to what God has authorized and we teach the same to others, we are contributing to their future punishment.

    The next few chapters of Leviticus continue the laws God gave to His people concerning many topics. God expected His people to obey those laws. In Leviticus 18 God began to prepare the Israelites for living in the land which He was giving them. In verse 3, He told the people not to live like the people of Egypt, from where they had just come, had lived. He told them not to live like the people of the land of Canaan, where they were headed, were living. Instead, His people were to do His judgments and keep His ordinances. In Leviticus 18:5, the promise was made to the people if they kept God's statutes and judgments, they would live in them. Throughout the rest of the book of Leviticus many other commands were given always with the promise, if the people obeyed God He would be with them, but if they disobeyed Him, God would no longer help them.

    Some of the events in Numbers are also included in Genesis, Exodus, or Leviticus, but more information is sometimes provided in the accounts found in Numbers. In reading the book of Numbers, it appears from Chapters 1-10 the people were obeying God's commands. Several of the chapters actually end with a statement to this effect. Beginning in Numbers 11, the people have been complaining as we saw earlier in Exodus. According to verse 1, their complaining displeased God. He actually sent fire among them to consume them. Then in verses 4-6, the author gave more details concerning the quail God sent when the Israelites complained about their food. He sent so many quail they were piled two cubits high. With a cubit being about eighteen inches, they had around three feet of quail. As the people began to eat the quail, God smote them with a plague.

In Chapter 12 of Numbers, even Miriam, Moses' sister, and Aaron spoke against Moses because of the Ethiopian woman he had married. Miriam became leprous and God refused to heal her even though Moses cried to God begging Him to do so. God said she needed to follow the same rules that applied to others and be shut out for seven days and then she could return to the camp.

These many accounts show us the severe side of God. This is the side of God about which all too many preachers will not preach. Instead, in so many sermons, we hear only about the goodness of God and how He has given us eternal life just like He gave the Israelites manna in the wilderness. What the preachers forget to tell us is if we want that eternal life, we must, like the children of Israel, do something to get it. God gave the Israelites manna but they had to go out and collect it in the manner authorized by God. Remember from Exodus how they were to collect only enough for the day except on the sixth day they were to collect enough for the seventh day. That was God's authorized plan. The manna was free just like salvation, but the people had to do something according to the plan to get it. When we get into the New Testament, we will see how salvation is free, but we have to do something to get it.

Continuing in Numbers 13, God was ready to give the Israelites the Promised Land. He told Moses to send out twelve spies to look over the land. Ten of the twelve spies came back with a report telling how wonderful the land was but stating the Israelites would not be able to go up against the people because the people were stronger than the Israelites. In Numbers 14:1-4, the people were murmuring because of the report of the ten spies. Two of the spies, Joshua and Caleb brought a good report and said they could take the land (verses 6-9). Because of the continued murmuring of the people, God told Moses the people who were twenty years old and upward which had murmured against Him would not enter the Promised Land. Instead they would wander in the wilderness for forty years which was a year for each day the spies had searched out the land. Joshua and Caleb, the two spies who brought the good report, would be allowed to enter the Promised Land.

God destroyed with a plague the ten spies who brought the evil report. The people mourned greatly and even after seeing God's power from the past when the people had complained or disobeyed God, the next morning the people rose up and said they would go and take the land. Moses tried to persuade them not to because God was not with them, but they would not listen. Moses told them in Numbers 14:43 the Lord was not with them because they had turned away from

Him. This is another important point for us today. We turn from God. We leave Him. He does not turn from us until we make the choice to leave Him. These Israelites who decided to go it on their own were killed by the Amalekites and Canaanites who dwelled in the land.

Again in Numbers Chapter 16, there was more rebellion against God. Korah, Dathan, Abiram, and On along with 250 other famous men in the congregation rose up against Moses and Aaron. The men accused Moses and Aaron of trying to take on too much power. In verses 9-10, Moses indicated which men had been chosen by God to do the service of the tabernacle. He told them to take their censers and put fire therein before the Lord and those the Lord chose would be holy. When Moses called for Dathan and Abiram, they refused to come up to him and accused Moses of bringing them out of a land that flowed with milk and honey to kill them in the wilderness.

Moses was very angry with these men and God must have been too for in the rest of Numbers Chapter 16 it is indicated God not only destroyed the 250 men, but after Moses warned the people to remove themselves from being near the tents of Korah, Dathan, and Abiram, God also caused the earth to open up and swallow them and all that pertained to them. One would think seeing what happened to these evil men would have been enough to stop the murmuring of the people, but in verse 41 the very next day, the children of Israel were accusing Moses of killing the people of the Lord. Before Aaron could go into the congregation with his censer and fire to offer an atonement, God had already killed 14,700 of them.

The murmuring continued and in Numbers Chapter 20 came the downfall of Moses. To this point he had done very well in being patient with the people. Previous to this event, on another occasion back in Exodus 17, you may remember when the people complained to Moses about water, God had told Moses to smite the rock and water would come forth. Moses did smite it and the people had water. Here in this account in Numbers 20, God told Moses to speak to the rock. Instead of speaking to the rock, according to verse 11, Moses smote the rock twice. God allowed the water to flow abundantly, but He told Moses and Aaron because they believed Him not to sanctify Him in the eyes of the children of Israel, neither of them would be allowed to lead the children into the land of promise. Can you imagine how Moses must have felt after all this time of dealing with the complaints of the people?

In Chapter 20 of Numbers, the accounts of the deaths of both Miriam and Aaron are recorded. Then in Chapter 21, the people were again complaining to Moses for bringing them out of Egypt in the wilderness to die. God sent fiery serpents among them to bite them. The people went to Moses and told him they had sinned. They wanted him to pray to the Lord to deliver them. Moses did pray and God told him to make a serpent and put it on a pole and when the people looked on it, they would live. What a strange command, but in verse 9 we can read when they looked upon the serpent of brass, they lived. Why did God make such a command? We are not told why. It does not appear from the reading that the Israelites were told why. But if they obeyed they were saved. The same is true for us today. God has told us what to do to be saved. If we obey, we will be saved. How simple.

Numbers 22-24 provides a very interesting account of a man who wanted to be able to prophesy against God's people in order to gain an earthly reward, but he obviously knew it was not a smart thing to do. In Chapter 22, Israel was moving on through the wilderness. They had already wreaked havoc on the Amorites and were headed to Moab. Balak, the king of the Moabites, knew what the Israelites had done and he wanted Balaam, a prophet, to come and curse the Israelites. When the men went to ask Balaam to go and curse the Israelites, he told them to stay there that night and as the Lord would speak to him, he would have to do what God said. Sure enough that night God told Balaam he was not to go with them and he was not to curse the Israelites because they were blessed. Balaam got up the next morning and told the men who had come for him to go on back to their land because the Lord refused to let him go with them. The men went back to Balak and told him what Balaam had said. Balak was not satisfied so he sent more princes to Balaam. These princes were to tell Balaam if he would come to Balak, he would promote him with great honor.

Instead of Balaam refusing to go with them like he knew God had told him to do, he told the men to stay the night there and he would find out what God had to say.

Sure enough this second time, God came to Balaam. This time, God told Balaam that if the men came to call him, for him to rise up and go with them but to only do whatever it would be God would say to him. The next morning, Balaam got up and saddled his animal and away he went with the princes. God was mad because he went and if it had not been for the donkey seeing the angel of God standing in the way, Balaam could have been killed. The donkey two times turned out of the way of the angel and Balaam, not seeing the angel, smote the donkey. On the second time, the donkey thrust herself into the wall and crushed Balaam's foot. He hit her again. On the third time, the angel stood in a place where there was nowhere to turn. The donkey fell down under Balaam. When Balaam began to hit her this time, she spoke to him. She asked him what she had done to him that he was hitting her. Balaam actually talked to the donkey and told her if he had a sword he would kill her. She told him how good she had been to him and asked him if she had ever done him wrong. About that time, God opened Balaam's eyes and he saw the angel of the Lord with the drawn sword. He bowed his head and fell flat on his face.

One would think this would have been enough for Balaam, and he did tell the angel he would go back, but the angel told him no, he was to go on. So he went. When he got to

Balak, and Balak reprimanded him for not coming sooner, Balaam told Balak he had no power to say anything other than whatever God would tell him. The next day, Balak took Balaam up to a high place to see the people of Israel. Balaam offered to God seven rams and seven bullocks. God told Balaam to say to Balak (Numbers 23:8), "How shall I curse, whom God hath not cursed? Or how shall I defy, whom the Lord hath not defied?" Balak took Balaam to another place to see the Israelites in hopes he would curse them from that place. Again, Balaam was not allowed by God to curse them and he told Balak they were blessed. Balak did not give up easily and took Balaam to one more spot. For the third time, Balaam offered offerings and while he looked upon the Israelites in their tents, the spirit of God came upon him and he blessed Israel. Balak was very mad and told Balaam to flee to his place. Before leaving, as recorded in Numbers 24:17, Balaam told Balak a prophecy concerning the Christ who was to come. He said there would come a Star out of Jacob and a Sceptre out of Israel.

In Numbers 26, the children of Israel were numbered. Their number was 601,730. According to verses 64-65 there was not in this number even one man other than Joshua and Caleb, who had been in the number above twenty years of age when leaving Egypt. If you remember, God had said earlier due to the report of the spies and the continued complaining, only Joshua and Caleb of the original men above the age of twenty would enter the Promised Land. In Chapter 27 Joshua was given the responsibility to complete the trip into the Promised Land.

Deuteronomy begins with the children of Israel in their fortieth year of wandering in the wilderness and they were ready to go in and possess the land. Deuteronomy is a review of the history of the people and of the laws of the Lord. In Chapter 11, Moses again warned the people of the importance of obeying God's laws and in verses 18-19, he stressed the need to teach the words of the Lord to their children. Concerning His words, God said in verse 19, "And ye shall teach them your children, speaking of them when thou sittest in thine house, and when thou walkest by the way, when thou liest down, and when thou risest up." They were told in verse 20 to write them upon the door posts of their house and upon their gates. In verse 22, the people were once more told to "diligently" keep all of the commands which Moses had commanded them. The people were promised to be blessed when they did as Moses said, but in verse 28, they were also promised a curse if they did not obey God's commands. In verse 32 of Chapter 12, Moses again warned the people not to add to or take from the commands they had been given.

Throughout Deuteronomy are many laws and commands the people of Israel were expected to follow. These were the laws that were to be taught to the children. It is very interesting to read these laws which appear to be expanded information related to the Ten Commandments. Within these many verses, there are commands for the king given in Chapter 17 beginning in verse 14 and continuing through the end of the chapter. God told the people here once they arrived in the land He was giving them, they would say, "I will set a king over me, like as all the nations that are about me." God went on to tell them that He would be the one who chose their kings and the kings were to follow God's rules. Those rules included the king was not to multiply horses to himself nor was he to send to Egypt for horses. He was not to multiply wives to himself so he would not turn his heart from God. He was not to greatly multiply silver and gold to himself. He was supposed to write a copy of the law given by God into a book and he was to read from it all the days of his life so he would learn to fear the Lord his God, to keep all the words of the law and the statutes to do them. Keep these verses in mind as we move into the days of the kings later in this book.

In Deuteronomy Chapter 20, is another interesting command from God which will again be ignored as the Israelites take possession of the land God gave them. In the rules for warfare with those near and those far from the land God gave the people, according to verses 13-18, there were some cities that were to be destroyed completely and others where only the men had to die. If the city was far from them and not a city of one of the specific nations God named, the Hittites, Amorites, Canaanites, Perizzites, Hivites, and the Jebusites, then the Israelites could have of the spoil for themselves. But if the city was of one of those nations, nothing could be left alive. God's reason for commanding the Israelites to destroy everything from these nations was so His people would not do after the abominations of these people in worshipping false gods or idols. Again, keep these verses in mind when we get to the book of Joshua and the Israelites claim their land.

In Deuteronomy 29-30 are some very important points we need to always keep in mind. In Deuteronomy 29:29, is recorded: "The secret things belong unto the Lord our God: but those things which are revealed belong unto us and to our children forever, that we may do all the words of this law." From this verse it is clear there were some things God chose not to reveal to mankind, but He revealed all man needs in order to do His will. In Chapter 30, Moses told the Israelites once the blessing and curse had come upon them and they returned unto the Lord and obeyed His voice, God would turn their captivity and have compassion upon them. The fulfilment of that prophecy comes later in this book. It is so important to know when this prophecy was fulfilled since many today say it is yet to be done.

In Chapter 31 of Deuteronomy, Moses was at the end of his life. He was 120 years old and he knew he would not be allowed to go over Jordan. This had to be a sad time for him. He had given the last forty years of his life in service to God, but he had messed up at the rock where God said to speak to the rock and he chose to smite the rock. In Chapter 31 it is recorded God told Moses what the people would do after his death. He told Moses the people would go after the gods of the land and God would forsake them. In Chapter 32, just before his death, Moses spoke of the Lord as the Rock in verse 4. There will be more about the Rock in the New Testament. Finally in Chapter 34 after Moses was allowed to look from Mt. Pisgah and see the Promised Land, he died and was buried in the valley in the land of Moab by God. Joshua became the leader of this great nation of Israel whom we commonly refer to as the Jews.

The next book of the Old Testament, Joshua, begins with God speaking to Joshua, one of the two spies who said forty years prior the Israelites could take the Promised Land. God told Joshua to arise and go over Jordan and take the land which God had given the people. In Joshua 1:7-8, God told Joshua, "Only be thou strong and very courageous, that thou mayest observe to do according to all the law, which Moses my servant commanded thee: turn not from it to the right hand or to the left, that thou mayest prosper withersoever thou goest. 8. This book of the law shall not depart out of thy mouth; but thou shalt meditate therein day and night, that thou mayest observe to do according to all that is written therein: for then thou shalt make thy way prosperous, and then thou shalt have good success."

Meditate night and day on the book was what God told Joshua to do. If God's people today were to meditate night and day on the book and spend less time on the TV or on the games or on the worldly literature, would the people not have a much greater knowledge and be better prepared to teach the word? Sometimes it is just a matter of setting priorities. When a day seems not to have enough hours, something must be left off. All too often, it is the study of God's word that gets left out while ball games or participating with friends in some worldly activity can be done. While there may be nothing wrong with these activities, God must always come first.

As the book of Joshua unfolds, the Israelites began to possess the land the Lord had given them. It is so important to note here they began to "possess" the land. God had promised to give the Israelites the land just as He has promised to give salvation. But, they had to possess it just as people today must possess salvation. In the case of the Israelites, they had to possess it by physically fighting for it, but God would win their battles. Today's people possess salvation by spiritual battles which are won through God's word.

In Joshua 2, Joshua sent out two spies who went to a harlot's house and spent the night. The harlot, Rahab, who is in the lineage of Christ, realized what was about to happen to her country and she showed the spies kindness in hopes they would agree to save her family. They did agree to save her family, if she placed a scarlet thread in the window by which she had let them escape from those who were looking for them. Needless to say, Rahab placed the thread in the window and when Jericho was destroyed, she and her family were saved. If she had chosen to ignore the one element by which she and her family could be saved, they too would have been destroyed.

God gave the Israelites the city of Jericho. In Joshua 6:2 it is recorded: "And the Lord said unto Joshua, See, I have given into thine hand Jericho, and the king thereof, and the mighty men of valor." If we just stopped there, it would sound like there was nothing to do. They had the land. But going on to the next verses, "And ye shall compass the city, all ye men of war, and go round about the city once. Thus shalt thou do six days. And seven priests shall bear before the ark seven trumpets of rams' horns…" So this means although God said He had given them the city, the men had to do something to get it. God gave further instructions recorded in Joshua 6, but the important point to understand when teaching others is God gives in His own way and in order to get what He gives, one has to obey what He says. God gives salvation, but does that mean there is nothing to do to obtain it? If these Jews had just said, well, there is nothing we have to do to take Jericho, would they have had Jericho?

Even though God gave the Jews Jericho, they were not allowed to take of any of the bounty. All of the silver, gold, and vessels of brass and iron were to go into the Lord's treasury and the people were to take nothing for themselves. But in Joshua 7, Achan chose to disobey God and take some of the bounty for himself. While no one knew what he had done, in the next battle at Ai, it became evident. While Ai was just a small place which should have been able to be taken by a few men, instead the men of Ai won the battle. Joshua was beside himself. He asked God why He had brought them out there to destroy them. God told him to get up. He said Israel had sinned and He was not with them anymore unless they destroyed the accursed among them. After searching out the problem it was discovered Achan had taken gold, silver, and a Babylonian garment and hid them in his tent. Israel stoned Achan and his family and burned them. At that point, God was again with the Jews and told them He had given them Ai. Once more, though, the Jews had to do something to get Ai.

In Joshua 8:34-35, Joshua read all of the book of the law to the people. He read these words not just to the men but to the women and the children and even to the strangers that were among them. He read the blessings and the cursings. The people at this point had no excuse for not knowing what God had promised if they obeyed and if they disobeyed. Yet, as one continues to read the book of Joshua, it is obvious the Israelites either had a short memory, did not believe what God said, or just plain chose to be disobedient.

Remember, God had very clearly told the people as recorded back in Deuteronomy 20:17 when they entered the Promised Land they were to destroy the Hittite, Amorite, Canaanite, Perizzite, Hivite, and the Jebusite. But when the

Gibeonites who were descended from Amorites (2nd Samuel 21:2) heard Israel had arrived, they tricked the Israelites into making an agreement with them to let them be servants to the Israelites and not to kill them (Joshua 9). The Gibeonites showed Joshua their moldy bread and told him when they left home they had fresh bread. They said their clothes and shoes had worn out on the trip. Joshua believed them and made an agreement with them in direct opposition to what God had told the Israelites to do to the Gibeonites.

This is a perfect example of how we can be tricked into believing something that is false. Had Joshua consulted God first on the matter, the agreement would not have been made. The Israelites would have obeyed God. How often do we make mistakes because we do not pray about our decisions or consult God's word concerning our decisions? How important is it when we teach others, we teach them to pray about all decisions and to use God's word as their guide?

In Joshua 11:23, is a very important fact. God had promised the Jews the land of Canaan. Many today will tell us this prophecy is still to be fulfilled, but according to this verse, Joshua took the whole land just like God had told Moses and he gave it to Israel. The promise was fulfilled. While the land was taken, there was much of it still not possessed. In Chapter 13, Joshua was old. God told him to divide the land by lot to the Israelites for an inheritance. In Joshua 18:2 there were still seven tribes that had not received their inheritance. According to verse 3, God had given it to them. Think about what this is saying. God had given them the land. They had not received their inheritance. God has given us His grace that brings salvation according to Titus 2:11 which we will study when we get to the New Testament. But, has everyone received their inheritance? No, and we will see why later in this book.

In Joshua 21:43, God gave Israel all the land which He had sworn to give them AND they possessed it and dwelt therein. According to verse 45, everything God had promised Israel had been delivered. In Joshua 23:15-16, Joshua warned the Israelites of what was to come: "Therefore it shall come to pass, that as all good things are come upon you, which the LORD your God promised you; so shall the LORD bring upon you all evil things, until he have destroyed you from off this good land which the LORD your God hath given you. 16. When ye have transgressed the covenant of the LORD your God, which he commanded you, and have gone and served other gods, and bowed yourselves to them; then shall the anger of the LORD be kindled against you, and ye shall perish quickly from off the good land which he hath given unto you."

In Joshua Chapter 24, Joshua told the people if serving the Lord seemed evil to them, they needed to choose that day who they would serve whether the gods their fathers served or the gods of the Amorites, but he and his house would serve the Lord (verse 15). The people said they too would serve God since He was the one who had brought them up out of Egypt and He was their God. Joshua's death was recorded in this chapter and in verse 31 the record says the people served God all the days of Joshua and all the days of the elders who lived longer than Joshua. But after the death of those leaders, we have a different story, as we will see in our next chapter which begins with the book of Judges.

Chapter 4
God's People United under Judges and Kings

The book of Judges opens with God's people once more not obeying His commands. Earlier you will remember, God had told His people in Deuteronomy 20:16-17 they were to leave nothing alive but they were to utterly destroy the Hittite, Amorite, Canaanite, Perizzite, Hivite, and the Jebusite. Here in Judges 1:27-28 the Canaanites were allowed to remain in some of the land. In verse 35 the Amorites remained, and of course from verse 21 we see the Jebusites remained. In Chapter 2, the angel of the Lord came to the people and brought them a message from God. The angel told them God had promised the fathers never to break His covenant with them, but God had commanded the people not to make a league with the inhabitants of the land. Now they had disobeyed God so instead of driving them out, God was going to make them as thorns in the sides of the Israelites and the gods of the inhabitants would become a snare to the Israelites. The people were sad, but they went on their way.

One of the saddest passages in the Bible is found here in Judges 2:10-13. After Joshua died, the rest of his generation died and there arose a generation that "knew not the Lord, nor yet the works which he had done for Israel." How could this happen? What happened to the commands God had given the fathers to teach their children His laws and to talk about His words in the morning and the evening and to write them upon the door posts? Once no one knew the Lord or His works, doing evil was easy. In verses 11-13 the Israelites totally forsook God and began to bow themselves to the gods of the people. How is their behavior any different from what we see today in those people whose families used to be Christians but today the children are running after the gods of this world not knowing anything about the God of heaven?

God was against Israel like He promised them He would be. In Judges 2:14-15, God was delivering the Israelites to the enemies. Yet, God still had one promise left. He was going to bring forth one of the seed of Abraham through which all the nations of the earth would be blessed.

Beginning in Judges 2:16, God raised up judges to deliver His people. Even then, the people would not listen and according to verse 17, they would not obey God. Throughout the book of Judges, we find a repeating cycle. The people disobeyed God. Their enemies overcame them. God sent a judge to deliver them. They served God for a while and then they disobeyed God. Their enemies overcame them. God sent a judge to deliver them. This cycle repeated through at least fifteen judges who ruled anywhere from three to forty years each and included a period of about three hundred fifty years beginning around 1400-1350 B.C. and ending when Saul became the first king around 1050 B.C. Othniel was the first judge and Samuel was the last one. Five of the most famous judges were Deborah, Gideon, Samson, Eli, and Samuel.

Judges 3 begins with the people doing exactly what God told them not to do. In verse 5 they were dwelling among the Canaanites, Hittites, Amorites, Perizzites, Hivites, and Jebusites. In verse 6 they were intermarrying with these people that God had told them to destroy. God was angry in verse 8, and He had delivered the people to the king of Mesopotamia and they had to serve him eight years. Then in verse 9, God gave the people the first deliverer or judge, Othniel. The land had rest for forty years and then the judge died. The people again did evil and God allowed another king to come against them. This time the Israelites served eighteen years and in verse 15, they were crying to God again.

After Othniel, the next two judges were Ehud and Shamgar. While the author of the book of Ruth did not actually say when the events of the book took place, some historians have placed it around the time of Ehud (The Interactive Bible). So we will look at this beautiful story of love here before going on with the next judge, Deborah.

The little book of Ruth has only four chapters but these four chapters show us a love that needs to be taught to our children and grandchildren and all the women we know. According to the account, there was a famine in the land of Israel and Elimelech and his wife Naomi along with sons, Mahlon and Chilion left their land and went to Moab. Elimelech died and the two sons married women of Moab. In a while both of the sons died and left Naomi and the two daughters-in-law,

Orpah and Ruth. Naomi heard God had provided the Israelites with bread again, so she planned to go back to Judah. She told the two daughters-in-law to each return to her own mother's house. Her desire was for the Lord to deal kindly with the women just as they had dealt kindly with Naomi. At first both women said they would return with Naomi to Judah and to her people, but Naomi told them to go on to their own people. She said she had no more sons in her womb for them and she was grieved for them. Both women cried and Orpah kissed Naomi and left her but Ruth refused to leave.

What Ruth said to her mother-in-law in Ruth 1:16-17 is very well known and is often included in weddings. She said, "Intreat me not to leave thee, or to return from following after thee: for whither thou goest, I will go; and where thou lodgest, I will lodge: thy people shall be my people, and thy God my God: 17. Where thou diest, will I die, and there will I be buried: the LORD do so to me, and more also, if ought but death part thee and me." Imagine having that kind of love for your own mother-in-law. If all of us had love of this nature, wouldn't we have more peace in our families?

The two, Naomi and Ruth, continued on the journey to Bethlehem and arrived at the beginning of barley harvest. God had commanded His people to take care of the poor among them and one of the commands was when the landowners harvested their crops, they had to leave some for the poor. Ruth went out to glean in the fields behind the reapers. She was going to pick up what they had left. She ended up in the field of Boaz who was kin to Elimelech, Naomi's dead husband. When Boaz saw Ruth gleaning he asked his workers who she was. They told him who she was and Boaz told Ruth not to go to any other field but to continue to abide there near his maidens. He charged the men not to touch her and he even told them to let some of what they had harvested fall to the ground for her to glean.

Why would Boaz do such a thing? For one, he was a believer in God. Notice in Ruth 2:4 and 12 how Boaz called upon the Lord to bless the reapers and to bless Ruth. Second, according to verse 11, he had heard how Ruth had treated her mother-in-law. Ruth continued to glean in his fields through the barley and wheat harvests and was treated very well.

At the end of the harvests, Naomi who knew the law of the land, told Ruth what she needed to do. The rule of that time taken from Deuteronomy 25:5-6 was when a man died and left his wife childless, the next brother was to take the woman for a wife and the first child born would bear the name of the dead brother. In this case, there was not a brother left. Naomi told Ruth to wash herself, put on her perfume and her clothes, and go to the threshing floor where Boaz would be cleaning the barley harvest. Once he had laid down for the night, Ruth was to uncover his feet and lay down with him and then she was to do whatever Boaz told her to do.

Ruth went to the threshing floor and did what Naomi had said for her to do. At midnight, Boaz realized she was at his feet. He asked who was there and Ruth told him. Ruth asked him to spread his skirt over her for he was a near kinsman. Again, Boaz blessed Ruth and told her how kind she had been in not following after a young man whether poor or rich. He told her he would do by her what was right but there was a closer kinsperson who would have to be dealt with first. Boaz promised to take care of it. The next morning before it was light, Ruth got up. Boaz did not want anyone to know she had been there. He gave her more barley and she went back to Naomi. Naomi told Ruth to wait because Boaz would take care of it before the day ended.

Sure enough, Naomi was right. Boaz went to the nearer kinsman and told him Naomi had returned from Moab and was selling the parcel of land belonging to Elimelech. He offered the nearer kinsman the opportunity to redeem the land and when he said he would, Boaz told him the day he bought the field of the hand of Naomi, he must also buy it of Ruth the Moabitess to raise up the name of the dead. The kinsman changed his mind due to not wanting to mar his own inheritance, so he thus gave Boaz permission to take Ruth. The people of the city were happy and in Ruth 4:11-12 you can read how they blessed Boaz.

Boaz and Ruth married and they had a son. Now Boaz and Ruth could have left Naomi out of the picture, but that love

Ruth had for her mother-in-law was still strong. The son was given to Naomi to nurse. Think how this must have made Naomi feel. This son was Obed who was the father of Jesse, who was the father of David who we will be studying when we get to the section on the kings. Interestingly, through Obed's progeny, Ruth is in the ancestry of Jesus Christ. What a beautiful love story the book of Ruth is.

Now, back to Judges 4, where Deborah who was a prophetess judged Israel. At this time, the people were having to serve Jabin, King of Canaan. Deborah told Barak to go and fight the battle against Jabin, but he told her he would only go if she went with him. She agreed to go but she told Barak that Sisera, the captain of Jabin's army, would be taken by a woman. Just as Deborah said, God delivered the people and Sisera fled on foot. He went to the tent of Jael the wife of Heber the Kenite because there was peace between the two houses. Jael went out to meet Sisera and told him to come into the tent where she gave him milk to drink and covered him up. He went to sleep because he was so tired and she nailed his head to the ground with a tent nail. When Barak arrived in pursuit, Jael delivered Sisera to him, dead. So Jael had the credit for killing the captain and was the star of Deborah's song recorded in Chapter 5 of Judges.

The land had rest again for forty years and then God allowed the Midianites to overcome them. The next judge, Gideon, started out a little like Moses in questioning God about his own ability to lead the people. He asked God for signs and God granted them. After seeing the angel consume with fire the flesh and cakes Gideon had placed on the rock, Gideon still needed other signs. He needed more proof God was going to save Israel by his hand. He put a fleece of wool on the floor and first asked God to let there be dew on the fleece only and the earth beside it be dry. When his request was granted, he put the fleece out again and asked for the fleece to be dry and the ground to be wet with dew. God granted both signs and only then did Gideon who was also called Jerubbaal agree to go after the Midianites.

When Gideon headed out to battle, God told him he had too many people with him (Judges 7). He had 32,000 and once they had won the battle, they would be bragging about what they had done. The battle was not theirs; it was God's. God told Gideon to tell the people anyone who was afraid was to go back. There were 22,000 who were afraid. Where was their faith? After what they had seen from God, why were they fearful? God said there were still too many people. God had Gideon take the 10,000 who were left to the water to get a drink. Everyone that lapped like a dog was allowed to stay in the fighting party. There were three hundred of them. God told Gideon by the three hundred men that lapped, He would deliver the Midianites into Gideon's hand. The men each took a trumpet and a pitcher with a light in it. When they got to the camp of the Midianites, they blew their trumpets and broke the pitchers they carried in their hands and God set the Midianites against each other and they fled. Other men of Israel pursued them and the battle was won by Israel. Gideon fought other battles, but later in life he made an ephod of gold. The ephod was most likely a garment like the priests wore, but in this case, Israel fell to worshipping it and according to Judges 8:27, it became a snare to Gideon and his house.

How easy it is even today for people to take on some seemingly innocent activity only to find out the end result is a snare to themselves and others. One example is the activities of our children. Many parents want their children to be involved in school and community affairs and events. They even encourage such engagement often without checking into the fine details only to discover the child's drama group practices on Wednesday from five to seven o'clock making it impossible to attend mid-week worship service or the basketball team wears clothing that is not appropriate, or even the music group sings religious songs to the accompaniment of mechanical instrumental music as entertainment for an audience.

Can you see how the problems come about all so innocently? By the time an unknowing parent finds out the details, it can be very painful to tell the child he or she can no longer be part of the group. It is much better to have taught our children about the Lord and His expectations so that they are not upset when earthly schedules conflict with the Lord's work. They know which to choose. I once had a young lady in my

Bible class who although she was not a Christian, when she was given the opportunity for a class at school which would have given her an advantage but was only offered on Wednesday night, she told the teacher she would not be attending because doing God's will was more important. Don't we all wish for such teenagers?

The next seven judges, Abimelech, Tola, Jair, Jephthah, Ibzan, Elon, and Abdon, continued in the same manner to deliver God's people. Jephthah is remembered because of the foolish promise he made if God would deliver the Ammonites by his hand he would sacrifice whatever came out of his house first upon his return from battle. His daughter came out first to meet him, and he kept his vow according to Judges 11:39.

After Abdon, the children of Israel did evil again and God delivered them to the Philistines for forty years. An angel of the Lord appeared to Manoah's wife who was barren and told her she was to conceive and bear a son. He was to be a Nazarite unto God and no razor was to come on his head. According to Judges 13:5, he would begin to deliver Israel out of the hand of the Philistines. The woman told her husband who asked God to send the angel to talk to him. God sent the angel back to Manoah's wife and she ran and got Manoah. The angel told Manoah the same things he had told Manoah's wife. After the angel left, Manoah was afraid and he told his wife they were going to die because they had seen God. Now why would God do such to them and why would Manoah even think it was going to happen? The woman, in this case, just like the case of Deborah, had the good sense. She told Manoah if God had been going to kill them, He would not have showed them what was going to happen with the birth.

The son born to Manoah and his wife was Sampson who grew up to be one of the most famous judges. In Judges 14, Sampson took his mom and dad to Timnath of the Philistines to get him a wife. His mom and dad were not happy he was getting a wife of the Philistines, but they did not know the plan was from God as noted in verse 4. On the trip down, Sampson killed a lion but he did not tell his parents. Then on another trip with them, he found honey in the body of the dead lion and gave some to his parents to eat. Sampson made a marriage feast and he put a riddle to thirty men. The riddle as recorded in Judges 14:14 was: "Out of the eater came forth meat, and out of the strong came forth sweetness." They had the seven days of the feast to figure out the answer. When they could not figure it out, they told his wife if she did not get the answer for them, they would burn her and her father's house. She got the answer out of Sampson by crying and telling him he hated her. Can't you just see this picture?

When the men answered the riddle, Sampson had to come up with thirty changes of garment because that was the deal. If they got it right, he had to give them thirty sheets and thirty change of garments but if they did not get it right, they had to give Sampson thirty sheets and thirty changes of garments. The Spirit of the Lord came upon Sampson and he went out and killed thirty men at Ashkelon and brought the garments to the men. Sampson was mad so he went back home and his wife was given to another man. In Judges 15, Sampson appeared to be over his mad spell and he went back to get his wife. But her father told him he had given her to Sampson's friend and Sampson could have her sister. Sampson caught three hundred foxes and tied them together by their tails with fire between them. He let them go in the standing corn of the Philistines and burned up their corn, vineyards, and olives. The Philistines were mad and they retaliated by burning Sampson's wife and father.

Sampson continued to fight the Philistines and then he went to the area where Judah was settled at the top of Rock Etam. The Philistines came to Judah and wanted Sampson. The men of Judah went to the top of Etam and told Sampson they had come to bind him and deliver him to the Philistines. Sampson let them bind him and he went with the Philistines for a distance and then the Spirit of the Lord came upon him and he broke loose, found a jawbone of an ass, and slew 1,000 men (Judges 15:16).

In later years, Sampson became involved with Delilah which finally ended in his death as recorded in Judges 16. The Philistines persuaded Delilah to find out where Sampson's strength was. First he told her if he was bound with seven green withs or vine tendrils he would lose his strength. When that failed and she asked him again, he said if he was bound with new ropes that were never used before he would lose his strength. She tried that and it failed. The third time he said if his hair was woven into seven locks he would lose his strength. Again, Delilah reported to the Philistines and they carried out the plan but Sampson's strength remained. Finally, after Delilah continued to cry and beg, he told her a razor had never come on his head and if his hair was cut, he would lose his strength. He went to sleep and Delilah had a man cut his hair. When Sampson awoke, he had no idea the Lord had departed from him. His strength was gone.

The Philistines took Sampson and put out his eyes and put him to work grinding in a prison house. His hair grew back and on a certain day when the Philistines had come together to offer sacrifice to their god, Dagon, they had Sampson called out of the prison so they could make fun of him. He was set between the pillars the house was standing on. He took hold of the two middle pillars and pulled the house down killing himself and the Philistines gathered there for the sacrifice.

In Judges 17:6 it is recorded "In those days there was no king in Israel, but every man did that which was right in his own eyes." According to Psalm 47:7 "For God is the King of all the earth..." If the fathers had done as they were commanded to do earlier and taught their children about God, King of all the earth, there would have been a king in Israel. Instead, not only did the people not recognize God as their king, they refused to obey the judges God had put in charge. This same discouraging statement is presented again in Judges 18:1, 19:1, and 21:25. There was no king in Israel. Thus ends the book of Judges. The account of the final judges begins in 1st Samuel Chapter 1. Here another barren wife, Hannah, was loved so much by her husband, Elkanah. In this chapter, it is recorded Elkanah and Hannah had gone up to Shiloh for the yearly offering and Hannah prayed to the Lord for a son. Eli, the priest who was also according to 1st Samuel 7:15 the judge in Israel, saw her lips moving but heard no sound. He accused her of being drunk in 1st Samuel 1:14, but Hannah told him she was not drunk but had poured her soul out to the Lord. Eli told her to go in peace and the God of Israel would grant her petition. Hannah had asked God for a male child and she had promised God if He gave her a child, she would return the child to God for all of his life.

Hannah conceived and when the child, Samuel, was weaned, Hannah took him to the yearly sacrifice and presented him to Eli to work for the Lord. Samuel remained in the house of the Lord and ministered before Eli. Each year, Hannah went up to Shiloh and took the child a coat. As Eli got older, his sons were wicked men, but Samuel continued to grow in the Lord and the people liked him.

According to 1st Samuel 3, the Lord was not giving visions to men as He had done in the past. But on a certain night, the Lord called Samuel. Samuel thought it was Eli and he went to him to see what he wanted. Eli told him he had not called him. This happened again a second and third time. On the third time, Eli realized it was God calling Samuel so he told him to go and lie down and if he heard the call again he was to say (1st Samuel 3:9), "Speak, Lord; for thy servant heareth." Samuel did as Eli had told him to do and the Lord appeared again, this time with a message. God told Samuel that Eli's house was going to fall because of the wickedness of Eli's sons. The next morning when Eli asked what the message was, Samuel told him everything. Eli said (verse 18), "It is the Lord: let him do what seemeth him good."

Samuel continued to grow in the Lord and the Lord was again in Shiloh. In 1st Samuel 3:21 the statement is: "And the Lord appeared again in Shiloh: for the Lord revealed himself to Samuel in Shiloh by the word of the Lord." But in Chapter 4, the Israelites were badly beaten by the Philistines. Even the ark of God was taken and Eli's sons were killed. When Eli found out about the ark of God being taken, he fell off of his seat backwards and died. He was ninety-eight years old and had judged Israel for forty years. The Philistines only kept the ark of the Lord for seven months, because of the many misfortunes that befell them from the destruction of their idol, Dagon, to the people being smitten with emerods, and mice marring the land. The Philistines put the ark on a new cart and put offerings inside of it and hooked two cows to it to pull it home. The cows took the ark straight to Bethshemesh and the Philistines knew the act was from God. While the ark was in Bethshemesh, some of the men looked into it and God smote 50,070 men because of it. The people of Bethshemesh sent word to the people of Kirathjearim also known as Baale-judah to come and get the ark.

The people of Kirathjearim took the ark to the house of Abinadab and sanctified Eleazar to keep the ark of the Lord. It remained there for twenty years. Samuel, who was then the judge of Israel told the people if they would return to God with all their hearts and put away the strange gods from among them and prepare their hearts to the Lord and serve Him only, God would deliver them from the Philistines. The people agreed and a fight with the Philistines soon occurred. God thundered with a great thunder upon the Philistines and they were smitten before Israel. Samuel set up a stone between Mizpeh and Shen where the battle had taken place and called it Ebenezer which means hitherto hath the Lord helped us.

Many of you may have sung the song O, Thou Fount of Every Blessing that has the words, "Here I'll raise my Ebenezer." Did you ever consider from where that phrase may have come and what it means? The author of the song, Robert Robinson, in the next sentence of the second verse of the song wrote, "Hither by Thy help I'm come." Thus when you raise your Ebenezer, you are acknowledging the help God has given you in your life. It is always important that we know what the words in the songs we sing mean. Why does it matter? It matters because we could be singing in an unscriptural manner or an unscriptural song. We will look more at this in the New Testament section of this book, but for now, give some thought to the songs you sing and teach to others. Make sure you can explain what they mean if anyone should ask you.

When Samuel aged, he made his sons Joel and Abiah judges over Israel, but his sons, like Eli's sons before him, were evil. The elders of Israel went to Samuel and told him they wanted a king to judge them like the other nations. Samuel was not happy with this request, but according to 1st Samuel 8:7, God told him to go ahead and give them a king because they were not rejecting Samuel but they were rejecting God as they did not want Him to reign over them. God told Samuel to protest solemnly to the people and show them the manner of king who would reign over them. Samuel told the people what kind of king they would have and in 1 Samuel 8:18, he told them they would cry to the Lord because of their king but the Lord would not answer.

In 1st Samuel 9, a young man by the name of Saul was out looking for his father's mules. When he and the servant could not find the mules, the servant suggested they go and see the seer or prophet, Samuel. They did and Samuel was waiting for them because God had told him they were coming. Samuel was to anoint Saul as the first king of Israel. Samuel told Saul and the servant the mules had been found and the next day he would tell Saul something. At the appointed time,

Samuel told Saul to send the servant on and Samuel took oil and poured it upon Saul's head and anointed him to be the king. He told Saul the Spirit of the Lord would come upon him and he would prophesy and be tuned into another man.

As Saul began his reign, in 1st Samuel 12, Samuel again warned the people about how they should live and serve God. He told them in verse 14 if they would serve God and obey His voice, it would be good for them but if they rebelled against the commandments of the Lord, His hand would be against them. God then sent thunder and rain upon their wheat harvest to show them how wicked they had been. The people wanted Samuel to pray for them and he did. Then he told them he would teach them the good and the right way but they needed to fear the Lord and serve Him with all their hearts.

When Saul had reigned two years, he went after the Philistines. In 1st Samuel 13, Saul was supposed to be waiting at Gilgal for Samuel to come but when Samuel was late, Saul took it upon himself to offer a burnt offering. As soon as he had made the offering Samuel came. Samuel was not happy with what Saul had done in making the offering. What was wrong with Saul offering this offering? We are not really told here in this passage, but we know the offerings were to be done by the priest. Saul was a king and not a priest. Was Saul trying to make himself equal to God's priest? How did Saul react to Samuel when Samuel asked him what he had done? Was he repentant? No, instead he tried to blame Samuel. Saul accused

Samuel in 1st Samuel 13:11 of not coming to him at the planned time. In verse 12, Saul indicated he forced himself to make the offering. Why did he have to force himself? Was it he knew he should not be making the offering? We may not have answers to the questions, but here again is an example of a man going beyond what God commanded and getting himself into trouble. Samuel told Saul he had done foolishly in not keeping the commandment of the Lord God and now God would take the kingdom from Saul and give it to a man after God's own heart.

In Chapter 14 of 1st Samuel, Saul's son, Jonathan wanted to go over to the Philistine camp and see what was happening there. He told his armor bearer God might work for them and they might be able to take the Philistines. Sure enough, God gave Jonathan the battle and saved Israel from the Philistines. While Jonathan was gone, Saul had commanded the people not to eat anything until evening, but Jonathan not knowing of the order had eaten honey along the way. When Saul found out what Jonathan had done, he was prepared to kill him, but the people rescued Jonathan.

Continuing through 1st Samuel, Saul and his army kept fighting the battles the Lord commanded. In Chapter 15, God told King Saul through Samuel to go smite the Amalekites and to utterly destroy all they had. Saul was to destroy everything. Saul and his men fought the battle and smote the Amalekites, but he took Agag the king alive along with the best of the sheep, oxen, fatlings, lambs, and all that was good. Everything considered vile, he destroyed. It sounds like Saul did a pretty good job until you really think about what God said in relation to what Saul did. God said in verse 3, "...utterly destroy all that they have, and spare them not."

God sent Samuel back to Saul with a message. When Samuel got to Saul, Saul told him, "I have performed the commandment of the Lord." Did he really think he had done what God said? In 1st Samuel 15:14 Samuel asked Saul what the bleating of the sheep and the lowing of the oxen meant if he had done what God commanded. Saul told Samuel the people spared the best to sacrifice to God but the rest they had utterly destroyed. What Samuel said in verses 22-23 is just as appropriate today as it was when Samuel said it. "Hath the Lord as great delight in burnt offerings and sacrifices, as in obeying the voice of the Lord? Behold, to obey is better than sacrifice, and to hearken than the fat of rams. For rebellion is as the sin of witchcraft, and stubbornness is as iniquity and idolatry."

At this point, Samuel told Saul because he had rejected God, God had rejected him from being king. Finally, Saul admitted he had sinned and transgressed God's commandments. He said it was because he was afraid of the people and he obeyed their voice. He asked Samuel to pardon his sin and to turn again with him so he could worship God. At first Samuel refused, but then he did turn with him and worshipped God. Afterward, Samuel himself cut King Agag into pieces. Samuel left Saul and did not go to see him again.

In the meantime, God had plans for a new king over Israel. Samuel was still sad and mourning over Saul according to 1st Samuel 16:1, but God told him to go to Jesse the Bethlehemite and anoint a new king. Samuel went to Bethlehem and called Jesse and his sons to the sacrifice. Each of Jesse's sons were called to pass before Samuel but God chose none of them. When one of the sons, Eliab, passed by, Samuel was sure he was the one God had chosen because of his appearance, but God told Samuel not to look at the outward appearance because God looks on the heart. Finally when seven of Jesse's sons had passed by and God had not chosen any of them, Samuel asked Jesse if all of the sons were there. Jesse said the youngest one was keeping the sheep. Samuel told Jesse to send for him. They waited for the final son and when he got there, God told Samuel he was the one and to anoint him. Samuel anointed this son, David, and from then on, the Spirit of the Lord came upon David.

Back at Saul's place, the Spirit of the Lord had departed from Saul and an evil spirit from the Lord troubled him. When the evil spirit troubled him, his servants suggested he find a man who could play on a harp to come and play before him so he would be well. Saul told his servants to find him such a man and they found, of all people, David, the son of Jesse. When Saul met David, he loved him and took him as his armor bearer. When the evil spirit was upon Saul and David played with the harp, Saul was refreshed and the evil spirit departed.

First Samuel 17 has caused some concern among Bible commentators. Lyons (2003) reported some believed it is out of place, some believed the events are in the right order but Saul was just pretending not to realize who David was, while others have said nowhere does the text indicate Saul did not know who David was, but he was asking who his father was so he would be sure to provide tax relief to the right family since in verse 25 there is an indication the house of whoever slew the giant would be free of taxes. Whatever the case may be, the chapter opens with the Philistines gathered in battle against Israel.

Saul and his men were afraid of the champion of the Philistines who happend to be a giant of over nine feet in height named Goliath. In reading the description of Goliath and what he had to say to Saul and his men in 1st Samuel 17:4-10, one can almost picture this tall and large man with his body covered in armor standing over the people. His deep voice can be imagined rumbling through the air and the fear of the Israelites who failed to trust in God is evident.

Not one of Saul's men could stand up to this giant. In 1st Samuel 17:11 the record says they were greatly afraid. Three of Jesse's sons were in the army of Saul and they must have been afraid too because they did nothing to stop the giant. It sounds like in verses 14-15 David had been there at the battle but had returned to feed his father's sheep in Bethlehem. His dad told him to take some food to the camp for his brothers, to see how they were doing, and to bring something back to their father to indicate their safety. David went to his brothers and while he was talking to them, Goliath came out as he had done for forty days and delivered his speech to the army of Saul. All the men of Israel fled when they saw him and David started asking questions. He wanted to know who this uncircumcised Philistine was and why he should defy the armies of the living God.

When David's oldest brother, Eliab, heard David talking to the others about Goliath, he got mad at David and spoke rather meanly to him as recorded in 1st Samuel 17:28. David continued to talk to others about Goliath and when Saul heard what David was saying, he sent for him. David told Saul he would go and take care of this Philistine. Saul told David he was too young to go against this man of war, but David convinced Saul he was able to do so. He told Saul about killing a lion and a bear that were after his father's flock and he would do the same to this uncircumcised Philistine. He said the Lord who had delivered him out of the paw of the lion and the paw of the bear would deliver him out of the hand of this Philistine. Saul gave his permission for David to go forth.

Saul provided his own armor for David, but once he got it on, not being used to such uniform, he told Saul he could not wear it and he took it off. Instead, he took up his staff and got himself five smooth stones out of the brook. He put them in a shepherd's bag and took his sling in his hand. David headed out toward Goliath and when the Philistine looked at him, he was rather insulted to think Saul would send such a youth out to do battle with him. Goliath cursed David by Goliath's gods and told David he would give his flesh to the birds and the beasts. David replied back to Goliath even though he was coming at David with a sword, a spear, and a shield, David was coming to him in the name of the Lord of hosts, the God of the armies of Israel, who Goliath had defiled. David went on in 1st Samuel 17:46 to tell Goliath on this day the Lord would deliver him into David's hand and he would give the carcasses of the host of the Philistines unto the birds and the beast so all the earth would know there was a God in Israel and all the assembly would know the Lord saves not with sword and spear. David said the battle was the Lord's and he ran toward the Philistine army to meet Goliath. David took one stone from his bag and slung it toward the Philistine where it sunk into Goliath's forehead and he fell upon his face to the earth. David then took the Philistine's sword and cut off his head and the Philistines fled.

In 1st Samuel 17:55 is where the question concerning whether Chapter 17 is in the right place comes in. One would think Saul would have known the lad who played for him when an evil spirt came upon him, but Saul enquired of Abner the captain of his host concerning whose son David was. When Abner did not know, Saul told him to find out and in verse 58, David told King Saul he was the son of Jesse the Bethlehemite.

We learn in 1st Samuel 18 that beginning then, Saul did not let David go back to his father's house but kept him with him.

Saul's son, Jonathan, loved David as his own soul. He loved him so much, he gave David his own robe, sword, bow, and girdle. David did whatever Saul wanted him to do and Saul set him over the men of war. But trouble was brewing for David because the people began to honor David above Saul with the women saying Saul had slain his thousands and David his ten thousands. Saul was not happy with this turn of events and when the evil spirit came upon him the next time, and David played the harp, Saul cast the javelin at him. David dodged the javelin twice. Saul realized the Lord had departed from him and was now with David and Saul was afraid.

Saul gave David his daughter Michal to wife in exchange for the foreskins of two hundred Philistine men. The required dowry was only one hundred, but David killed two hundred men and delivered to the king (1st Samuel 18:27). Saul realized David would eventually take his place. He told Jonathan and his servants they should kill David, but Jonathan told David to go hide and he would bring him word. Jonathan talked to Saul and Saul agreed not to harm David. David fought another battle against the Philistines and they again fled. Once more, the evil spirit of the Lord came upon Saul and he tried to kill David. David fled and his wife bought him some time by tricking the men who were looking for him into thinking he was in bed sick (1st Samuel 19).

The conflict between Saul and David continued and on at least two occasions, David had an excellent opportunity to kill Saul, but David refused to harm God's anointed. One of the times as recorded in 1st Samuel 24, David was in a cave and Saul did not know it. Saul went in and David cut off the skirt of his robe. Saul did not know David had cut off his robe and he left the cave and went on his way. David went out after him and called to him and told him how God had delivered Saul unto David but he would not put forth his hand against Saul because he was the Lord's anointed. He showed Saul the skirt of his robe David had cut off and he told Saul the Lord was the judge between him and Saul. Saul actually called David his son in verse 16 and he lifted up his voice and wept. Saul told David in verse 20 he knew David would be the new king and the kingdom of Israel would be established in his hand.

Even though Saul promised no harm to David, he continued to plan evil for him. The second occasion where David could have killed him is recorded in 1st Samuel 26. Saul and his men were sleeping in camp. Abner should have been watching out for the king but he too was asleep. David and one of his men, Abishai, went to the camp and Abishai wanted to kill Saul. David refused but instead he told Abishai to take the spear and the cruse of water from beside Saul. He did and they left and once they got to the other side of the hill, David called out to Saul and his men. He asked Abner where the king's spear and the water were. Saul recognized David's voice and he again called David his son and promised him he would no more try to do him harm because David had saved him from harm. According to 1st Samuel 27:4, Saul did not look for David any more.

But back in 1st Samuel 25 we have another interesting account of something happening to David. First, in verse 1 is the account of Samuel's death. After his death, David went to the wilderness of Paran where Nabal, a very rich man lived. It appears from verses 14-16 David and his army had at some point offered protection to Nabal's shepherds and now David was asking for a favor in return. In verse 8, David told his ten men they were to ask Nabal for some food. Nabal, rich as he was, must have been like some of today who are rich but have no intent of sharing. He refused to give the men anything and would not even acknowledge the good David and his men had done for him. When the men returned to David, David prepared for battle with Nabal, but one of Nabal's men told Nabal's wife, Abigail, what had happened and in her wisdom, she prepared a great feast for David and his men. She delivered the feast with her servants, but she did not tell her husband. When she delivered the food, she asked David when the Lord had dealt well with him to remember her. Abigail left and went back home. When she got home Nabal was drunk so she did not tell him anything until the next morning. When she told him what she had done, his heart died within him and he became as a stone according to verse 37. Then about ten days later, he died. When David heard of his death, he sent and took Abigail as his wife. Saul had given Michal, David's wife to another man.

In 1st Samuel 28, the Philistines were again getting ready to fight against Israel. Samuel had been dead for a while and God would not answer Saul when he enquired of Him. Saul had previously had all of the wizards and mediums removed from the land, but from the account in Chapter 28, Saul was desperate. When his servants told him of a medium in Endor, Saul disguised himself and went to her. When he asked her if she could bring up someone from the dead she told him if she did she would be in great trouble due to what Saul would do. She obviously did not know she was talking to Saul. Saul swore to her she would not come to any trouble so she asked who he wanted her to bring up. He told her Samuel and when she saw Samuel, she realized it was King Saul in her presence.

Samuel spoke to Saul and asked him why he had bothered him. Saul told Samuel how God would no longer answer him and he needed so badly to know what to do about the Philistines. Samuel asked Saul why he would even think of asking Samuel since God had left Saul and was become his enemy. Samuel told Saul because he had disobeyed God in not executing fierce wrath upon Amalek, God had rent the kingdom from Saul and given it to David. He also informed Saul the very next day God would deliver Israel along with Saul into the hand of the Philistines and Saul and his sons would be with Samuel.

The very next day, the Philistines went against Israel and in the fight Saul was wounded. When his armor bearer would not kill him, he took a sword and fell upon it. His armor bearer did the same and Saul's three sons were killed in the battle. According to 1st Chronicles 10:13, Saul died because of his sins against the Lord and for asking counsel of one with a familiar spirit.

Meanwhile, David who had been living in the Philistine's land was going to have to go into the battle on the side of the Philistines, but thankfully, some of the princes of the Philistines who knew David had previously been involved in killing many Philistines insisted he not be allowed to go to the battle. David and his men were returning to Ziklag but when they got there they found the Amalekites had invaded and taken captives including David's two wives. David's men were ready to turn on him, but David did what we should all do when disaster strikes in that he consulted God. Upon God's answer, David and his men went after the invaders, recovered all that was taken from Ziklag, and took much additional spoil. They took so much spoil David was able to send an abundance to Judah and particularly to Hebron which later was his capital when he became king which happened in just a few days.

Second Samuel begins with David being told of the death of Saul. In Chapter 2, David asked God if he should go up and God told him to go up to Hebron. David took his wives and did as God told him to. There were battles between David's house and Saul's house, but after the death of Saul's son, Ishbosheth, it is recorded in Chapter 5 all the elders of Israel came to Hebron to David and anointed him as king over Israel.

In 2nd Samuel 6, David set out to retrieve the Ark of God or the Ark of the Covenant from the house of Abinadab in Kirjathjearim where it was left back in 1st Samuel. Remember, the Ark was to be moved only by the priests carrying it on poles. David and his men loaded it upon a cart and when the oxen shook the cart, Uzzah put forth his hand to steady it and God immediately smote him. David was unhappy because God had killed Uzzah, but if David had moved the ark like he was supposed to, it would not have happened. According to 1st Chronicles 13:12, maybe David really did not know how he was supposed to carry the Ark since he was afraid of God and was asking how was he going to bring the Ark home. Yet, if he had been doing what he was supposed to do, he would have known the law of God. Remember the earlier command for the king to copy the law of God and read it. How often today does God get blamed when someone ends up hurt because of some sin he or she committed?

David left the Ark at the house of Obededom, the Gittite for three months, but when David was told the Lord had blessed the house of Obededom because of the Ark, David had it brought up. This time he did it right for In 1st Chronicles 15:2 David was reported as saying only the tribe of Levi could carry the Ark. Once it was delivered to the tent David had set up for it, David thanked God with a psalm. The psalm is recorded in 1st Chronicles 16:8-36. In the psalm, in verse 13, David called Israel God's chosen ones. He told the people to always be mindful of God's word and of the covenant He made with Abraham, Isaac, and Jacob.

In 2nd Samuel 7, David had peace. God had granted him rest so David was ready to do something for God. David told the prophet of that day, Nathan, he wanted to build God a house. Nathan told him to go ahead and the Lord was with him, but that night, the word of the Lord came to Nathan and told him to go and tell David something else. The Lord said for Nathan to tell David the Lord had not dwelt in any house since the time He brought the children out of Egypt and He was the one who had brought David to where he was. In verse 16 the Lord said David's house and kingdom would be established for ever and in verse 12 He said once David's days were fulfilled He would set up his seed after him and establish his kingdom. According to 1st Chronicles 17:12-14, God went on to say David's son would build the Lord a house and the Lord would establish His throne forever. God said He would be this king's father and this king would be His son. God said He would not take His mercy away from this king. Little did David understand while this promise would be fulfilled physically on earth through David's earthly son, it would be fulfilled years later spiritually through his descendent, Jesus Christ.

While David was a man after God's own heart according to 1st Samuel 13:14, he was not a perfect man. We find in 2nd Samuel 11 how David let lust get the best of him when he saw Bathsheba bathing herself. After finding out she had become pregnant through their union, David found a way to put her husband, Uriah, the Hittite, on the front line of battle where he was killed. Then he took Bathsheba for his wife. According to 2nd Samuel 11:27, this displeased the Lord who sent Nathan to David with a parable.

Recorded in 2nd Samuel 28, Nathan told David about the rich man with many herds who when a traveler came by and the rich man wanted to entertain him with food, instead of killing one of his own, he sent and got the one little lamb a poor man had and used it for the meal. David was furious with the rich man and said he should restore the lamb fourfold because he had done such a thing with no pity. When Nathan told David he was the man and God had given him everything but in turn David had taken the wife of Uriah for his own David immediately acknowledged his sin. David said he had sinned against the Lord. David's heart was what made him a man after God's own heart. We too must have a tender heart and be repentant when we realize we have sinned. We must be willing to acknowledge our frailty and ask God to forgive us when we sin. In Psalm 51 David acknowledged his transgression and asked God to wash him from his iniquity.

God promised David the sword would never depart from his house. In addition, Bathsheba's child once born was very sick and on the seventh day he died. While the child was living, David fasted and prayed but when he received word the child was dead, according to 2nd Samuel 12, he arose, changed his clothes, went to the house of the Lord and worshipped, and ate. The people could not understand this behavior, but David explained while the child was alive there was a chance God would allow him to live, but once he was dead he could not return to David, but someday David would go to him. What a lesson for us on the death of our loved ones.

Just as God promised, the sword was always present in David's house (2nd Samuel 12:10). Another son Absalom had a sister, Tamar (2nd Samuel 13), who another son, Amnon, loved. He tricked her into bringing him food and when she did, he had sex with her. Absalom did nothing at the time but he was very angry to the point he hated Amnon. Two years later, Absalom worked out a plan and killed Amnon but then Absalom could not go back home to David. David longed to go to him but would not. Eventually David did call for Absalom to come to his own home but he was not to see King David. Absalom stayed in Jerusalem for two years and after he set David's servant Joab's field on fire because Joab would not come to Absalom, David consented to see Absalom.

Absalom began to scheme to take the kingdom from David. When anyone had a problem for the king, Absalom met them and told them there was no one to hear their case but if he were judge of the land, he would do them justice. Eventually Absalom had many followers and by the time David realized the situation, it was almost too late. A messenger went to David and told him what Absalom was doing. The king prepared himself and his men for battle but even as the soldiers were going out after Absalom and his men, David commanded his leaders to deal gently with Absalom. Absalom was riding upon a mule in the battle and when he went under a great oak, his head caught hold of the oak and he was taken up between heaven and earth according to 2nd Samuel 18:9. There, Joab, one of David's men, killed Absalom. When David found out what had happened, he cried, "O my son Absalom, my son, my son Absalom! Would God I had died for thee, O Absalom, my son, my son!" Does this ending remind you of how we sometimes react to the death of a person even when we know the person was in the wrong and was responsible for his or her own death? It does not seem to matter how evil one is, love covers a multitude of sins and even seems to cause us to forget the evil done to us by others.

David continued to have wars until the end of his reign. When his death drew near as recorded in 1st Kings 1, he could not get warm. His servants found a very beautiful virgin, Abishag, who they brought in to minister to David. David was not intimate with her. During this time, Adonijah, David's son by one of his wives, Haggith, decided he would be the next king.

David had already promised Bathsheba her son Solomon who was born after their first baby died, would be king in David's place. When David found out what Adonijah had planned, he called Zadok the priest and Nathan the prophet and had them anoint Solomon. When Adonijah found out Solomon had been crowned as king, he was afraid and caught hold to the horns of the altar for safety. Solomon said if Adonijah showed himself to be a worthy man, he would not harm him but if he was wicked, he would die. Adonijah went to Solomon and bowed himself and Solomon told him to go to his own house.

Before David's death, he gave orders to Solomon. Recorded in 1st Kings 2, David told Solomon to keep the charge of God by walking in His ways and keeping His statutes, commandments, judgments, and testimonies as written in the Law of Moses. He told Solomon to do God's will so the promise God had made to David that the king of Israel would always be a man from David's family, if his children would walk before God in truth, would be fulfilled. David instructed Solomon to get rid of Joab because he had killed two captains of the host of Israel and to kill Shimei because of his curse to David. In addition, David gave Solomon complete directions for building the temple as recorded in 1st Chronicles 28.

During David's lifetime, he wrote many of the Psalms. While there are 150 Psalms, at least seventy-three are attributed to David. In some of these Psalms, David showed his love for God and his dependence upon God as in Psalm 63. In many of the Psalms David offered thanks to God for blessings and sometimes he asked for deliverance as in Psalm 4 where David asked God to hear him when he called upon Him and at the end he indicated a sense of satisfaction his prayer would be answered as he said he would lie down in peace knowing the Lord made him dwell in safety. In Psalm 51, David asked God to forgive him of his transgressions. In verse 4, David said it was against God he had sinned when he went in to Bathsheba. If we today would consider when we sin it is against God, would we be less likely to go astray?

The shortest Psalm which is also the shortest chapter in the Bible is Psalm 117 which has only 2 verses and it is a praise to God. In the next psalm, Psalm 118:22 was given a prophecy concerning the coming Christ and His church. This verse says: "The stone which the builders refused is become the head stone of the corner." Then the longest psalm is Psalm 119 with 176 verses which was mentioned in Chapter 1 of this book.

After David died, Adonijah persuaded Bathsheba to ask Solomon for Abishag, for his own wife. This was another attempt to prove Adonijah had a right to the throne. Bathsheba asked Solomon and his response was to send Benaiah to kill Adonijah. Around the same time, Solomon took care of killing Joab and three years later when Shimei left the area where Solomon had told him he could live and be safe, Solomon had him killed. Abiathar a descendent from Eli's family was cast out from being priest in fulfillment of the 1st Samuel 2:31 prophecy the priestly line of Eli would end.

Recorded in 1st Kings 3, Solomon loved the Lord and walked in the statutes of his father David. Solomon realized he had a big job to do and when God asked him in a dream what he wanted God to do for him, Solomon told God he was as a little child (verse 7) and he did not know how to go out or come in. Solomon asked God in verse 9 for an understanding heart to judge the people and to discern between good and bad. It is recorded in 2nd Chronicles 1:10 he asked God for wisdom and knowledge so he could come in and go out before the people and judge them. God was pleased with this request and in 1st Kings 3:11-14 God promised Solomon a wise and understanding heart and in addition because he had asked only for wisdom, God said He was giving him riches and honor. God told him if he would walk in God's ways and keep his laws as David had done, He would also give him a long life.

When Solomon went up to Jerusalem to make his offerings, he had his first recorded opportunity to use the wisdom God had given him. Two women came to him with an awful story. The two women were harlots and both had a child, three days apart. According to the woman telling the story, the other woman's child died in the night so that woman took the live baby of the woman telling the story and claimed him as her own. Of course, the other woman said the story was not true and the live child was hers. Solomon asked for a sword and made as if he would have the live child divided into two parts with a part for each woman. The woman to whom the child belonged told the king not to kill the baby but to give him to the other woman. The other woman said to divide the child. Solomon knew then whose child the baby was. When the people of Israel heard of the king's judgment they saw the wisdom of God in him and they feared the king.

When Solomon had peace and rest on every side, he contracted with Hiram the King of Tyre to provide the cedar trees so Solomon could build the temple his father David had wanted to build for God. According to 1st Kings 5:5, God had authorized the building of this house. The building of the temple is recorded in 1st Kings 5-6 and in 2nd Chronicles 3-4. It took seven years to build and based upon the description provided, it must have been a beautiful building. Then in 1st Kings 6:12-13, God promised Solomon if he would walk in God's statutes and execute His judgments, and keep all of His commandments God would dwell among the children of Israel and not forsake them. It is so important to notice the little word "if" upon which the whole promise to Solomon was dependent.

Once the temple was complete, Solomon had the Ark of the Covenant placed inside in the most holy place. Inside the ark were the two tables of stone Moses had placed there at Horeb when God made the covenant with the children of Israel. Solomon had a great sacrificial service in which he dedicated the temple to God. In his dedication prayer to God recorded in

1st Kings 8:23-53 and 2nd Chronicles 6, Solomon asked God to keep His eye toward the temple day and night. He asked God to continue to forgive the people when they sinned. He asked for deliverance from their enemies. Solomon realized his dependence upon God and he was very humble in his petition.

After Solomon's humble prayer, God came to him and told him He had heard his prayer and had hallowed the house Solomon had built to put His name there forever. In addition, God told Solomon if he walked before Him as David had done in the integrity of his heart and in uprightness to do all God had commanded in keeping His laws and judgments then God would establish the throne of his kingdom upon Israel forever like He promised David. But God said if Solomon or his children turned from God and served other gods and worshipped them, then God would cut off Israel out of the land He had given them and the house He had hallowed for His name would be cast out of His sight. In addition, Israel would be a proverb and a byword among all people who would be astonished when they saw what had happened to the temple (1st Kings 9:2-9). Keep these verses in mind because they are so important as we look later at what happened when the nation of Israel forgot God and went about serving idols.

Word of Solomon's riches and wisdom spread across the land. In 1st Kings 10 there is an account of one queen, the Queen of Sheba, who heard about his fame. She went to Solomon herself to see if what she had heard was true. While she was there, Solomon showed her his wealth and answered her questions. In verse 5, once she had seen all of his wealth, there was no more spirit in her. She said his wisdom and prosperity exceeded even what she had heard. She commented on how happy Solomon's servants were and she even blessed Solomon's God who she said delighted in Solomon.

Continuing in Chapter 10 of 1st Kings, beginning in verse 26, Solomon gathered together chariots and horsemen. He had 1,400 chariots, and 12,000 horsemen. He had horses brought out of Egypt. Recall back in Deuteronomy 17:16 the command from God that the king should not multiply to himself horses nor cause the people to return to Egypt to get horses. If the king truly trusted in God for deliverance, there would be no need for these horses for battle.

When 1st Kings 11 began, Solomon was doing exactly what God had said His people would do. Solomon loved many strange women. He had seven hundred wives and three hundred concubines. He had women from many countries including those from Egypt, Moab, Ammon, Edom, Zidon, and Heth. Remember God's previous command to the Israelites if the city was a city of one of the specific nations God named, the Hittites, Amorites, Canaanites, Perizzites, Hivites, and the Jebusites, then, nothing could be left alive. Obviously the Israelites did not keep this command either.

Solomon's failure to keep God's commands led to his downfall. According to 1st Kings 11:3-11, these women turned Solomon's heart to other gods and his heart was not perfect with the Lord as was the heart of David. Solomon even built worship places for these other gods for all of his strange wives and he burned incense and sacrificed to their gods. Can you even imagine how this could happen to a person with the wisdom of Solomon?

God had promised Solomon as long as he continued to obey, God would keep His promise to David that there would always be a son of David on the throne. After Solomon denied God, God was angry with him and told him as recorded in 1st Kings 11:11 because he had not kept God's covenant and statutes, God would rend the kingdom from him and give it to his servant. Because of David though, God said He would not take the kingdom from Solomon but from his son. God said He would give one tribe to Solomon's son for David's sake and for Jerusalem's sake which God had chosen.

God then began to stir up other rulers against Solomon. In addition to these rulers, one of Solomon's own servants Jeroboam who was a mighty man of valor (1st Kings 11:28) turned against Solomon. One day when Jeroboam went out of Jerusalem, the prophet Ahijah went to him in a field where they were alone. Ahijah had on a new garment which he took off and tore into twelve pieces. He told Jeroboam to take ten pieces of the garment which represented the ten tribes that God was giving to Jeroboam. Two tribes, Judah and Benjamin, would be left for Solomon's son Rehoboam. Note Ahijah told Jeroboam in verse 31 he would have ten tribes and in verse 32 the other ruler would have one, but according to 1st Kings 12:21, both Judah and Benjamin followed Solomon's successor, Rehoboam. Since Rehoboam was of the tribe of Judah that tribe would have already been his so God gave him the tribe of Benjamin. In 1st Kings 11:13 God had told Solomon He would give one tribe to his son for Jerusalem's sake which He had chosen. Jerusalem was in the territory of Benjamin according to Judges 1:21. When Solomon knew what was going to happen, he tried to kill Jeroboam, so Jeroboam fled to Egypt.

Like his father David, Solomon was a writer. Much of the book of Proverbs, the book of Ecclesiastes, and the book of Song of Solomon are generally attributed to Solomon. Proverbs is a collection of wisdom sayings to help in dealing with everyday life. There are several passages in Proverbs telling parents how to deal with their children and giving children advice for listening to parents. The last chapter of Proverbs details a godly woman but it is attributed to King Lemuel. Ecclesiastes is a book which shows us how impossible it is to live a full and rich life without God. The preacher, Solomon, told all about his life and how in the end nothing really mattered except fearing God and keeping His commandments (Ecclesiastes 12:13) which is the whole duty of man. The Song of Solomon is usually thought of as a love story about a bride and her husband. The deeper meaning of this book revolves around Israel as God's betrothed bride and the church as the bride of Christ. The book clearly shows the love of God for His people.

With the death of Solomon, God's people were no longer united under one king. They chose to follow two different men with ten tribes going to one and two tribes to the other. Keep in mind, God had promised His people blessings if they followed His commands and punishment if they chose not to.

Chapter 5
God's People Divided

Chapter 11 of 1st Kings ended with Solomon's death and Rehoboam his son reigning. Jeroboam, Solomon's servant who had run away when Solomon tried to kill him, heard of Solomon's death, so he returned to King Rehoboam and on behalf of the people he asked Rehoboam to make things better for the people and if he would, they would serve him. Rehoboam asked the older men who had been with Solomon what they thought and he asked the young men he grew up with what they thought. The old men told him if he would be a servant to the people and speak good to them, they would be his servants forever but the young men told Rehoboam he should tell the people his little finger would be thicker than his father's loins and he would add to their burdens. Rehoboam listened to the younger advisors because it was actually an act of God as part of taking the kingdom from Rehoboam. When Israel saw how they were going to be treated by the new king, they rebelled and followed Jeroboam. When Rehoboam brought together the tribe of Benjamin and the tribe of Judah as recorded in 1st Kings 12:21 to fight against Israel, God spoke to Shemaiah and told him to tell Rehoboam not to go up and fight against Israel because this was from the Lord. They actually listened to Shemaiah and did not have war.

Jeroboam built Shechem in Ephraim as the capital of the northern tribes while Jerusalem remained the capital of the southern tribes of Judah and Benjamin and was the place of worship ordained by God. We learn from 1st Chronicles 9:3 the children of Judah and Benjamin, and the children of Ephraim and Manasseh (Joseph's children) lived in Jerusalem. Jeroboam was afraid with the temple in Jerusalem, and the people being required to go there for sacrifices, the people might turn again to Rehoboam, so he made them two other places to worship. He set up golden calves in Dan and Bethel. He installed priests who were not of the house of Levi. He established feasts like the ones God had authorized. In 1st Kings 12:33 is the sad statement concerning Jeroboam's worship: "…which he had devised of his own heart." How often today we find religious people who have devised worship of their own heart. Remember God's command back in Deuteronomy 4:2 not to add to His commands. Jeroboam is another perfect example of an Old Testament figure who ignored this command.

  In 1st Kings 13, a man of God came out of Judah to the place where Jeroboam offered at Bethel and he prophesied a child would be born of the house of David by the name of Josiah and he would offer the priests of the high places upon this very altar where Jeroboam was making his offering. The prophet promised the sign would be the altar would be rent and the ashes poured out. When Jeroboam put forth his hand toward the prophet, the hand dried up, the altar was rent and the ashes poured out from the altar just like the prophet had said. Jeroboam asked the man to pray for him so his hand would be restored. The man prayed and the hand was restored. Jeroboam did not turn from his evil ways but continued the same religion which he had devised of his own heart.

This man of God who prophesied against the altar had been instructed by God not to eat bread or drink water in that place. There was an old prophet in Bethel and when he heard from his sons what had been done in Bethel by the man of God, he rode after him and when he found him, he told him to come on home with him and eat bread. When the man of God told him he could not return with him nor eat with him because of what God had commanded him, the old prophet lied to him and told him an angel had spoken to him by the word of the Lord telling him to go and get this man and bring him to his house to eat and drink. The man of God believed the lie and as a result of his failing to obey God, while he was eating with the old prophet, the word of the Lord came unto the old prophet and he told the man from Judah because he had disobeyed God and not kept His commandment his carcass would not be buried with his fathers.

Sure enough, when the prophet from Judah headed home, a lion slew him and his carcass was cast in the road where a lion and donkey stood by it. The old prophet heard about it and went and took the body and buried it in his own grave. The death of this prophet who listened to another prophet and believed him may seem so harsh to us. But remember, the prophet from Judah had the word from God and he rejected it. Looking at today's situations, something similar could easily happen when we listen to a preacher and truly believe he is telling us the truth even though it seems contrary to what we already know. Only by diligent study will we know the truth and be able to distinguish it from something sounding so good to our ears.

Jeroboam's son became sick and Jeroboam had his wife disguise herself and go to Shiloh where Ahijah, the prophet who had told Jeroboam he would be king, was living and to ask him what would happen to the child. Ahijah was old and could not see, but God told him Jeroboam's wife was coming in disguise to ask about the son. When Ahijah heard Jeroboam's wife coming, he called to her as the wife of Jeroboam and asked her why she was pretending to be someone else. He told her he had heavy tidings. He told her to go back and tell Jeroboam God had exalted him among the people and made him prince over Israel but since he had done evil even above those before him God was going to bring evil upon his house. Because Jeroboam had made other gods and images and caused Israel to sin as recorded in 1st Kings 14:16, God was giving Israel up. Ahijah also told Jeroboam's wife when her feet entered the city of her house, the child would die. Just as Ahijah said, when she entered the city, the child died.

According to 1st Kings 14:30, there was war between Rehoboam and Jeroboam all of their days. When Rehoboam died, his son Abijam became king and there was continued war between him and Jeroboam. Abijam continued in the sins of his father Rehoboam. When Abijam died, his son Asa became king over Judah and he did what was right in the eyes of the Lord like David had done. He removed the idols his father and grandfather had created. He even removed his mother from being queen because she had made an idol in a grove. These groves were places where idol worship took place. He did not remove the high places though. The wars continued between Israel (the ten tribes) and Judah (the two tribes). There was not another king over the ten tribes noted as "doing what was right" in Israel. In Judah, there were some kings over the two tribes who did right and some who did not do right. The rest of 1st Kings contains an account of the reign of these kings including the wickedness and once in a while acts of goodness of these kings.

In 1st Kings 16 during Asa's thirty-eighth year of reigning over Judah (verse 29) and after several other kings had reigned over Israel, Ahab became the king of Israel. According to verse 30, Ahab did evil above all the kings that were before him. We find in verse 31 Ahab took Jezebel for his wife. Because of her, Ahab began to serve Baal. In 1st Kings 17:1, another famous prophet of God, Elijah, warned Ahab there would be no dew or rain.

God sent Elijah to the brook of Cherith to hide out and the ravens brought him bread and flesh both morning and evening and he drank from the brook. When the brook dried up because of the lack of rain, God told him to go to Zarephath where God had commanded a widow there to take care of him. Elijah went to the city and a widow woman was there gathering sticks. He asked her for a little water to drink and a morsel of bread. She told him she did not have anything but a handful of meal and a little oil and she was gathering two sticks so she could fix the bread for her and her son and then they would die. Elijah told her not to fear but to go make him a cake first and then to make one for her and her son. He told her the barrel of meal and the cruse of oil would not run out until God sent rain. She believed him and did what he said. Neither the meal nor the oil ran out.

The woman's son became ill and there was no breath left in him. The woman asked Elijah if he had come to call her sin to remembrance and slay her son. Elijah took the boy and carried him up to the loft where he had been living and laid him upon the bed. He prayed to God to let the child's soul come to him again after he had stretched himself upon the child three times. God heard his prayer and the child revived. When Elijah gave him back to his mother, she said she knew by this act Elijah was a man of God and the word of the Lord in his mouth was true. One would think from the meal and the oil the woman would have known for a fact Elijah was a man of God.

In 1st Kings 18, three years had passed since Elijah told Ahab there would be no rain and God again sent Elijah to

Ahab. It appears Ahab had been looking for Elijah everywhere because when Elijah told Obadiah to go tell Ahab that Elijah was there, Obadiah was afraid. He asked Elijah what he had done to make Elijah deliver him into the hand of Ahab to slay him. Obadiah said Ahab had looked in every nation and kingdom for Elijah. Obadiah was afraid as soon as he left Elijah to go and tell Ahab Elijah was there, the Spirit of the Lord would take Elijah somewhere else. Obadiah then asked Elijah if he knew about Obadiah hiding one hundred of the Lord's prophets and feeding them thus showing he was on the Lord's side.

Elijah promised Obadiah he would show himself to Ahab (1st Kings 18:15), so Obadiah went to meet Ahab and told him Elijah was there. When Ahab met Elijah, he asked if he was the one troubling Israel. Elijah told him he had not troubled Israel but Ahab and his house had done so by forsaking the commandments of the Lord and following Baalim. Elijah told Ahab to gather the four hundred fifty prophets of Baal and the four hundred prophets of the grove which ate at Jezebel's table and bring them to Mount Carmel. Ahab gathered all the prophets to the mount and Elijah spoke to them. He asked them how long they would continue to halt between two opinions. He told them if the Lord was God then to follow Him but if Baal was God, then follow him. The people could not answer him so Elijah proposed a sacrifice.

Elijah asked for two bulls for the sacrifice (1st Kings 18:23). One was for the prophets of Baal to offer and one was for Elijah to offer. The prophets of Baal cut their bullock into pieces and laid it on the wood with no fire under it. Elijah did the same to the other bull. The prophets of Baal called upon the name of Baal from morning until noon but they got no answer. They leaped upon the altar and they cut themselves and they prophesied until the time of the evening sacrifice but they got no answer. Elijah then called unto the people to come near to where he was. The people came to Elijah where he took twelve stones to represent the twelve tribes of Israel and with those he repaired the torn down altar of the Lord. He made a ditch around the altar which would hold about two measures of seeds or about three gallons of water. He put the wood on the altar along with the cut up bullock and then he had the people fill four barrels with water and pour it on the sacrifice and the wood. He had them do this three times so the water ran around the altar and filled up the ditch he had dug.

Elijah then called upon the God of Abraham, Isaac, and of Israel to hear him so the people would know He was the Lord God. Fire from the Lord fell and consumed the sacrifice, the wood, the stones, and the dust, and licked up the water in the trench. The people fell on their faces and proclaimed God as Lord and God. Elijah told them to take the prophets of Baal and not to let any of them escape. They did so and Elijah took the prophets to the brook of Kishon and killed them. Elijah then told Ahab to get up and eat and drink because rain was coming.

Ahab went to eat and drink but Elijah went to the top of Mount Carmel. He sent his servant toward the sea to look and see what he could see. The servant came back and said there was nothing. Elijah sent him out seven times and on the seventh time, the servant came back and said he saw a little cloud out of the sea like a man's hand. Elijah told the servant to go and tell Ahab to prepare his chariot and leave so the rain would not stop him. Ahab headed back to Jezreel but the hand of the Lord was on Elijah and he ran ahead before Ahab to the entrance of the city.

When Ahab got to his wife, Jezebel, who had previously cut off the prophets of the Lord as recorded back in 1st Kings 18:4, and told her what Elijah had done, she was furious. She sent Elijah a message saying to let the gods kill her if she did not kill Elijah by the next day. Elijah ran away. He left his servant in Beersheba and he went on another day's journey and sat down under a juniper tree where he asked God to let him die. He went to sleep and while he slept an angel told him to arise and eat. He looked and there was a cake on the coals and water at his head. He ate and drank and laid back down. The angel came again and told him to arise and eat because the journey he was about to take was too great for him. He arose and ate and drank and on the strength of the food he made a forty day journey to Mount Horeb where he went into a cave to lodge.

The word of the Lord came to Elijah in the cave as recorded in 1st Kings 19 and asked him what he was doing there (verse 9). Elijah responded he had been serving God while the people of Israel had broken their covenant and torn down God's altars and killed His prophets. He said he was the only one left and now they were trying to kill him too. God told Elijah to go and stand upon the mount before the Lord. Elijah went out and as the Lord passed by him, there was a mighty wind and a great earthquake and then a fire. Then there was a gentle whisper and then a voice asked Elijah again what he was doing there. Elijah repeated his previous answer saying he had been serving God while Israel had broken the covenant and torn down the altars and killed the prophets and were now trying to kill him too. The Lord told him to go back the same way he had come and when he got to the wilderness of Damascus he was to anoint Hazael to be king of Aram, anoint Jehu to be king of Israel, and anoint Elisha to be the replacement for Elijah as God's prophet. God said anyone who escaped Hazael would be killed by Jehu and those who escaped Jehu would be killed by Elisha. God also told Elijah He had 7,000 in Israel who had not bowed unto Baal, so Elijah was not as alone as he thought he was.

Elijah headed back and on the way he found Elisha who was plowing with twelve oxen (1st Kings 19:19). As Elijah passed by Elisha, he cast his mantle upon him. Elisha left the oxen with which he was plowing and ran after Elijah. Elisha told

Elijah to let him go and tell his parents good-bye and then he would follow him. Elisha killed the twelve oxen and used the wood from his plow to build a fire to roast the meat. He gave the meat to the people around him and then followed Elijah for whom he ministered until Elijah's death.

In the meantime, Benhadad, the king of Syria, and some other kings declared war against Samaria (1st Kings 20). Benhadad sent word to Ahab he wanted his silver, gold, wives, and children, in addition to whatever Benhadad's servants wanted from Ahab's possessions. Ahab had agreed to give up the silver, gold, wives, and children, but he called the elders of Israel together and told them Benhadad wanted his own servants to be able to take what they wanted and the elders said no. Ahab sent word to Benhadad saying he would not agree to allow the servants of Benhadad to come and take what they wanted. Benhadad and his servants prepared to attack Ahab, but God intervened and saved Israel from Syria. The servants told Benhadad the gods of the Israelites were gods of the hills but if they were to fight them in the plain, his servants would win. Once again they went into battle, but God again delivered the Syrians into the hands of Israel. They slew 100,000 Syrian footmen in one day. The rest of the Syrians fled into Aphek where a wall fell upon 27,000 of them.

Benhadad's servants told the king to let them go and persuade Ahab to accept a surrender from Benhadad. He agreed and they went to Ahab where they made a covenant as recorded in 1st Kings 20. God was not pleased because Ahab had not killed Benhadad. He sent Ahab word because he had let go out of his hand a man whom God had appointed to utter destruction, Ahab's life would go for Benhadad's life and the Israelites for the Syrians. Ahab went home mad but the problem was of his own making. He refused to do what God wanted done. How often do we see this happening in our own lives when we know what God wants done but people refuse to obey Him?

At home, Ahab wanted something that was not his. He wanted the vineyard of Naboth who was a Jezreelite. Ahab offered Naboth another vineyard or money as payment (1st Kings 21). Naboth refused to give up the inheritance of his fathers and Ahab got mad again. He went home and went to bed where he pouted. He turned his face away and would not eat. Jezebel went to him to find out what was wrong. He told her and she told him not to worry, just be merry, and she would get him the field. She wrote letters in Ahab's name and signed them with his seal and sent them to the elders and nobles who lived around Naboth. She told them to proclaim a fast and set Naboth high among the people. They were to set up two men who would be false witnesses against him who were to say Naboth had blasphemed God and the king. Then they were to carry him out and stone him to death. The evil people did what Jezebel said and Ahab took possession of the vineyard. Then, Elijah came back into the picture.

The word of the Lord came to Elijah and told him to go meet Ahab who was in the vineyard of Naboth where he had gone to possess it (1st Kings 21:18). Elijah was to tell Ahab as he had killed and taken possession so would dogs lick up Ahab's blood in the very place where they licked up Naboth's blood. In addition, Elijah told Ahab dogs would eat Jezebel's body by the wall of Jezreel. Ahab tore his clothes and put sackcloth upon his flesh and fasted. God saw Ahab had humbled himself and even though he had been so sinful in his days, God told Elijah because Ahab had humbled himself before God, He would not bring the evil to pass in Ahab's days but in the days of his sons.

There was peace between Syria and Israel for three years and then Jehoshaphat the King of Judah went down to visit Ahab and while he was there Ahab said to his own servants that Ramoth in Gilead was really theirs and they should go take it from Syria. He asked Jehoshaphat if he would help him. Jehoshaphat told him he would but first they should check for word from the Lord. Ahab called together the prophets and asked if he should go against Ramothgilead. They told him to go because the Lord would deliver into his hand. Jehoshaphat asked if there was a prophet of the Lord other than these four hundred men. Ahab said there was one other one, Micaiah, but Ahab hated him because he did not prophesy good concerning Ahab. Jehoshaphat wanted to hear from Micaiah too, so Ahab called for him. As he was coming the messenger who had gone after him told him what the prophets had said to Ahab and encouraged Micaiah to say the same (1st Kings 22:13). Micaiah said he could only say what the Lord said to him.

When Micaiah arrived where the kings were, he told them to go and prosper for the Lord would deliver Ramothgilead into the hand of the king. Ahab replied to him he wanted to know nothing but what was true in the name of the Lord. Micaiah told him he saw all Israel scattered upon the hills as sheep without a shepherd. Micaiah said he saw the Lord sitting on his throne and all the host of heaven was standing by Him. The Lord asked who would persuade Ahab to go up so he would fall at Ramothgilead. Different ones said different things but there was a spirit who came up and said he would persuade him. The Lord wanted to know how and the spirit promised to become a lying spirit in the mouth of the prophets. One of the other prophets then smote Micaiah on the cheek and asked which way the Spirit of the Lord went from him to speak unto Micaiah. Micaiah told him he would find out on the day he went into the inner chamber to hide himself.

Ahab told the servant to put Micaiah into prison and not let him out until Ahab returned from battle. Micaiah told Ahab if Ahab returned at all then the Lord had not spoken by Micaiah. The two kings went into battle anyway with Ahab disguising himself but Jehoshaphat wearing his kingly garments. The King of Syria had commanded his captains not to fight with anyone except Ahab. When the captains saw Jehoshaphat coming in his chariot, they thought he was Ahab, but as they turned to fight him they realized it was not Ahab so they left off fighting him. Then one of the men drew his bow and randomly shot into the Israelite troops where he hit Ahab and wounded him (1st Kings 22:34). Ahab told his chariot driver to carry him out of the battle because he was wounded. Ahab died at evening and the blood ran out of his wound into the chariot. When they washed the chariot, the dogs licked up his blood like God said would happen.

At Ahab's death, Ahaziah began to reign over the ten tribes while Jehoshaphat continued to reign over Judah. Jehoshaphat made peace with the king of Israel but when Ahaziah wanted to send his men with Jehoshaphat's men in sailing vessels, Jehoshaphat refused. Ahaziah continued to reign in the manner his father Ahab had and was not pleasing to the Lord, while Jehoshaphat did God's will.

Around this time Obadiah prophesied against Edom, the descendants of Israel's brother Esau, because of the way they had treated the Israelites. In this prophecy God promised to bring Edom down. In Obadiah verse 10 a reason for their promised destruction was because of their violence against Jacob.

When the events of 2nd Kings began, Ahaziah had fallen through a lattice and had been seriously injured. He sent his messengers to enquire of Baalzebub, the god of Ekron, concerning whether he would live or die. The angel of the Lord sent Elijah to meet the messengers and ask them why they were going to the god of Ekron instead of the God of Israel. Elijah told them to go and tell Ahaziah he would not get up from the bed but he would die there. When the messengers got back to Ahaziah and told him what the man had told them to say, Ahaziah wanted to know what the man looked like. They described him as a hairy man with a girdle of leather about his loins. Ahaziah knew it was Elijah and he sent a captain and fifty men to get him. When the captain got there, he called to Elijah and told him the king had said for him to come down. Elijah answered him and said if Elijah was a man of God, then let fire come down from heaven and consume the captain and his men. It did. So the king sent another captain and fifty men with the same message. Elijah responded with the same response and fire came down and consumed them. The king sent a third captain with fifty men, but this captain fell on his knees before Elijah and begged him to spare his life and the life of the servants. The angel of the Lord told Elijah to go with this captain, so he did. The message he gave to Ahaziah was because he had sent messengers to enquire of Baalzebub instead of the God of Israel, he would surely die. Ahaziah died and because he did not have a son, his brother, Jehoram reigned in his place. His reign began in the eighteenth year of Jehoshaphat's reign over Judah.

Elijah's time on earth was coming to an end and remember earlier, he had already anointed his successor, Elisha. When the Lord was about to take Elijah away to heaven in a whirlwind, he and Elisha were going from Gilgal to Bethel as recorded in 2nd Kings 2. Elijah told Elisha to stay at a certain place for he was going to Bethel. Elisha refused to leave him so they went on together. A group of prophets from Bethel asked Elisha if he knew God was about to take Elijah away. Elisha said he knew it and for them to be quiet about it. Again Elijah tried to get Elisha to remain in a place because the Lord had told Elijah to go to Jericho. Elisha again refused to stay so they went together to Jericho. Again a group of prophets asked Elisha if he knew God was going to take Elijah and he told them to be quiet about it. This time Elijah told Elisha to stay there because he was going to the Jordan River. Elisha refused but wet on with Elijah. When they got to the river, Elijah folded his mantle or coat and smote the waters which divided so they could go over on dry ground. Elijah asked Elisha what Elisha wanted Elijah to do for him before he was taken up and Elisha asked for a double portion of Elijah's spirit to be on him. Elijah told him if he saw him when he was taken from him, what he requested would be done.

As they continued their journey, a chariot of fire and horses of fire appeared and parted them asunder. Elijah went up by a whirlwind into heaven and Elisha saw it. He cried to Elijah, but he saw him no more. He took Elijah's coat which had fallen and went back to the bank of the Jordan where he smote the waters and asked where the Lord God of Elijah was. When he did, the waters parted and the prophets which were watching saw what happened and knew the spirit of Elijah was upon Elisha. They went to meet him and bowed themselves before him. They wanted to go look for Elijah and at first Elisha refused them but finally he let them go. They could not find Elijah.

The prophets came back to Elisha and told him how the city was having problems with its water. Elisha told them to bring him a new cruse or a bowl with salt in it. When they did, he put the salt into the spring which supplied the water and the water was healed. Elisha headed to Bethel but on the way, there were little children who mocked him because of his bald head. He cursed them in the name of the Lord and two female bears came out of the woods and attacked the children.

When the events in 2nd Kings 3 began, Mesha, king of Moab, was rebelling against Jehoram, king of Israel. Jehoram asked Jehoshaphat, king of Judah, to go with him against Moab. Just as before when Ahab wanted Jehoshaphat to go with him to war, Jehoshaphat wanted to hear from a prophet of the Lord. They called for Elisha who asked the king of Israel why he did not call on the prophets of his foreign gods instead of him. Elisha went on to tell Jehoram if it was not for his respect for Jehoshaphat, he would not even look at Jehoram. The hand of the Lord came upon Elisha and he told the kings to make the valley full of ditches because even though there would be no wind nor rain, the valley would be filled with water and the Lord would deliver the Moabites into their hand. They were to smite every fenced city and stop the wells of water and mar every good piece of land.

The next morning, like Elisha said, the valley was full of water. When the Moabites saw the water with the sun shining on it, the water looked like blood. The Moabites thought the two kings had war between them and had smote each other so they headed out to raid the camp. When they got to the camp, the Israelites rose up and killed the Moabites. The Israelites chased the Moabites and destroyed their country like God had said for them to do.

Chapters 4-7 of 2nd Kings are filled with accounts of Elisha's activities as God's prophet. In Chapter 4, a wife of one of the prophets cried to Elisha because her husband who feared the Lord had died and the creditor had come to take her two sons as bondmen. Elisha asked her what she had in her house. She only had a pot of oil. Elisha told her to go and borrow a lot of empty containers from her neighbors. Then she was to go in her house with her sons and close her door and pour oil from the pot into each of the vessels. She did what Elisha told her to do and filled all of the containers. Elisha told her to sell the oil and pay her debt.

On another occasion recorded in 2nd Kings 4, Elisha had gone to Shunem where a woman invited him to come in for food. After that, each time he passed by, he went in to eat. The woman told her husband she was sure Elisha was a holy man of God and she wanted to make him a room with a bed, table, stool, and light so when he came to them, he could have a place to stay. I always find this passage interesting because when I was growing up, my dad and mom kept the preachers who held our gospel meetings. Mom always made sure the preacher had a bed, chair, table, and ample lighting so he would be comfortable and could study for his next sermon in the privacy of his room. I wondered if this verse was part of the reason for her preparations or if it was just a woman thing. Anyway, this man and woman in 2nd Kings 4 made Elisha the room and he stayed there from time to time.

One day while Elisha and his servant, Gehazi, were at the Shunammite's house, Elisha had Gehazi call the woman to come to the room. He wanted to know what he could do for her because she had been so good to them. She did not have need of anything, but Gehazi knew she had no children and her husband was old. Elisha called her back to the room and told her about the same time the next year she would have a son. She asked him not to lie to her and did not seem to believe him, but sure enough the next year she had the son.

One day the son went out with his dad and the reapers. His head hurt so badly his dad told a lad to carry him to his mother. She held him until noon and he died. She placed his body on Elisha's bed and she headed out with one of the young men to find Elisha. She went to Mount Carmel where Elisha was. When she got there, and grabbed Elisha by the feet, he knew something had to be wrong but God had not revealed it to him. The Shunammite questioned Elisha as to why she had even had this son when she had not requested a child. Elisha sent Gehazi straight to the child with Elisha's staff to lay upon him, but the woman insisted Elisha had to go to. Gehazi got there first, but laying the staff on the child did nothing. When Elisha got to the child, he went in and closed the door with just the two of them there. Elisha prayed to God and then he stretched himself upon the child until the child's flesh got warm. Elisha walked back and forth in the house and then laid upon the child again. The child sneezed seven times and opened his eyes. Elisha called Gehazi to call the woman. She came and he told her to take up her son. She fell at Elisha's feet and then took her son and went out.

Still in 2nd Kings 4, Elisha went to Gilgal where there was nothing much to eat because the crops had failed. Elisha told his servants to cook some stew for prophets who were there with Elisha. One of the servants gathered wild gourds and shredded them into the stew. They were poison, but the servant did not know it. When the men began to eat from the pot, they realized it was poison. They called to Elisha saying there was death in the pot. He told them to bring him meal. He put the meal in the pot and the poison was gone.

On even another occasion, a man from Baalshalisha came and brought Elisha twenty loaves of barley and full ears of corn. There were one hundred people with Elisha at this time. Elisha told the man to give it to the people to eat. The man questioned Elisha concerning whether twenty loaves would be enough for so many people. Elisha assured him the Lord said there would be plenty with some left. Sure enough, the man gave the people the bread and there was some left.

Chapter 5 of 2nd Kings has a most beautiful account of faith and lack of faith. A mighty man in valor by whom the Lord had given the king of Syria deliverance from his enemies, Naaman, was a leper. The Syrians had taken captives from Israel and among those captives was a little maid who had become a servant of Naaman's wife. The maid told Naaman's wife if Naaman was in Samaria there was a prophet there who would heal him of his leprosy. The Syrian king heard about the conversation, so he sent Naaman along with a letter, ten talents of silver, 6,000 pieces of gold, and ten changes of raiment to the king of Israel. In the letter he told the king of Israel he was sending his servant Naaman to him so he could recover him of his leprosy.

When the king of Israel read the letter, he was very upset. He tore his clothes. He said the king of Syria was seeking a quarrel with him. When Elisha heard about what had happened, he sent to the king and told him to send Naaman to him and Naaman would see there was a prophet in Israel.

Naaman went to Elisha's house but instead of Elisha going out to see Naaman, he sent a messenger to him. The messenger told Naaman to go and wash seven times in the Jordan River and his flesh would be clean. Naaman was angry because he thought the prophet would at least come out and call on the name of the Lord and strike his hand over the leprosy. Naaman also did not like the choice of the Jordan River. He said the Albana and Pharpar Rivers of Damascus were better than all the waters in Israel. He left in a rage.

Thankfully, Naaman's servants had more faith than Naaman. They asked him if the prophet had told him to do some great thing, would he have not done it. They persuaded him to do what Elisha had said to do. He dipped in the Jordan seven times like Elisha said to do and his flesh was clean like a little child. I love using this example when I talk to someone about how God's ways are not necessarily like we think they should be. Our job is to know His will and do it but not to question it. If Naaman's servants had not believed the words of the prophet, Naaman would not have done what he needed to do in order to be healed.

Naaman was then convinced there was no God in all the earth but the God of Israel. In 2nd Kings 5:15, Naaman tried to get Elisha to accept a blessing from him. Elisha refused and Naaman tried again to get him to accept. Elisha would not accept a gift. Naaman then asked for two loads of earth to take with him. Remember he previously thought the waters of Israel were bad but now he was asking for the dirt of Israel. In the context, he was telling Elisha from then on, he would only worship the Lord, so he may have been thinking of using the dirt for an altar. But even in his promise to worship only the Lord, he made an exception for when he went with his master into the house of Rimmon he must still bow.

Elisha told Naaman to go in peace, but Elisha's servant, Gehazi thought Elisha let him off too easy so he followed Naaman and told him Elisha had sent him to ask for a talent of silver and two changes of garments for a couple of young men who had just come to him. Naaman gave him two talents of sliver and two garments and even had his servants carry them for him. When the servants had left and Gehazi went in to Elisha, Elisha asked Gehazi where he had been. Gehazi told Naaman he had not left. Elisha told him his heart had gone with him. He knew what Gehazi had done and as punishment, Gehazi received the leprosy of Naaman.

Chapter 6 of 2nd Kings begins with a very short account of an axe that floated. One day the prophets who lived with Elisha told him the place where they were dwelling was too small. They wanted to make a bigger place. Elisha agreed with them and he went to help them. While one of the prophets was cutting a tree, the axe head fell into the water. The prophet called to Elisha and told him it was borrowed. Elisha cut a stick and cast it into the water where the axe head met with it and floated to where the prophet who lost it was able to pick it up.

Next in 2nd Kings 6, an account of the king of Syria again warring against Israel was recorded. It seemed every time the Syrian king decided where he was going to place his camp, the Israelite king, Jehoram, knew about it. He was very upset because he thought some of his men were telling the Israeli king about his plans. When his men told him it was Elisha telling his plans, he sent men after Elisha. When they got to Dothan where Elisha was, they surrounded the city and when Elisha's servant saw them the next morning, he was afraid. Elisha told him not to be afraid. Elisha prayed to God to open the servant's eyes so he could see the horses and chariots of fire around Elisha. Elisha asked God to smite the Syrians with blindness and He did. Elisha led them right into Samaria where the king of Israel was. Jehoram asked Elisha if he should kill them. Elisha told him no, he had not taken them in battle. Instead, Elisha told him to feed them and let them go. He did and there was peace between Israel and Syria for a while.

After the Syrian event, Benhadad king of Syria, besieged Samaria. There was a famine in Samaria and as the king was passing by, a woman cried to him for help. She and another woman had already boiled her own son and eaten him but now it was time to boil the other woman's son and the other woman had hidden her son. Jehoram rent his clothes when he heard the story and the people saw underneath his outer clothes he had sackcloth which was a sign of sorrow and mourning. But it is obvious from the next few verses Jehoram was not in sorrow for his own sins. In verse 31, he was determined to cause harm to Elisha. He sent a messenger to get him, but Elisha knew he was coming. In Chapter 7, Elisha promised the next day things were going to be better in Samaria. There would be barley and fine flour in abundance. A man upon whose hand the king leaned showed his disbelief and Elisha told him he would see it with his own eyes but he would not eat of it.

There were four leprous men outside the gate of Samaria. They decided among themselves to go over to the Syrian camp where they would either be killed or not. So they went to the Syrian camp but there was no one there. God had made the Syrians hear a noise of chariots, horses, and a great host and they thought Israel had hired kings against them so they had fled. The lepers went on inside and ate and drank and gathered what they wanted and hid it. Then they decided they had better tell the king. They did but the king thought it was a trick by the Syrians. He let some of his men go and check it out and when they returned with the good news the Syrians had left, the people went and took what they wanted from the camp. The king placed the man who had earlier told Elisha it could not happen in charge of the gate and the people ran over him so he died. Elisha's prophecy from the previous day came true.

Then Elisha told the woman whose son he had raised from the dead she and her household needed to go somewhere else because there was going to be a famine for seven years. The woman took her family and went to the land of the

Philistines. At the end of the seven years, she returned to her land and went to the king to ask for her house and land back. When she got to the king, he was talking with Elisha's servant, Gehazi, and asking him about the great things Elisha had done. Gehazi saw the woman and told the king she was the woman whose son Elisha had restored to life. When the woman agreed with Gehazi, the king restored all of her possessions to her.

Elisha went to Damascus where the King of Syria, Benhadad, was sick (2nd Kings 8:7). When the king found out Elisha was there, he sent Hazael to Elisha with a present carried by forty camels to ask Elisha if Benhadad was going to get well. Hazael took the present and found Elisha. He asked Elisha if the king would recover. Elisha told Hazael to go and tell the king he would recover but really he would not for Elisha went on to tell Hazael God had told Elisha the king would die. Elisha stared at Hazael until Hazael was ashamed and Elisha began to cry. Hazael asked him why he was crying and Elisha told him he knew the evil Hazael would do to the people even to setting the walled cities on fire and killing babies and ripping open pregnant women. Hazael asked how he could do such a thing as he was only a servant. Elisha told him God had showed him how Hazael would be king over Syria. Hazael went back to the king and told him Elisha said he would recover but the next day Hazael took a thick cloth dipped in water and spread it over Benhadad's face so he died. Just as Elisha said, Hazael became king in Damascus.

Jehoshaphat's son Jehoram became the new king in Judah while Jehoram the son of Ahab was king in Israel. Jehoshaphat and Jehoram reigned together for a while which would explain what appears to be contradictory information concerning when Jehoram began to reign. This Jehoram in Judah was married to a daughter of Ahab who if you will remember was one of the worst kings of all Israel in the way he led the people to worship false gods. This Jehoram walked in the same manner but God would not destroy Judah for David's sake as he had promised to keep someone from his family always ruling in Judah. When Jehoram died, his son, Ahaziah became king in Judah during the twelfth year of Jehoram's rule in Israel. (If you are following this in your KJ Bible, you will note sometimes Jehoram is spelled Jehoram and sometimes Joram.) Ahaziah also acted like Ahab's family and disobeyed God.

Ahaziah went with King Joram of Israel to attack King Hazael and the Syrian troops at Ramothgilead where King Joram was wounded (2nd Kings 8:28). He went to Jezreel to heal from his wounds and while he was there, Ahaziah the king in Judah went to see him. It was at this time Elisha was at work again getting ready to anoint a new king for Israel. Elisha sent one of the prophets out toward Ramothgilead to look for Jehu. When he found him, he was to anoint him king over Israel and then the prophet was to open the door and run for his life (2nd Kings 9:1-3). The young prophet found Jehu and once he had poured the oil on his head to anoint him, he told Jehu he was to smite the house of Ahab his master in fulfilment of the prophecy from Elijah in which it was prophesied Ahab's house would perish and the dogs would eat Jezebel in Jezreel.

Jehu prepared to obey the prophet and headed to Jezreel. When messengers came out to see if he was coming for peace, he would not tell them. When Joram heard Jehu was coming, he and Ahaziah, king of Judah, went out to war against him, if necessary. When they met, Joram asked if it was peace and Jehu replied to the negative. Joram fled but Jehu killed him with an arrow. Jehu told his men to take his body and cast it into the plot of ground where Naboth's blood was shed as God had said would happen years earlier. Ahaziah tried to flee, but Jehu followed him and told his men to kill him too. They did.

When Jehu got to Jezreel and Jezebel knew about it, she looked out the window and Jehu saw her. Jehu called out and asked who was on his side. Two or three eunuchs looked out at him and he told them to throw Jezebel down from the window (2nd Kings 9:32). They did and her blood sprinkled on the wall and the horses walked right over her. After Jehu had a meal he told his men to go get her body and bury it since she was a king's daughter, but the only thing left of her was her head, feet, and palms. The word of Elijah was fulfilled.

Ahab still had seventy living sons and Jehu's job was to destroy the family of Ahab so he wrote letters to the rulers of Jezreel telling them to pick out the best of Ahab's sons and set him on the throne and fight for his house. The men were very afraid knowing two kings had just been killed by Jehu. They sent word back to Jehu saying they were Jehu's servants and would do whatever he wanted. He wrote to them again and told them if they were his servants they needed to come to him by the next day with the heads of the seventy sons. They did what Jehu ordered. Jehu proceeded to go to Samaria where he killed all of the rest of Ahab's family. Then he gathered all of the people of the place together and pretended like he was going to serve Baal more than Ahab had. He called all of the prophets of Baal to a great sacrifice to Baal. All of the worshippers of Baal came and went into Baal's house for the sacrifice. Meanwhile, Jehu told eighty of his men they were to kill every one of Baal's worshippers and if they let anyone go it was life for life. Jehu's men went in and killed all of the worshippers of Baal and tore down the house of Baal and burned all of the images.

What a marvelous work this man Jehu did in putting to death the worship of Baal, but yet, we find recorded in 2nd Kings 10, he departed not from the sins of Jeroboam as he left the two golden calves at Dan and Bethel (2nd Kings 10:29). God promised him because he had obeyed God in the matter of Ahab, Jehu would have children to the fourth generation on the throne, but Jehu did not walk in the law of the Lord with all his heart. God allowed other nations to begin smiting the Israelites. Jehu died and his son Jehoahaz reigned in his place. God allowed Hazael, that King of Syria from before, to oppress

Israel but Jehoahaz begged God to deliver them. God did, but according to 2nd Kings 13:6, the Israelites continued to sin. When Jehoahaz in Israel died, his son, Joash (also spelled Jehoash) began to reign. He too was an evil ruler.

Back over in Judah, when Athaliah, the mother of the slain king Ahaziah, saw he was dead, she proceeded to kill all of the royal seed making herself Queen. But one of Ahaziah's sisters, Jehosheba, realized what was happening and she hid Joash, the son of Ahaziah, so he was not killed. He was hidden for six years and in his seventh year, the priest Jehoiada, had the captains and officers kill Athaliah, and he placed Joash (also spelled Jehoash) in as the next king in Judah.

Most likely it was during the time of Joash's rule the prophet Joel penned the short prophecy to Judah bearing the name Joel. Joel began the prophecy with "The word of the Lord that came to Joel the son of Pethuel." This was God's word to the people living then telling them what was going to happen in the future. Not only were the people to hear these words (Joel 1:2-3), but they were to tell their children who were to tell their children who were to tell their children. Does this remind you of anything we have looked at previously where the word was to be taught to each generation?

In this prophecy, Joel told the people how things were going to get really bad. He began with a physical illustration of a palmerworm having eaten the vegetation. What was left by the palmerworm the locust ate. What was left by the locust, the cankerworm ate. What was left by the cankerworm, the caterpillar ate. If you are familiar with what a tree infested with caterpillars looks like, then you see we have an ugly picture of destruction. In addition, everything was going to be dried up. The food was in trouble as was the seed for planting. The animals would have no pasture and a flame would burn the trees. In Joel 1:5 the people were told to wake up and in verse 14 Joel told them to call a solemn assembly and cry to the Lord. He said alas for the day of the Lord is at hand and it would come as a destruction from the Almighty. It should be mentioned here many times in the Old Testament we read about the day of the Lord being at hand. This is not always a reference to the end of time or the judgment but often the phrase is used to mean some type of awful destruction before that final Day of Judgment. An interim time of punishment seems to be the meaning here in Joel.

In Chapter 2 of Joel the prophet continued with more warnings to the people of how bad things were going to be. There would be darkness and gloominess with clouds and thick darkness like never before or after. Joel told the people in Joel 2:12 the Lord said to turn back to Him with fasting and weeping and mourning. He said God is gracious and merciful. If the people would turn back to Him, according to verse 19, the Lord would answer and send them blessings again. In verse 25, Joel said God would restore what the locust, cankerworm, caterpillar, and palmerworm had eaten. In verse 27 the people would know God was in their midst and He was the Lord their God.

After these events, according to Joel 2:28-32, God was going to pour out His spirit upon all flesh and there would be prophesies and visions and wonders in the heavens and the earth. Whoever would call on the name of the Lord would be delivered with a deliverance coming from Jerusalem and it would be for the remnant the Lord would call. We know this part of the prophecy was fulfilled on the day of Pentecost as recorded in Acts 2:17 where Peter told the people who had accused the apostles of being drunk they were not drunk but the prophecy of Joel was being fulfilled. Peter then went on to quote Joel 2:28-32.

The last chapter of Joel is one that has caused people a lot of problems in trying to understand its meaning. Coffman (n. d.) has summarized the chapter well in his commentary on this chapter where he says the chapter does not pertain to physical Israel but to the spiritual Israel or the church. According to Coffman, the first section refers to the forgiveness of sins for the true Israel and the punishments of those in opposition. The prophecy in Joel 3:9-13 refers to the same gathering noted in Revelation 16 for the final judgment. Christ's reign is indicated in Joel 3:14-17 when the church finds safety in God. Coffman saw the last part of the chapter (verses 18-21) as the blessings in the kingdom.

Joash listened to the prophets at least as long as Jehoiada was the priest (2nd Kings 12:2). Joash tried to get the house of the Lord repaired. The workers were so honest no one had to watch over the money collected. The money was in a box and the workers used it for its intent. But Joash seemed to forget God when Hazael the king of Syria was about to attack Jerusalem and instead of going to God for help, Joash gathered all of the hallowed items including the gold from the king's house and from the temple and gave it to Hazael. Hazael accepted the gift and did not attack. At the end of Joash's rule, two of his servants killed him and Amaziah, his son, reigned.

Elisha became sick while Jehoash was still king in Israel. Jehoash went to Elisha and cried over him. Elisha told Jehoash to take a bow and arrows and shoot an arrow. As he shot the arrow, Elisha put his hands upon the king's hands. After he shot the arrow, Elisha told him it was the arrow of the Lord's deliverance and Jehoash would smite the Syrians until he had consumed them. Then Elisha told Jehoash to take the arrows and smite the ground. Jehoash smote the ground but only three times. Elisha was upset with him and told him he should have hit the ground five or six times because now he would only smite the Syrians three times. Sure enough, Jehoash beat the Syrians three times and recovered the cities of Israel which had been taken previously by the Syrians.

Elisha died and they buried him. At the beginning of the next year, when some men were burying a man and were interrupted by a band of Moabites invading the land, the men cast the body of the dead man into the place where Elisha had been buried. When the dead man's body touched Elisha's bones, he came back to life.

The next prophecy was most likely the one to Nineveh by Jonah who prophesied around the time of Amaziah, the next king of Judah, and Jeroboam II, the king in Israel. In 2nd Kings 14:25 is mention of this same Jonah, the son of Amittai, and he was called the prophet. Jonah 1 begins with the word of the Lord telling Jonah to go to Nineveh and cry against it because their great wickedness had come up before God.

Jonah did not want to go to Nineveh simply because he knew if the people repented, God would not go forth with His planned judgment against them. Jonah chose to get on a ship headed to Tarshish to flee from the presence of God. Do we ever have a job we know we should do but we do not want to do it, so we try to flee from the presence of God? Well, it did not work for Jonah and most likely will not work for us either. In Jonah's case, God sent a great storm upon the sea so the sailors cried to their gods for help. Jonah was on a lower floor of the ship asleep and the shipmaster woke him up and told him to pray to his God to see if He would save them.

According to Jonah 1:10, Jonah had already told the sailors he was running from God. The shipmen cast lots to see whose fault the storm was and the lot fell on Jonah. Jonah confessed to them he was a Hebrew and he feared the God of heaven who had made the sea and the dry land. He told them to throw him overboard and the sea would be calm. The men did everything they could to get the boat to land, but they could not, so they threw Jonah into the sea. The sea ceased raging and the men feared the Lord. They offered a sacrifice and even made vows to the Lord.

The Lord had prepared a great fish to swallow Jonah. He stayed in the fish's belly for three days and nights and in Chapter 2 Jonah prayed to God a most beautiful prayer recorded in verses 2-9. God heard his prayer and spoke to the fish who vomited Jonah out on dry land. This time in Chapter 3 when God told Jonah to go to Nineveh, he went. The record says Nineveh was an exceedingly great city of three days journey. Jonah entered the city and began telling the people in forty days Nineveh would be overthrown. The people from the smallest to the greatest even to the king believed Jonah and they repented. The king took off his robe and put on sackcloth and sat in ashes. He commanded man and beast to fast and be covered with sackcloth. They were to cry to God in hopes He would repent of His decision to destroy them. God saw their works and that they had turned from evil and in Jonah 3:10, the record says God repented and did not do to them what He had said He would do.

One would think the prophet, Jonah, would have been happy his prophecy had saved so many people but remember from earlier in the book of Jonah, the reason he did not want to go and prophesy against Nineveh was he knew they would repent and God would not destroy them. Sure enough when the record in Jonah 4 began, Jonah was very angry and in verse 3 he asked God to take his life from him. God asked him why he was angry. Jonah went out from the city and made himself a little place to sit so he could watch and see what happened to the city. God made a gourd to come up over Jonah and be a shadow for him. Jonah was pleased about the gourd, but the next day God prepared a worm that killed the gourd and it withered. Then He sent a strong east wind so the sun beat hot upon Jonah and he again wanted to die. God shamed him in asking why he had pity on the gourd for which he had not worked at all but he had no care for the 120,000 people in Nineveh who did not even know the difference between their right and left hands. The book of Jonah ended there. How sad for a prophet of God to have no more care for the people than what Jonah appeared to have had. How sad today when children of God for whatever reason fail to tell sinners about God so they can have a chance to repent and become servants of the Most High.

Back in 2nd Kings 14:8, Amaziah sent a message to Jehoash to come out and fight with him. Jehoash warned Amaziah if he came, he was going to defeat Judah. Amaziah would not listen so Jehoash came out for battle. Jehoash and his men won. They took all of the gold and silver and vessels from the Lord's house along with hostages. Jehoash died and his son Jeroboam II became king. Amaziah, king in Judah, lived fifteen more years and he died through a conspiracy and his son Azariah took over in Judah. Upon Azariah's death Jotham reigned, and when he died Ahaz took over. When Jeroboam II died, his son Zechariah became the king in Israel as recorded in 2nd Kings 15:7-8.

Jeroboam II did as Jeroboam I had done in his evil ways. Although he restored the lands Israel had lost and he recovered Damascus and Hamath, God was not important to him in his reign for if He had been, Jeroboam would have served him. During the reign of Jeroboam II, two other prophets were active in Israel, Amos and Hosea. Amos prophesied while Uzziah was king in Judah and Hosea's prophecy was for a longer time during the reigns of Judah's kings, Uzziah, Jotham, Ahaz, and Hezekiah.

According to Amos 1, Amos was a herdsman. Later in the book (Amos 7:14-15), he described himself more fully to Amaziah, the priest. Amos began his prophecy with judgments against Damascus, Gaza, Tyrus, Edom, Ammon, Moab, and then Judah and Israel. Judah's judgment, recorded in Amos 2:4, was because they had despised the law of the Lord and had not kept His commandments. The judgment against Israel takes up most of the rest of the book. God was angry with Israel because they had sold the righteous for silver and the poor for a pair of shoes (2:6). Amos went on to explain in Amos 3-6 why Israel's punishment was deserved and what they could expect as punishment. In Chapter 7 Amaziah, the priest of Bethel came on the scene. Amaziah sent a message to Jeroboam as recorded in Amos 7 beginning in verse 10 in which he told the king Amos had conspired against him and the people could not endure what Amos was saying about the woes to come upon them. Amaziah also went to Amos asking him to go away from Israel to Judah and prophesy there. Amos told Amaziah he had to do what God sent him to do and because of Amaziah's request that Amos not prophesy in Israel, Amaziah was going to have troubles in his house and Israel would go into captivity (7:17). In Amos 9:8 God said His eyes were upon the sinful kingdom and He would destroy it from the face of the earth but He would not utterly destroy the house of Jacob. Instead as recorded in Amos 9:11-15, Amos ended with a Messianic hope.

Just a few years after Amos prophesied, the Lord spoke through Hosea. This prophecy was recorded in the book of Hosea. God commanded Hosea to take a wife of the harlots as a demonstration of the harlotry the Israelites had committed in departing from God. Throughout the book, Hosea gave examples of God's judgment upon the people of Israel because of their rejection of God. In Hosea 6:4, God said the goodness of Judah was like the morning dew that vanishes. In verse 6 God said He had desired knowledge more than burnt offerings. Remember how God had previously commanded the people to know and do His word, but in verse 7 He said they had transgressed the covenant. In Chapter 7 God made it so plain how He wanted to heal Israel but they refused. In 11:7, the Lord said His people were bent on backsliding from Him. In Hosea 14, God begged Israel to return to Him. In the very last verse, there was hope given for those who were wise and would walk in the ways of the Lord.

With such strong prophecies being proclaimed among the people, one would think there would have been great repentance but it did not happen. Zechariah was the fourth generation of Jehu to sit on the throne. Remember God had promised Jehu four generations so Zechariah was the last of Jehu's family to be king. Shallum conspired against Zechariah and killed him and became the king (2nd Kings 15:10). He was king for a month before Menahem killed him and reigned in Israel. When Menahem died, his son Pekahiah reigned. One of his own captains, Pekah, conspired against him and killed him and took over as king. Azariah (also called Uzziah) was still reigning in Judah while all of these kings came and went in Israel.

When Azariah died, his son Jotham began to reign in Judah. When Jotham died, Ahaz, his son, reigned. Pekah, the king of Israel, and Rezin, the king of Syria went together to war against Jerusalem. They were not able to overcome Ahaz, but Ahaz ended up becoming a servant of Assyria so the Syrian king Tiglathpileser would save him from the hand of Israel. When Ahaz died, his son Hezekiah reigned in Judah.

While Ahaz was still king in Judah, Hoshea became the king in Israel. The king of Assyria, Shalmaneser, came up against him and Hoshea became Shalmaneser's servant and gave him presents. Shalmaneser was upset with Hoshea one year because instead of sending Shalmaneser presents, Hoshea had sent messengers to King So of Egypt. In the ninth year of Hoshea's reign, 725 B.C., Assyria invaded Samaria and three years later in 722 B.C. Assyria took Samaria and carried Israel away into Assyria. According to 2nd Kings 17:7-18 God did this because His people had failed to keep His commands and His laws. They had worshipped other gods and sold themselves to do evil in the sight of the Lord. Note in verse 19 Judah did likewise, but Judah remained a nation for several more years.

In 2nd Kings 17:20 is a most important verse making it clear physical Israel is no longer God's chosen people. According to this verse, the Lord rejected all the seed of Israel. In verses 21-22 the record says He took Israel from the house of David because they followed after the sins of Jeroboam. I do not know how it could be made any plainer God rejected physical Israel because they first rejected Him.

Continuing in 2nd Kings 17, is the account noted in Chapter 1 of this book where the Assyrian king took people from other areas and settled them in the land of Israel. When they first began their settlement, they had no fear of the Lord as they did not know the Lord. God sent lions among them which killed some of the people. The people being worshippers of many gods thought they needed to know something about the God of this place so they told the king how they did not know the ways of this God. The king told them to get one of the priests who had been carried away to come back to the land and live and teach the people the ways of the God of the land. A priest came back and taught them how they should fear the Lord as recorded in 2nd Kings 17:28, but note in verses 29-31 how the people made them gods according to their previous nations and cities. Then the verses I find so amusing are verses 32-33 and 41. They feared the Lord and served their own gods, both their children, and their grandchildren, as did their fathers. How is that any different than what we see today? People say they fear God and they love God, yet if there is a school function or a ball game on TV or overtime work for extra pay, they serve their own gods. Ladies, how do we use this history of Israel to show people what is going on today?

    Judah was not taken in 722 B.C., but was able to survive another 135 years. Hezekiah, who had begun to reign in the third year that Hoshea was king in Israel, was doing right in the sight of God. He had removed the high places and gotten rid of the images and groves again. According to 2nd Kings 18:5, there was none like him among all the other kings of Judah. After the Assyrians took Israel, they came up against Judah too, and Hezekiah paid the Assyrian king with much gold and silver but he was not satisfied. He sent his men to Jerusalem to tell the people Assyria was going to take them over. Hezekiah tore his clothes and covered himself with sackcloth. He went to the house of the Lord himself and he sent his men to Isaiah the prophet to get help.

Isaiah sent Hezekiah back a message saying he did not need to fear the Assyrian king because God would send a blast upon him and he would hear a rumor and return to his own land. Hezekiah begged God to save the people and God promised him he would. In 2nd Kings 19:30-34 God promised a remnant of the house of Judah would take root and bear fruit. He promised Hezekiah the Assyrian king would not even shoot an arrow into Jerusalem. That night the angel of the Lord went out and smote the Assyrian camp and killed 180,000 men. The Assyrian king left and as he was worshipping in the house of his god, Nisroch, his own sons killed him.

Hezekiah became very sick and the prophet Isaiah told him to set his house in order because he was going to die. Hezekiah again prayed to the Lord and asked Him to remember how he had walked before Him with a perfect heart. He cried to God and God's word came to Isaiah telling him to go back and tell Hezekiah God had heard his prayer and He would heal him. On the third day Hezekiah would go up to the house of the Lord and God would add fifteen years to his life. He would also deliver him and his city out of the hand of the king of Assyria for His own and His servant David's sake. Hezekiah wanted a sign he would be able to go up to the house of the Lord on the third day. Isaiah asked if he wanted the shadow to go forward or backward ten degrees. Hezekiah said it would be a normal thing for the shadow to go down ten degrees but to let it back up ten degrees. Isaiah asked God and sure enough, He brought the shadow backward ten degrees on the dial. Can you imagine the shock to any of the sundial watchers when the shadow went backward?

Isaiah had been prophesying in Judah from the days of Uzziah through the reign of Hezekiah covering at least forty years. In the book of Isaiah is recorded God's pronouncement of judgment against not only Judah and Israel but against the other countries of that time period. In Isaiah 2 is a wonderful promise of a time when the mountain of the Lord's house was going to be established and nations would flow unto it. In verse 2, Isaiah said it shall come to pass in the "last days..." In verse 3 Isaiah wrote when this happened, people would say "Come ye, and let us go up to the mountain of the Lord, to the house of the God of Jacob; and he will teach us of his ways, and we will walk in his paths: for out of Zion shall go forth the law, and the word of the Lord from Jerusalem." We will see later when we get into the New Testament when this was fulfilled.

In Chapter 7 of Isaiah, God gave King Ahaz a sign concerning the Christ. In 7:14 the prophecy was: "...Behold a virgin shall conceive, and bear a son, and shall call his name Immanuel." Again in Chapter 9 there is more prophecy concerning the birth of Christ. In Isaiah 11:10, it was prophesied there would be a root of Jesse who would stand as a banner to the people and the Gentiles would seek it. From Chapter 9 on through 39 the book of Isaiah is filled with promised destructions to different nations with a little hope scattered here and there concerning a coming kingdom. In Chapter 40 verse 3 is a prophecy of John the Baptist which we will look at more closely when we get to the New Testament. From Chapter 40 on through 66 are many prophecies concerning the kingdom that was to come and the salvation for the remnant who would obey God, along with a few more condemnations to those who refused to give heed to God's word. The prophet in Isaiah 44:28-45:1 gave a particularly important prophecy concerning the restoration of the temple which would be destroyed. Through Isaiah, years before it happened, God said Cyrus would be the one who would be ruler when the city and temple would be rebuilt.

Another prophet who prophesied in Judah from the reign of Jotham through the reign of Hezekiah was Micah. Micah's prophecy was against Samaria and Judah (Micah 1:1), against those who used their power against those who were powerless (2:1-2), and against princes and prophets who caused the people to sin (3:1-7). While he pronounced judgment upon these people, he also included the promise of a future kingdom (2:12, 4:1-2). Micah prophesied the birth of the Messiah (5:2) and went on to show how God pleaded with His people to return to Him. In the very last verse, Micah again reminded the people of the promise God had made to Abraham and unto the fathers from the days of old which was the promise concerning how in Abraham's seed all the earth would be blessed.

When Hezekiah died, his son Manasseh became king (2nd Kings 20:21). He destroyed the good his father had done by rebuilding the high places and the altars. He used enchantments and dealt with spirits and wizards. He was so wicked God spoke by the prophets to say because of his wickedness, God would bring evil upon Jerusalem and Judah so whoever heard about it, both his ears would tingle. God said He would forsake the remnant of His inheritance and deliver them to the hand of their enemies. Manasseh died and his son Amon became king. He too did evil. His servants killed him.

During the reign of Amon, Nahum prophesied to Nineveh. Remember about one hundred years before the time of Nahum, Jonah had prophesied to Nineveh they were going to be destroyed in forty days, but they along with their king repented in sackcloth and ashes and God chose not to destroy them. Now here again in Nahum, we have recorded God's judgment that was to befall the city. In 1:3 Nahum said the Lord was slow to anger and great in power but He would not at all let the wicked by with their evil. In Nahum 3:1-4, some of the sins of the city were noted including robbery, lying, harlotry, and witchcraft. Does that sound like any places of today? In 3:19 Nahum said there was no healing of their bruise and their wound was grievous. Historians (Padfield, n.d.) believed

Nineveh was destroyed in 612 B.C. Padfield noted the different prophecies by Nahum and how they were fulfilled in the destruction.

When King Amon died, Josiah, his son who was only eight years old, began to reign. He did what was right in the sight of God. He repaired the temple. According to 2nd Kings 22:2, he walked in the ways of David and turned not aside to the right hand or the left. Under the reign of Josiah, Hilkiah, the high priest, found the book of the law in the house of the Lord. Hilkiah gave the book to Shaphan the scribe and after Shaphan read it, he took it to the king and read it before him. When Josiah heard the words of the book of the law, he was upset. He commanded Hilkiah and some other men to go and enquire of the Lord for him and the people of Judah concerning the words in the book. Josiah said the wrath of the Lord was kindled upon them because their fathers had not hearkened unto the words of the book to do what was written therein.

Hilkiah and the other men went to the prophetess, Hulda and asked her about the book. She told them the Lord God of Israel said to tell them He was going to bring evil upon the people just as was recorded in the book which had been read to the king because the people had forsaken Him and burned incense to other gods thus provoking Him to anger. God said His anger would be kindled against Judah and would not be quenched. He said to tell the king because his heart was tender and he had humbled himself before the Lord and had rent his clothes before Him and wept, God would not bring forth the evil upon the place until Josiah had died.

Josiah then had all the people of Jerusalem go up to the house of the Lord where Josiah read to them all the words of the book of the covenant which had been found in the house of the Lord. Josiah made a covenant before the Lord to walk after Him and to keep His commandments and testimonies and statutes and the people all agreed. Josiah proceeded to destroy everything causing Judah to sin (2nd Kings 23). Josiah had Hilkiah, the high priests, and the other priests and keepers of the door take out of the Lord's temple all of the vessels made for Baal and for the grove and for all the other gods. He had them burned outside of Jerusalem. He destroyed the idolatrous priests and tore down the houses of the sodomites. He removed the altar Jeroboam had built at Bethel. Josiah saw a particular burying place with a title over it and he asked what the title was. He was told it was the sepulcher of the man of God who had come from Judah and prophesied all Josiah had just done against the altar of Bethel.

Remember back in 1st Kings 13:2 a man of God had prophesied against the altar at Bethel set up by Jeroboam. The man of God said one named Josiah would come to the throne and would do just what this Josiah did. Passages such as this can be so beneficial when we are trying to show others why we believe the Bible is true. There are so many fulfilled prophecies we must know the Word is from God.

During the time Josiah was king in Judah, both Zephaniah and Jeremiah were prophets for Israel. While Zephaniah prophesied only during Josiah's reign, Jeremiah prophesied until Israel went into exile during the reign of Zedekiah and even for a while afterwards. Both prophets shared a message of doom and gloom for the people of God who had gone astray after other gods.

In Zephaniah's short book of only three chapters are found promises of judgment upon the whole earth with special emphasis upon Judah (1:4). According to Zephaniah 1:6, judgment would be coming to both those who had turned back from the Lord and those who had not sought after the Lord. The punishment was described as one in which the gold or silver would be of no benefit and the Lord would make a speedy end of all who dwell in the land (1:18). The people were called to repentance in 2:1-3. In the final chapter, a promise was again made to save a remnant.

While Jeremiah's prophecy began during the days of Josiah, he continued to prophesy throughout the reign of Jehoiakim, and unto the end of the eleventh year of Zedekiah unto the carrying away of Jerusalem as captives (Jeremiah 1:2-3). God told Jeremiah to go and speak unto the people all God commanded him and not to be dismayed when they would not listen because God would be with him (1:17-19). God said His people had committed two evils. They had forsaken Him, the fountain of living water, and they had made themselves broken cisterns not able to hold water (2:13). Throughout the book, Jeremiah reminded the people of their sins and continued to tell them they would be destroyed because of them.

Under Josiah, Jeremiah condemned the people for their idolatry and their willful sins. He tried to show them what Israel had done as backsliders (Jeremiah 3:6) and they were following in the same steps. Jeremiah showed the people in 11:3-4 what was going to happen to those who continued to disobey the commands God had given the fathers. In Jeremiah 14-17 in addition to continuing to tell the people what was going to happen, Jeremiah prayed for their sins and asked God for mercy. Eventually in Chapter 20 Jeremiah was put in jail for his preaching. When Pashur, the governor who had put Jeremiah in jail, let him out, Jeremiah told him his house would be taken into captivity by Babylon.

Even though Josiah did several great acts in an attempt at bringing the people back to the Lord, this time the Lord was finished with the people. In 2nd Kings 23:27 the writer recorded the Lord said He would also remove Judah out of His sight just as He had removed Israel. He said He would cast off Jerusalem which He had chosen and the house of which He had said, "My name shall be there." Again, this is in fulfillment of what God told David He would do if the people did not obey Him.

While Josiah was king, Egypt went against Assyria and Josiah fought against Egypt. Josiah died in battle and the people made Jehoahaz, his son, king (2nd Kings 23:30). Jehoahaz followed after the ways of the evil kings and did evil in the sight of the Lord. Pharaohnechoh, the king of Egypt, took Jehoahaz out of power and gave the throne to Eliakim another son of Josiah. Pharaohnechoh changed Eliakim's name to Jehoiakim. Egypt demanded money from Judah and Jehoiakim taxed the people to get the money. Jehoiakim also did evil in the sight of the Lord.

In Nebuchadrezzar's first year as king of Babylon which was the fourth year of Jehoiakim's reign in Judah, the word of the Lord from Jeremiah recorded in Jeremiah 25 was a reminder to the people of Judah concerning how Jeremiah had been prophesying to them since the thirteenth year of Josiah and telling them they had to turn to the Lord. Jeremiah told them they had continued to refuse to turn from their sins and because of their continued refusal, he said in verse 9 God was going to bring Nebuchadnezzar against the land of Judah. This king would destroy them and the whole land would be a desolation.

Sure enough, Nebuchadnezzar, king of Babylon took control of Judah. Jehoiakim obeyed him for three years but then he rebelled (2nd Kings 24). The Lord sent armies from other countries to destroy Judah just as He had promised by the prophets. When Jehoiakim died, his son, Jehoiachin, became king. There was no more trouble with Egypt because the king of Babylon, Nebuchadnezzar had defeated Egypt and taken control of the land all the way to the Euphrates River and now Babylon had control of Judah too. King Nebuchadnezzar had Jehoiachin arrested and he ordered his men to strip the temple as the Lord had warned earlier would happen. Nebuchadnezzar took the military leaders, skilled workers, and officials as prisoners and left in Judah only the poorest of the people. He appointed Mattaniah as king of Judah and changed his name to Zedekiah.

Under Zedekiah, Jeremiah continued to prophesy. Zedekiah sent messengers to have Jeremiah enquire of the Lord concerning what was going to happen when Nebuchadnezzar had laid siege to Jerusalem (Jeremiah 21:1-2). God through Jeremiah gave them the choice of staying in the city and dying (verse 9) or going with the Chaldeans and living.

In Jeremiah 22 beginning with verse 24, a most important prophecy concerning Coniah was recorded. Here God declared no descendent of Coniah, also called Jeconiah, would sit upon the throne of David and rule in Judah. This prophecy completely does away with the idea Christ will return to this earth and sit upon David's throne in Jerusalem since we know from both the genealogies of Christ, one recorded in Matthew and one in Luke, Jesus was definitely from the lineage of Coniah. In Matthew 1:12 Jechonias is listed and in Luke 3:27, Jeconiah's son Salathiel and grandson Zorobabel are both mentioned. Thus while Christ can be king over His spiritual kingdom, the church, He cannot rule physically from Jerusalem. These are some more of the very important passages from the Old Testament we need to remember so when we talk to those who are still looking for Christ to come and reign on this earth, we can show them why that is not going to happen.

Another prophet of the time period before the Judean captivity was Habakkuk. In the book bearing his name, Habakkuk asked God why He had not punished the wicked. God told him punishment was on the way. In Habakkuk 1:6, he recorded God would raise up the Chaldeans (those who lived in the southern part of Babylon) to march through and possess the land of Judah. Habakkuk begged God in Chapter 3 to remember mercy and in the end of the chapter, Habakkuk said God was his strength.

Even with all of the available prophecies, Zedekiah did not obey the Lord any more than his forefathers had done. In his ninth year as king, Nebuchadnezzar led his army to attack Jerusalem (2nd Kings 25). They held the city for a year and a half and there was no bread left for the people in the city. Zedekiah and the men of war fled. The Chaldees chased the king and overcame him. They killed all of his sons and then put out his eyes and carried him off to Babylon in or around the year 586 B.C.

The Babylonians burned the house of the Lord, the temple that God promised to dwell in as long as the people obeyed, and the king's house, and all of Jerusalem (2nd Kings

25:9). They took more prisoners and left only the poor people to be vinedressers. Nebuchadnezzar made Gedaliah the ruler of those people who were left and set Jeremiah free from the imprisonment which had been inflicted upon him due to his prophesying. Gedaliah told the people if they obeyed the Babylonian rule everything would be fine, but not long after he began his rule, people led by one named Ishmael killed Gedaliah and the Jews with him at Mizpah (2nd Kings 25:25). The people who were left fled to Egypt because they were afraid of what might happen next. They took Jeremiah with them and while in Egypt, Jeremiah continued to prophesy concerning the punishments to come upon the people. Chapters 50-51 of Jeremiah are prophecies concerning the doom of Babylon. According to Jeremiah 51:59-64, they were to be read and then bound to a stone and cast into the middle of the Euphrates River as a sign of what God would do to Babylon. In addition to the book of Jeremiah, the book of Lamentations also written by Jeremiah around the time of Jerusalem's fall in 586 B.C., provides a description of the desolation of Jerusalem and the anger of God toward the city. He described the conditions of the city during the siege and in the end asked God to remember them again and turn the people back to God.

According to 2nd Chronicles 36:20-23, Babylon continued to rule over the land for seventy years when the king of Persia, Cyrus, made a proclamation to build God a house in

Jerusalem. Recall Isaiah had prophesied in Isaiah 44:28-45:1 concerning this one Cyrus. During the seventy years of captivity or exile, Ezekiel and Daniel prophesied.

Daniel's prophecy covers the time from the first deportation of the captives all the way to the first return. He began the book of Daniel with a recounting of how God had given Judah over to the hand of Nebuchadnezzar king of Babylon. Daniel explained he had arrived in Babylon as one of the young men the king had requested be brought there so they could be taught the ways and the language of the Chaldeans or Babylonians. The king wanted children of royal birth and those in whom was no blemish but who were skillful and smart. They were to be given a daily provision of food and drink for three years and at the end of the three years, they were to be brought to the Babylonian king to serve him.

Daniel requested his keeper not to force him to take of the king's food and drink because he did not want to defile himself. His keeper was at first afraid to allow this, but Daniel persuaded him to give Daniel and his three friends Hananiah, Mishael, and Azariah better known to us as Shadrach, Meshach, and Abednego ten days to prove themselves (Daniel 1:12). Daniel and his friends ate vegetables while the others ate the king's portion. At the end of the ten days, Daniel and his friends looked much better than those who had eaten the king's food, so they were allowed to continue eating as they chose. God had given Daniel favor with the king's servants and He gave Daniel and his three friends knowledge and skill in all wisdom and learning (Daniel 1:9, 17). At the end of the three years when they stood before the king, the king found them to be ten times better than all the magicians and astrologers as far as wisdom and understanding. According to Daniel 1:21, Daniel continued in the king's service until the first year of Cyrus.

The first account in the book of Daniel concerning Daniel's involvement with the king was when the king had dreamed a dream and had forgotten what it was (Daniel 2). His servants could not tell him what he had dreamed and he determined to destroy all of them. When Daniel found out what was happening, he asked the king for a little time. He went to his three friends and they prayed to God for help. God gave Daniel the dream and the meaning and he reported back to the king. The dream was of a great image which Daniel explained to the king represented four great kingdoms or kingdom periods and it would be in the last of these periods or kingdoms when the God of heaven would set up a kingdom that would never be destroyed. It would break in pieces and consume all kingdoms and it would stand forever. We know today this prophecy had its fulfillment in the kingdom of Christ. In Luke 1:33, Luke wrote, "And he (Christ) shall reign over the house of Jacob for ever; and of his kingdom there shall be no end."

Because of Daniel's interpretation and prophecy, the king made him a chief ruler in Babylon and at Daniel's request, the king set Shadrach, Meshach, and Abednego over the affairs of the province of Babylon. The king, Nebuchadnezzar, made a huge gold image and required all to fall down and worship it (Daniel 3). Of course Shadrach, Meshach, and Abednego could not do so. The report was made to the king they had refused to worship the image. The king had them thrown into a fiery furnace heated seven times hotter than usual. It was so hot the flame slew those men who threw them in. The king looked in and saw a fourth figure in the fire and the king said the fourth was like the Son of God. The king went to the furnace and called for Shadrach, Meshach, and Abednego, servants of the most high God, to come forth. They came forth and had no harm at all not even to their clothes. The king then made a decree that anyone who spoke anything against the God of Shadrach, Meshach and Abednego would be cut into pieces and their houses destroyed. He also promoted the three men.

  Nebuchadnezzar had a vision afterwards (Daniel 4) and his men could not tell him the meaning. He called in Daniel whose name he had changed to Belteshazzar. Daniel told the king the meaning of the vision was because of his sins, he was going to be driven from among men and would dwell with the animals in the field. Daniel told him in Daniel 4:27 to stop his sinning and show mercy to the poor. The king did not heed Daniel's words and in 4:31 a voice told him the kingdom was departed from him. Sure enough, what Daniel had told the king was going to happen to him did and he went around like the beast of the field eating grass. When Nebuchadnezzar was restored by God, he praised God (Daniel 4:34).

Nebuchadnezzar's son Belshazzar became king and during a great feast he had made, he and those feasting with him drank wine in the vessels taken earlier from the temple of God at Jerusalem. While they were drinking, the fingers of a man's hand wrote upon the wall causing the king to become very afraid. When his men could not read the writing and explain it to him, the queen told him about Daniel. He called for Daniel who came and told him he was just like his father in not humbling his heart even though he knew what had happened to his father (Daniel 5:22). Daniel read the writing for him, MENE, MENE, TEKEL, UPHARSIN (verse 25) and told him the meaning was God had numbered his kingdom and finished it and he, the king, had been weighed in the balances and found wanting. His kingdom was going to be divided to the Medes and Persians. The king made Daniel third ruler in the kingdom and that night the king was slain and Darius the Mede who was an uncle of Cyrus took over.

Darius raised Daniel even higher in the kingdom making him first president over the princes of the kingdom (Daniel 6). The princes and other presidents tried to find something against Daniel but they could find no fault. They prepared a royal law saying whoever asked anything of any god other than the king for thirty days should be cast into the den of lions. The king agreed and signed the decree. When Daniel knew of it

(Daniel 6:10) he went as he was used to doing into his house three times a day with the window open toward Jerusalem and he prayed to God.

The king's men reported Daniel to the king and the king was very upset with himself for signing such a decree. He had Daniel cast into the den of lions, but he told Daniel he knew Daniel's God would deliver him. The king fasted all night and early the next morning he went to the den and cried out, "O Daniel, servant of the living God, is thy God, whom thou servest continually, able to deliver thee from the lions?" (6:20). Daniel was fine and the king was so happy. He had the accusers brought and thrown into the den of lions where the lions destroyed them. King Darius then made a decree unto all people and nations in every dominion of his kingdom, men were to tremble and fear before the God of Daniel because He is the living God (6:26). Daniel did well under the reign of Darius and in the reign of Cyrus according to Daniel 6:28.

Daniel also had visions in the book of Daniel as recorded in Chapters 7 and 8. In Chapter 9 Daniel prayed to God, confessing the sins of the nation. During his prayer, Gabriel came to him to give him revelation. In the last chapter of Daniel, the resurrection was prophesied (12:2) and Daniel was told to shut up the words and seal the book.

Another prophet, Ezekiel, was part of the second captivity which occurred in 597 B. C. His work covers a period going beyond the destruction of Jerusalem by about sixteen years. He spoke to those of the captivity in Telabib (Ezekiel 3:15). Through Ezekiel, God let the people know their captivity would be a long one. He showed them the reasons for their captivity and he tried to get them to change their ways. The chapters of Ezekiel contained various judgments against both Judah and other nations. Hamilton (n.d.) has written an excellent set of study notes concerning the book of Ezekiel as noted in the reference section of this book.

In Chapter 2 of Ezekiel, God told Ezekiel to go and tell the people what God had said but He warned Ezekiel the people were stiff hearted and impudent children (2:4) and they might not hear Ezekiel's words. In Chapter 3 God continued to warn Ezekiel of the likelihood the people would not hear him but in verses 17-22, God told Ezekiel if he did not warn the people of what was coming, then God would hold him accountable for not warning them but still the people would be punished. If Ezekiel did warn them and they chose not to repent, they would be punished, but Ezekiel would be free because he had warned them. God repeated this warning to Ezekiel in Ezekiel 33:1-9 and extended it to anyone who was a watchman. Will God hold us responsible if we have the truth and fail to share it with others?

In Chapter 18 Ezekiel made it very clear the children were not responsible for the sins of the parents or in other words, children did not inherit the sins of Adam and Eve. In verse 4 God told Ezekiel the soul that sins is the one that will die. Then in verses 20-28, He expanded upon that idea to say the son shall not bear the guilt of the father nor the father the guilt of the son. If the wicked turns from his sins and obeys God, then he shall live and his sins will not be mentioned. On the other hand, according to verse 24 when a righteous person turns from his righteousness and sins, then all the righteousness he has done will not be mentioned and he will die in his sins. In verse 32 God said He had no pleasure in the death of him that dies so turn yourself and live.

It seems no matter how many times Ezekiel and the other prophets appealed to the people to put their sinful ways aside and come back to the Lord, the people refused. God had set their time to be in captivity at seventy years as recorded in Jeremiah 29:10. Remember in Isaiah 44:28, about two hundred years previously, God had said in seventy years from the first captives being taken, King Cyrus would release them. Sure enough, Cyrus conquered Babylon and freed the Jews.

The book of Ezra picked up where 2nd Chronicles left off with this King Cyrus and his proclamation of freedom for the Jews. The first six chapters of Ezra are concerned with the first return of the Jews from Babylon led by Zerubbabel. In this return, fewer than 50,000 of the captives chose to go back to Jerusalem (Ezra 2:64). In Ezra 3-6 the prophet was concerned with the renewal of the worship in feasts and sacrifices and the construction of the new temple. In Chapter 4 of Ezra, the Jews met with opposition to their building program and construction ceased for a time. According to Ezra 5:1, it was during this time when Haggai and Zechariah were active in their work.

Haggai's message was concerned with how the people had taken care of their own needs (Haggai 1:4) but had left the temple to lie in waste. But God told Haggai to tell Zerubbabel even though this temple did not look like the first one, he was not to be discouraged because according to Haggai 2:4-9 God was going to do something great and shake all nations. The glory of the latter house would be greater than the glory of the previous one. Obviously, God was not referring to a physical temple in Jerusalem. In Haggai 2:21-23 the prophecy linked Zerubbabel to the coming Christ and in Matthew 1:12 Zorobabel (same person different spelling) was listed in the lineage of Christ.

While Haggai's message began in the sixth month of the second year of the reign of Darius, Zechariah's message began in the eighth month. The first part of Zechariah's work was also given as an encouragement to the people to complete the temple. Zechariah explained to the people how God was angry with them because of their inaction. But he went on to show God would provide for the people. In Zechariah 3:8, God promised to bring forth the BRANCH. Then in 8:12, He promised a remnant of the people would still receive a possession. Beginning in Chapter 9, God pronounced judgment against nations surrounding Judah. Then Zechariah prophesied concerning the coming Messiah and His rejection and being sold for thirty pieces of silver (11:12). He included the piercing of Christ (12:10-14) and the availability of cleansing (13:1). He noted prophets and unclean spirits would pass out of the land (13:2). In Zechariah 14:9, the prophet said, "And the Lord shall be king over all the earth: in that day there shall be one Lord and his name one."

The people listened to the words of Haggai and Zechariah and according to Ezra 5:1-2 work was begun again on the temple. Opposition to the building program continued until a search was made and the authorization from Cyrus to do the work was found as recorded in Ezra 6:1-3 and the temple was finished in Ezra 6:14-15. From Ezra Chapter 6 to Chapter 7 was a period of about sixty years. It was during this time Esther, a Jewess, became the queen of Persia. According to the information in the book of Esther, King Ahasuerus had made a feast and invited all the princes and servants. When the feast ended after 180 days, he made another feast lasting seven more days for all the people in the palace. When this feast was ending, and the king's heart was merry with wine (Esther 1:10), he called for Queen Vashti to come and let everyone see how beautiful she was. The queen refused to appear before the king and he became very angry. The king asked his wise men what he should do about the queen.

Memucan, one of the princes, told the king if he did not do something about Vashti's behavior, the rest of the women would follow her lead in not obeying their husbands. He suggested the king find a replacement for the queen. King Ahasuerus was pleased with the suggestion of Memucan, so he had letters sent to all the provinces saying every man should rule his own house and then he gave his servants permission to gather up all of the fair virgins so he could pick a new queen.

In their gathering up of virgins for the position of queen, Esther was included. Esther was an orphan being taken care of by her uncle Mordecai who had been carried from Jerusalem with the captivity (Esther 2:6-7). The keeper of the women, Hegai, liked Esther and helped her with all of the preparations the virgins had to go through before being presented to the king. Esther did not let anyone know she was a Jew because Mordecai had told her not to. Mordecai checked on her every day to see what was going to happen (2:11). After six months of purifications with oil of myrrh and six months with sweet perfumes and other preparations, it came Esther's turn to go in to the king. The king loved Esther above all of the other women. He placed the royal crown on her head and made her queen.

Now Mordecai sat at the king's gate and he heard some men plotting the king's death. Mordecai told Esther and she told the king. The men were hanged but nothing was done for Mordecai. The king had a man named Haman among his men and for some reason he promoted him above all the princes and commanded all the servants bow to Haman. Of course, Mordecai would not bow to him (Esther 3). When he continued to refuse to bow, some of the servants who knew Mordecai was a Jew reported him to Haman. Haman was mad and wanted to destroy not just Mordecai but also his people, the Jews. Haman went to King Ahasuerus and told him there was a certain people scattered abroad and dispersed among the Persians who had different laws and refused to keep the king's laws. He asked permission from the king to destroy them. The king agreed and allowed letters to be sent in his name to all the king's provinces ordering the Jews be destroyed.

When Mordecai and the Jews found out what was happening, they fasted, cried, and laid in sackcloth and ashes. When Esther found out Mordecai was outside the gate in sackcloth, she sent him raiment but he refused it. Esther sent Hatach to Mordecai to see what was wrong and Mordecai told him what Haman had done. Mordecai sent Esther a copy of the decree and sent her word she needed to go to the king and make supplication for her people. Esther was afraid to go before the king because she had not been called before him for a month and if she went to him when he was not inviting her, he might have her killed. In Esther 4:14, Mordecai sent her back word she would not escape if the Jews were killed and he said, "...who knoweth whether thou art come to the kingdom for such a time as this?"

Esther sent Mordecai back word (Esther 4:16) to gather the Jews and fast for three days and nights and then she would go in to the king and she said, "...if I perish, I perish." In three days, Esther went to the king and he held the scepter out to her. He asked her what she desired even to half the kingdom. She asked the king for him and Haman to come to a banquet she had prepared for them. The king agreed and called for Haman to come. Haman went to the banquet and went home bragging to his wife and friends about how he had been invited to the banquet and there was going to be another one tomorrow just for him and the king and queen. But Haman said none of this mattered to him as long as Mordecai the Jew was sitting at the king's gate. His wife and friends suggested to Haman he needed to build a gallows of fifty cubits in height and ask the king for permission to hang Mordecai.

In the meantime, the king could not sleep so he had the book of records brought in and read to him (Esther 6). In the book was the account of Mordecai having told the king about the planned attempt on his life. The king asked what had been done for Mordecai and when he found out nothing had been done for him, he decided something must be done. He asked who was in the court and Haman was there. The king said to send him in. The king asked Haman what should be done to a man the king wanted to honor. Haman, thinking it was himself the king wanted to honor, said the king should have one of the noblest princes put the king's clothes and crown upon this person and have him ride through the street of the city on the king's horse. The king liked the idea and told Haman to get the clothes and the horse and go and do this very thing for Mordecai, the Jew, who was sitting at the king's gate.

Haman and his friends knew there was trouble coming (Esther 6:12-13). While they were discussing the problem, the king's chamberlains or servants came to get Haman for the banquet. At the banquet, the king asked Esther what she wanted and she told him she and her people were going to be destroyed (7:1). The king wanted to know who was planning to do this and she told him it was Haman. The king was mad and left the room. While he was out, Haman thought to beg Esther for his life and he was on the bed where Esther was when the king returned. The king said (Esther 7:8), "Will he force the queen also before me in the house?"

One of the king's chamberlains told the king Haman had a gallows prepared for Mordecai who had helped save the king's life. The king said to hang Haman on that gallows. Mordecai was given the ring from Haman's hand and set over the house of Haman. The king asked Esther what she would like and she asked permission to destroy those who wanted to destroy the Jews. The king gave the Jews permission to destroy all of their enemies and many of the people became Jews because of their fear (Esther 8:17.) The Jews destroyed 75,000 enemies and then enjoyed two days of feasting. Mordecai was next unto the king and was a champion for his people (10:3).

Back in Ezra Chapters 7-10, the second group of Jews returned to Jerusalem being led by Ezra. According to Ezra 7:10, Ezra had prepared his heart to seek the law of the Lord and to do it and to teach in Israel the statutes and judgments. In Chapter 9, Ezra was very upset because he had found out the Jews had again taken wives of the children of the Canaanites, Hittites, Perizites, Jebusites, Ammonites, Moabites, Egyptians, and the Amorites. In 9:7 Ezra had prayed to God because of their sins and in verse 10, he admitted they had again forsaken God's commandments. In Chapter 10, others of the Jews admitted their sins and agreed to separate from the wives they had taken against God's laws.

Ezra's concern was mostly about the religious restoration of the Jews. During the same time when he lived but after his work, Nehemiah came on the scene. Nehemiah's concern was more with the restoration of Israel's government. Ezra 2 and Nehemiah 7 have some of the same information which helps to show Ezra and Nehemiah were writing about the same time period.

Nehemiah served in Shushan, the palace, under Artaxerxes who was the son of King Ahasuerus who married Esther. Nehemiah was the cupbearer for the king. In Nehemiah 2, the king asked him why he was so sad. Nehemiah told him the place of his fathers' burial grounds was in waste and the gates had been consumed with fire. Nehemiah asked the king for permission to go to Jerusalem in Judah and rebuild it. The king gave him permission and even sent letters requiring others to provide whatever Nehemiah needed.

Nehemiah went to Jerusalem and looked the situation over. He divided the work to the workers and they began the rebuilding of the walls. Just like the others had trouble rebuilding the temple because of ridicule and opposition, so did Nehemiah and his workers have trouble rebuilding the wall. But they succeeded and the wall was completed in 52 days (Nehemiah 6:15).

In Chapter 8 of Nehemiah, is an account where all the people gathered to hear Ezra, the scribe, read the book of the Law of Moses. In Nehemiah 8:3-4, Ezra read from a pulpit and the men and women were attentive to the book. In verse 8, the record said they explained the law to the people and caused them to understand the reading. The people were reminded of their great sins of the past and in Nehemiah 9:38 the people made a sure covenant and sealed it. Jerusalem was resettled by lots and the people promised to separate from the heathen. The Jews were once more settled in their promised land. Bible scholars including Coffman (n.d.) have indicated Nehemiah returned back to Persia around 433 B.C. which is when the book of Malachi is thought to have been written.

The last book of prophecy in the Old Testament, Malachi, is another short book of only four chapters. It seems there was no enthusiasm for doing the Lord's works. They despised the Lord, they were offering blemished sacrifices, and they had profaned the table of the Lord. They had neglected their tithes and were intermarried with the pagans. In Chapter 3, God once more reminded the people of His promise to those who serve Him (verses 16-18).

From Malachi to the New Testament, was a period of about 450 years of silence from God. The people had His word from the prophets. The Jews knew what they had gone through and those who knew the scriptures knew there was coming a Messiah who would be their new King. With the many prophesies in the scriptures concerning the new king to come, it is amazing how the priests and those who should have known the prophecies would not accept the Christ of the New Testament. In the next chapter, the many prophecies concerning this Christ will be reviewed.

Chapter 6
The Prophecies and their Fulfilment

In the last chapter of the book of Malachi, the last word of God from about 450 B.C. until the coming of Christ, there were two prophecies concerning one who would come before Christ and prepare the way for Him. The first prophecy in Malachi 3:1 says "I will send my messenger, and he shall prepare the way before me: and the Lord, whom ye seek, shall suddenly come to his temple, even the messenger of the covenant, whom ye delight in: behold, he shall come, saith the Lord of hosts." Then in Malachi 4:5 the prophet recorded a promise to send Elijah, the prophet, before the coming of the great and dreadful day of the Lord. In verse 6 is recorded this prophet would turn the heart of the fathers to the children and the heart of the children to their fathers.

In the New Testament account of the birth of John the Baptist, recorded in Luke 1, an angel announced to Zacharias his wife who was very old would have a son and many would rejoice at his birth. This one was to be great in the sight of the Lord and in verse 17 the angel was recorded as saying: "AND HE SHALL GO BEFORE HIM IN THE SPIRIT AND POWER OF ELIAS, TO TURN THE HEARTS OF THE FATHERS TO THE CHILDREN, AND THE DISOBEDIENT TO THE WISDOM OF THE JUST; TO MAKE READY A PEOPLE PREPARED FOR THE LORD."

In Isaiah 40:3-5, Isaiah had prophesied of one who would come to prepare the way for the Lord. Isaiah said in verse 3, "The voice of him that crieth in the wilderness, Prepare ye the way of the Lord, make straight in the desert a highway for our God." We know this prophet was John the Baptist because in Matthew 3:3 the writer said: "For this is He that was spoken of by the prophet Esaias, saying, The voice of one crying in the wilderness, Prepare ye the way of the Lord, make His paths straight," making it very clear this John was the one spoken of by Isaiah. We also know John the Baptist was the fulfillment of Isaiah's prophecy because in John 1:22-23 when the people asked him who he was, he said: "I am the voice of one crying in the wilderness, Make straight the way of the Lord, as said the prophet Esaias."

Many prophesies in the Old Testament referred to the coming of this One for whom John the Baptist was to prepare. Some of those prophecies have already been mentioned, but in this chapter, are more of these prophecies and their corresponding fulfillment in the New Testament. Interestingly not any one prophet in the Old Testament gave the complete prophecy of the coming Christ. Instead, God chose to deliver parts of the prophecy through different men and the enquiring mind needs to diligently study all of the prophecies to get the full picture of what God had planned for mankind. Jesus, Himself, told the people as recorded in John 5:39 to "Search the scriptures; for in them ye think ye have eternal life: and they are they which testify of me." Very clearly, one can again see the need for diligence in study. Jesus told the people to search the scriptures. In other words, they were not going to be able to go to just one book from the prophets or historians of the Old

Testament and understand the prophecies concerning Christ and neither can the modern day reader.

This One for whom John the Baptist was to prepare the way was the One who was in the beginning with God during creation and the One who was prophesied to come to establish His kingdom and to save His people. He was the One who fulfilled the seed promise from Genesis and the promise to Abraham, Isaac, Jacob, and David.

There are many websites providing excellent charts with prophesies concerning Christ and their fulfilment. Several of those are included in the reference section of this book (CBN, n.d.; Fairchild, 2016; New Testament Christians, n.d.; Palmer, n.d.; & Robinson, 2015). Once one is able to link the prophecies to their fulfillment in Christ, it is so hard to understand how there could be those who still do not believe in Him.

Throughout the Old Testament, the readers were reminded there was to be a seed coming. The first mention of this seed was in Genesis 3:15 as the seed of woman later revealed in Genesis 12:1-3 to be the seed of Abraham, then of Isaac (Genesis 17:19, 21:12), and Jacob (Genesis 28:13-15). He was to be of the tribe of Judah (Genesis 49:10). This seed would be one who blessed all nations of the earth.

The coming seed was to be a prophet like Moses (Deuteronomy 18:17-19), a priest (Psalm 110:4, Genesis 14:18), and a king who would be a descendent of David (2nd

Samuel 7:12-16). He was to come during the time of the Roman Empire, 490 years from when Daniel prophesied in Daniel 9:24.

He was to be born of a virgin (Isaiah 7:14) in Bethlehem (Micah 5:2) as a star out of Jacob (Numbers 24:17). Nations would come to Him bringing gold and frankincense (Isaiah 60:2-6). There would be lamenting due to deaths at His birth (Jeremiah 31:15). As a child, He would spend time in Egypt (Hosea 11:1).

This coming One was to be referred to by many different names that would indicate the work He would do, where He would live, and who He would be. Some of those were Immanuel (Isaiah 7:14), Son of man (Daniel 7:13-14), Son of God (Psalm 2:7), Wonderful, Counselor, Mighty God, Everlasting Father, Prince of Peace (Isaiah 9:6-7), the Christ (Messiah or Anointed) (Psalm 45:7-8), Emanuel or God with us (Isaiah 7:14).

He would bring light to Galilee (Isaiah 9:1-2), speak in parables (Psalm 78:1-4), that fell on deaf ears (Isaiah 6:9-10), and show signs of healing (Isaiah 35:5-6). He would be praised by little children (Psalm 8:2). He would come mounted on a donkey, even on a colt of the donkey (Zechariah 9:9).

Angels would protect Him from striking His foot on a stone (Psalm 91:10-12), but He would be rejected as a corner stone (Psalm 118:22-24). This Christ would have false accusations made against Him (Psalm 35:11), be betrayed by a friend (Psalm 41:9, 55:12-13), for thirty pieces of sliver (Zechariah 11:12-13). He would be spit on and struck (Isaiah 50:6), hated without a cause (Psalm 35:19), rejected by His own (Isaiah 53:3), and mocked (Psalm 22:7-8), but He would be silent amid it all (Isaiah 53:7) and would pray for His enemies (Psalm 109:4). He would be tried and condemned (Isaiah 53:8). He would be offered as a sacrifice for sin (Isaiah 53:5-12).

He would be crucified with criminals (Isaiah 53:12), would thirst (Psalm 22:15) and be given vinegar to drink (Psalm 69:21). In crucifixion, He would be pierced (Psalm 22:16, Zechariah 12:10) with blood pouring out (Psalm 22:14). As the animal sacrifices of the old covenant (Exodus 12:46, Numbers 9:12), His bones would not be broken (Psalm 34:20). The soldiers would gamble for His clothes (Psalm 22:18).

He would be forsaken by God (Psalm 22:1) but commit Himself to God (Psalm 22:20-21). He would be buried with the rich (Isaiah 53:9). He would be raised from the dead (Psalm 16:10, 49:15, 30:3), ascend to heaven (Psalm 68:18), and be seated at God's right hand (Psalm 110:1) as the heir to David's throne (2nd Samuel 7:12-13, Isaiah 9:7, Psalm 45:6-7, Daniel 2:44).

The promised seed would bring in a new covenant (Jeremiah 31:31). He would see His seed (Isaiah 53:10-11). He would establish an everlasting kingdom (Isaiah 9:7), and offer salvation to all (Joel 2:32). According to Daniel 9:24, the

Messiah would make an end of sin, make reconciliation for iniquity, bring in everlasting righteousness, seal up the vision and prophecy, and be anointed the Most Holy. According to verse 27, He would confirm the covenant with many and cause the sacrifice and offering to cease.

Having the ability to know all of these prophecies concerning the coming One does not at all mean the Jewish people of Jesus' day knew the prophecies. It is obvious few if any had made the connections between all of them. By putting together the accounts of His birth and life on earth given by Matthew, Mark, Luke, and John, it can be seen how Jesus Christ was definitely the fulfilment of the Old Testament prophecies. In the following pages, in nearly the same order as the previous prophecies, are the combined accounts of Jesus' birth, life, death, resurrection, and kingship.

According to the genealogy recorded in Matthew 1:1-2, and 6, Jesus Christ was the son of Abraham, Isaac, Jacob, Judah, and David. This would fulfill several of the prophecies concerning who Christ's ancestors would be and it placed Him in the correct tribe of Judah. In addition, Matthew said in Matthew 1:18-25 Christ was born of a virgin. According to Matthew 2:1, His birth took place in Bethlehem as Micah said would happen. At His birth, according to Matthew 2:2, the wise men saw His star and came to worship Him. They brought gifts of gold, frankincense, and myrrh as recorded in verse 11.

When King Herod found out about the birth, he made plans to kill Him. It was recorded in Matthew 2:16-18, how Herod had children two years old and under killed in hopes of killing Christ. According to verse 17 Jeremiah's prophecy concerning the lamenting was here fulfilled. To escape Herod, Joseph and Mary took the young child to Egypt as stated in Matthew 2:14 and they stayed there until the death of Herod. In Matthew 2:23, the author stated He lived in Nazareth that the prophecy concerning His being called a Nazarene would be fulfilled.

At His birth and throughout His ministry, Jesus was called by several names and in His work would have been known by even other titles. In Matthew 1:21, the angel said to call His name Jesus and in verse 25 the record says Joseph called His name Jesus. In verse 23 of the same chapter, Matthew mentioned the prophecy of Isaiah concerning calling Jesus Immanuel which is translated God with us. Peter pronounced Him as the Christ the Son of God in Matthew 16:16. The work He did fulfilled many of the other titles by which He was prophesied to be known. According to Matthew 21:15, the chief priests and scribes recognized the wonderful things Christ did thus fulfilling the role of wonderful. As a counselor or one who gave advice, Jesus fulfilled His role in every sermon. Finally, in John 14:27, Jesus said He left His peace with His disciples. Jesus came that we might have peace with God.

Matthew gave an account in Matthew 3:1-12 concerning John, the forerunner of Christ, and in verse 11, John told the people the One coming after him was mightier than John and John did not think himself even worthy of carrying the sandals of this One to come. In Matthew 3:13-17, Matthew recorded the baptism of Jesus by John and God Himself declared in verse 17, Christ was His Son.

After Jesus' baptism, He was led into the wilderness to be tempted by the devil. In Matthew's account of this event in Chapter 4, the second temptation by the devil was for Jesus to cast Himself down from the temple. The devil then told Jesus it was written about Him the angels would take care of Him if He dashed His foot against a stone. Even the devil knew it was Jesus about whom this prophecy was written. Later in Matthew 4:12-17, Matthew noted after the temptation, Jesus began to preach and He was the One who fulfilled the prophecy concerning bringing the great light to Galilee.

As Jesus continued His ministry, He often taught using parables. In Matthew 13:3 the author stated: "And He spake many things unto them in parables..." In verse 10, His disciples asked Him why He spoke in parables. He told them in verse 11 unto them was given to know the mysteries of the kingdom of heaven but to those outside of them, it was not given so He needed to speak in parables for them to understand. In Matthew 13:34-35, Matthew noted Jesus spoke in parables so the prophecy concerning Him speaking in parables would be fulfilled.

As Jesus taught the people, He also included signs of healing. When John the Baptist sent his disciples to ask Jesus if He was the One for whom they were looking, in their presence Jesus cured many diseases and He told the disciples of John to return to John and tell him what they had seen Jesus do with the healing of the sick, raising of the dead, and preaching of the gospel (Luke 7:17-22).

When Jesus was entering Jerusalem (Matthew 21:1-10), He sent two of His disciples into the village to get a donkey and her colt and bring them for Him to ride upon to enter the city. They brought the animals and put their clothes upon them and Jesus rode into Jerusalem where the people were chanting, "Hosanna to the son of the David. Blessed is he that cometh in the name of the Lord..." According to verse 11, the multitude said this Jesus was the prophet of Nazareth of Galilee.

Jesus continued His teaching and as recorded in John 12:32, Jesus clearly told the people if He was lifted up from the earth, He would draw all men to Himself. John explained in verses 37-40 even though Jesus had done all of these great miracles, the people did not believe, but this was in fulfillment of the prophecy of Esaias.

When Jesus went to the temple, and the money changers were there, Jesus drove them out and then healed a lame man. As recorded in Matthew 21:15-16, when the chief priests and scribes saw how the children were praising Jesus, they were very upset. They even asked Jesus if He heard the children calling out "Hosanna to the son of David." Jesus reminded them of the Old Testament prophecy and asked them if they had not read, "Out of the mouth of babes and sucklings thou has perfected praise." If these scribes had known the scripture as they should have, would they not have realized what was happening in their presence?

When the chief priests and Pharisees realized Jesus was speaking about them, in Matthew 21:42-44 when He told them the prophecy concerning Himself being rejected as the chief cornerstone, they wanted to lay hands upon Him. They were afraid to bother Jesus though because as noted in verse 46, the multitude believed Him to be a prophet. A prophet He was, but more than a prophet. As Jesus continued to preach to His followers, He explained to them in John 15:24-25 the hearers who had seen the works He had done hated both Him and His Father, but He said this had happened in fulfillment of the prophecy, "they hated Him without a cause."

Finally, the people could take no more of Jesus' teachings. One of His own apostles betrayed Him. In Matthew 26:14, Matthew recorded how Judas, one of the twelve, went to the chief priests and covenanted or agreed with them for thirty pieces of silver. Jesus Himself had warned His apostles this would happen as recorded in John 13:18 where after having eaten with the twelve, He quoted from Psalm 41, "He that eateth bread with me hath lifted up his heel against me," referring to His betrayal by Judas.

When Jesus was taken before the Sanhedrin to be tried, there were false accusations made against Him. In Mark 14:56, Mark stated many brought false witness against Him, but in verse 59, it seems they could not get their stories to agree. During the accusations, Jesus was silent as recorded in Mark 15:4-5. He was spit upon and struck as recorded in Matthew 26:67, He was mocked according to Luke 23:11 and 35, the voice of the people prevailed according to Luke 23:23-24, and He was led to be crucified. There on the cross, He prayed (Luke 23:34) "Father forgive them: for they know not what they do."

Jesus was crucified with two thieves (Mark 15:27-28). We know His hands were pierced because in John 20:25-29 after His resurrection, when Thomas had said he would not believe Christ was risen unless he could see the prints in His hands, He told Thomas to reach and feel them. While on the cross, He was thirsty and according to Matthew 27:34, they gave Him vinegar to drink. In His crucifixion, just like the Passover lamb, no bones were broken. According to John 19:33, when they came to check on Christ and the thieves and Jesus was already dead, instead of breaking His legs as was the normal process, they pierced His side and blood and water came forth. The soldiers cast lots to see who would get His clothes as noted in Matthew 27:35.

As Christ was the sacrifice for our sins (John 3:16), God forsook Him according to Matthew 27:46 where Matthew recorded Jesus as saying "My God, My God, why hast Thou forsaken me?" The centurion and those with him who watched the crucifixion were convinced Jesus was the Son of God when the earthquake came and graves were opened, and many bodies of saints arose according to Matthew 27:54. Then came Joseph of Arimathea, a rich man according to Matthew 27:57, and begged Pilate for the body of Jesus so he could bury the body in his own new tomb.

Christ Himself had told the people in Mark 8:31 He would be rejected and killed but He would be raised on the third day. Just as He said, recorded in Matthew 28:2-7, when the women went to the tomb on the first day of the week, there was not a body in the tomb. The Christ was risen. According to Mark's account in Mark 16:19, Jesus was received up into heaven where He sat on the right hand of God. He is reigning there now as promised to His mother in Luke 1:32-33; He is reigning over His everlasting kingdom which He promised to establish in Matthew 16:18-19. Here He told Peter, upon this rock or upon the confession Peter had made in saying Jesus was the Christ the Son of God, He would build His church. In verse 19, He told Peter he would be given the keys to the kingdom. Peter and the other apostles used the keys to the kingdom in Acts 2 when they preached the first gospel sermon and the Lord added those people who accepted the terms of obedience (Acts 2:38) to this kingdom or church (Acts 2:47). In the second recorded sermon Luke stated in Acts 3:20-23 that Peter showed the people this Christ was the prophet Moses promised.

In His death and shedding of His blood, Christ brought in the new covenant. In Matthew 26:28 when Christ was instituting the Lord's Supper, He told His apostles the cup was His blood of the new testament or covenant which is shed for many for the remission of sins.

As noted in previous verses, there were some who did believe Jesus was the Christ the Son of God. Peter confessed Him as being the Son of God. The devil knew He was the one to whom the prophecies of the Old Testament applied. Some of the scribes were convinced and the centurion and those with Him during the crucifixion knew He was the One. Yet, so many denied Him even having seen the miracles He did and having heard what He had to say. Is it any different today when people read these accounts and a few believe and obey but so many turn away? But for those who believe in the Christ, the Son of God, there is a great responsibility to share with others.

Hopefully some of the prophecies covered in this chapter along with their fulfillment will be useful when talking to others about belief in Jesus Christ as the Son of God. It should be obvious, He is the One God promised as the seed of Abraham, Isaac, Jacob, and David, and the One we need to trust and obey. In the next chapter, are several of Jesus' miracles which should have convinced the people He was the One sent from God and should convince our friends and neighbors He is all powerful.

Chapter 7
The Miracles of Jesus

The fact Jesus fulfilled so many of the Old Testament prophecies may not have been enough to convince the people He was the One they were looking for, but surely His miracles would do the job. It appears from Luke 3:23 Jesus began His earthly ministry when He was about thirty years old. In this passage, He had just been baptized by John the Baptist to fulfil all righteousness (Matthew 3:13-17), and in John 2:1-12, John recorded His first miracle of changing the water to wine.

One may ask why Jesus did miracles. The first thought in reply could be to help others because He loved them, but there seems to be another very different reason as stated in Matthew 8:16-17. Here Matthew said Jesus did these miracles in fulfillment of the Old Testament prophecies by Isaiah. In the Old Testament prophecies concerning the coming Messiah, it was indicated this One would do miracles. In Isaiah 35:5-7, Isaiah prophesied concerning the eyes of the blind being opened, the ears of the deaf unstopped, and the lame leaping. In Isaiah 53:4, the coming One was to carry the griefs and sorrows also called sicknesses. So for those who were present, these miracles served to prove to them Jesus was the Son of God. But what about us today who do not get to see the miracles but can read about them? According to John in John 20:30-31, the writers of the works of Jesus included these miracles in their writings so those who read would believe

Jesus is the Son of God. There truly was a reason for the miracles and for them being included in the writing of the New Testament. With this in mind, let us look at these miracles.

The first miracle recorded was at a wedding in Cana and the attendees had drunk all the wine. In John 2:1-11, Mary told Jesus they were out of wine as if she expected Him to do something about it. When Jesus asked her in verse 4 what her concern had to do with Him, she told the servants to do whatever Jesus told them to do. He told them to fill the six water pots with water. They did and then He told them to serve the guests. They did and when the ruler of the feast tasted the wine, he was very complimentary to the groom telling him most people set out the good first and then the inferior wine, but he had kept the best till last.

This miracle has been questioned by many because of the fact Jesus made wine, but we are taught we should not drink alcoholic beverages. The simplest explanation is found in the meaning of the word *oinos* which is the Greek word used in the passage for wine. This term can mean either fermented or unfermented juice of the grape. In keeping with the teaching of Christ and the apostles, I am firmly convinced the wine here was the pure unfermented juice of the grape. We know Christ lived under the Old Testament law and several passages such as Proverbs 20:1, Isaiah 5:11, and Proverbs 23:29-35 show the problems associated with drinking. In the New Testament, after Christ's kingdom was established, we have other verses telling us how we need to live. Among those are verses in Galatians 5:21 and Ephesians 5:18 telling us to not be drunk. Paul in 1st Thessalonians 5:8 said to be of a sober mind which one who is drinking cannot be. The best collection of definitions I have found in support of the conclusion the wine Jesus made was grape juice was from Lavista church of Christ and noted on the reference page.

This again is an excellent example of how we must make sure our understanding of any one passage of scripture is in agreement with the other scriptures. We cannot allow scriptures to contradict each other so when it seems we have a contradiction, the problem is never with the scriptures but with our understanding of them. According to 2nd Timothy 3:16, "All scripture is given by inspiration of God, and is profitable for doctrine, for reproof, for correction, for instruction in righteousness: that the man of God may be perfect (complete), thoroughly furnished unto all good works." By diligent study, we will get to the truth of all Bible subjects.

In John 4, Jesus had gone into Samaria where He sat down at the well. A Samaritan woman came to draw water from the well and Jesus began talking to her. If you remember back in Nehemiah, the opposition to rebuilding the walls of Jerusalem came from the Samaritans. These were the Jews left in Judah who intermarried with Gentiles who had been moved into the area by the king. The Jews hated them. So when Jesus began to talk to the woman, not only was she surprised (John 4:9), but His disciples were also shocked (John 4:27). The fact Jesus was able to tell this woman she had already had five husbands and the one she was with at the time of their discussion was not her husband led her to believe in Jesus. In verse 26 Jesus told her He was the Messiah. She went straight to the city and told the people Christ had told her all about her life. The people went out to see Him and in verse 39, John recorded many of the Samaritans believed on Him because of the woman's testimony. Jesus stayed with them for two days and more of the people believed (John 4:40-42). Then when He went into Galilee, the Galileans also believed on Him for what He did (John 4:45).

Here in John 4:46, Jesus was back in Cana where He had made the water into wine. One of the royal officials heard He was there and he went to Him asking Him to come and heal his son who was near death. Jesus told him his son lived and the man believed Him. Sure enough when the man got home, his servants told him the time of day the son revived and it was the very hour in which Jesus had told him his son lived.

Just as was prophesied in Isaiah, Jesus healed many people of sicknesses and cast out devils. In Matthew 8:14-17, Mark 1:29-31, and Luke 4:38-39 the writers gave the account of the healing of Simon's mother-in-law. In addition to being an important account of one being healed, this account also indicates Peter had been married which may be an important point to remember for some Bible discussions with our friends.

Another healing of a woman was recorded by the same three writers in Matthew 9:20-22, Mark 5:25-34, and Luke 8:43-48. This woman had been bleeding for twelve years and when she heard of Jesus, she thought to herself if she could touch only His garment, she could be healed. She touched the hem of His garment and in Matthew's account He turned to her and told her to be of good comfort for her faith had made her whole.

Remember from the Old Testament how lepers were considered unclean and there was no cure for the ailment. Naaman suffered from leprosy and Elisha was the prophet through whom God healed him. Jesus also healed those with leprosy. In Matthew 8:2-4, Mark 1:40-45, and Luke 5:12-15 is given the account of a leper who came to Jesus and worshipped Him asking Him to heal the leprosy. Jesus touched him and healed him. Jesus told the man to go and make his offerings according to the Old Testament law and to keep quiet about the healing. Instead the man went out and told everyone so even more people came to be healed.

In Luke 17:11-19, Luke gave the account of ten lepers who called to Jesus and asked for mercy. Jesus told them to go show themselves to the priests and as they went to do so, they were all healed. Only one of them, a Samaritan, returned to thank Jesus. Jesus commented in verse 18 concerning the fact that only one returned to give glory to God. How often today are people blessed only to continue living in their old life of sin and never thinking for a moment about the God from whom all blessings flow?

On several occasions, the writers recorded Jesus healed those we would today say were paralyzed. In both Matthew 8:5-13 and Luke 7:1-10 is given an account of such a man. He was a servant of a centurion and the centurion was sure Jesus could heal him. When Jesus was going to go with the centurion to heal the servant, the centurion told Jesus he was not worthy to have Jesus come under his roof, but if Jesus would just speak the word, his servant would be healed. Jesus said to the people He had not seen so great a faith in all of Israel and He told the centurion to go his way and for it to be done according to his faith. He servant was healed from that very hour.

Another account of a paralytic being healed was given in Matthew 9:2-8, Mark 2:1-12, and Luke 5:17-26. In this account, when those men who were bringing the paralytic to Christ could not get to Him because of the crowd, they took the roof off the house and let the man down. Jesus not only healed the man but proclaimed his sins forgiven him. Again, what faith those men who dropped this one down into the room must have had.

One other account of a man who must not have been able to move on his own was given in John 5:1-18 where the record indicates this man had been impotent for thirty-eight years. Jesus told him to take up his bed and walk and the man did. The problem was, it was the Sabbath Day and because of the law against working on the Sabbath, the Jews tried to kill

Jesus. Little did they realize Jesus was Lord of the Sabbath as recorded in Mark 2:28.

Again on the Sabbath, we have Jesus healing a man with a withered hand. This miracle is recorded in Matthew 12:9-14, Mark 3:1-6, and Luke 6:5-11. Since Jesus had already been doing miracles on the Sabbath, the people were watching Him to see if He would heal this man so they could accuse Him. He asked the people if it was lawful to do good on the Sabbath or to do evil, to save a life or to kill. The people did not answer Him and Jesus told the man to stretch out his hand. He did and the hand was made whole.

Another Sabbath miracle took place as recorded in Luke 13:10-17 where a woman who had been bent over for eighteen years was freed from her infirmity. Jesus laid His hands on her and she was immediately made straight. There was again indignation because Jesus continued to heal on the Sabbath.

In the very next chapter of Luke, Chapter 14, in verses 1-6 is given the account of a man with dropsy being in the house of a chief Pharisee where Jesus had gone to eat bread. There were lawyers and Pharisees there and Jesus asked them if it was lawful to heal on the Sabbath. They did not answer Him, so He healed the man and then He asked the lawyers and Pharisees if they had an animal that fell into the ditch on the Sabbath what they would do. They still did not answer him.

Jesus also healed the blind, deaf, and mute. In Matthew 9:27-31, He healed two blind men. He said for them to be healed according to their faith and both were completely healed from their blindness. In Mark 8:22-26 was recorded another account of a blind man healed. This time Jesus spit on his eyes and asked him if he saw anything. The man said he saw men as trees walking so then Jesus put his hands upon the man's eyes and his sight was restored and he saw clearly.

A whole chapter in John is devoted to an account of Christ healing a blind man. In John 9, before Jesus had restored the man's sight, Jesus' disciples wanted to know who had sinned causing the blindness, the man or his parents. Jesus made it clear the blindness was not the cause of the sin of either which is a very important point to remember when thinking about people who are sick or disabled. Once Jesus healed this blind man, the man had to tell his story several times and in the end, even his parents were involved. They would not admit Jesus had done the miracle because they were afraid of being cast out of the synagogue (verse 22), but the man confessed and was put out (verse 34).

Finally, in one other account Jesus healed two blind men near Jericho. This healing is recorded in Matthew 20:29-34 as two men but in Mark 10:46-52 and Luke 18:35-43 a similar if not the same healing was recorded as one man. Whichever the case, the multitude rebuked the blind for crying out, but Jesus stopped and had mercy and restored the sight. In Matthew

15:29-31, Matthew noted many were brought to Jesus to be healed including those who were lame, blind, dumb, and maimed. In each case when the multitude saw what Jesus did, they were amazed and glorified the God of Israel.

A deaf and dumb man received healing in Mark 7:31-37 and he was told not to tell anyone, but the more Christ told the healed not to broadcast it, the more they told others. According to verse 37, the people said of Christ, "He hath done all things well: He maketh both the deaf to hear, and the dumb to speak."

In addition to healing the sick, blind, lame, and those with other physical ailments, on many occasions, Jesus cast out devils. In Mark 1:21-28 and Luke 4:31-37, the evil spirit in the man knew Jesus was the Holy One of God and so confessed. Jesus rebuked him and commanded him to come out of the man. The evil spirit did come out.

Just after healing two blind men, Jesus met a man possessed with a devil. This account is given in Matthew 9:32-34. In Matthew 8:28-34, Mark 5:10-20, and Luke 8:26-40 is a most amazing account of Jesus casting out devils. Two men possessed with devils were so fierce no one could pass by the tombs where they were. These devils asked Christ if He cast them out to let them go into a herd of swine nearby. Jesus told them to go and they went into the swine. The pigs ran over a steep place and into the sea and were destroyed. The people of the city begged Christ to leave their city.

Then in Mathew 15:21-28 and Mark 7:24-30 is recorded the account of a Gentile woman begging Jesus to heal her daughter of a devil. At first Jesus would not answer her but when she persisted, He told her He was only sent to the lost of the house of Israel. He said it was not right to take the children's bread and cast it to the dogs. The woman was persistent and told Jesus He was right about the bread but the dogs do eat of the crumbs that fall from the master's table. Hearing her statement and seeing her persistence, Jesus admired her faith and granted her desire to make the daughter whole.

The scribes as recorded in Matthew 12:22-30, Mark 3:22-27, and Luke 11:14-23 accused Jesus of casting out devils by the power of Beelzebub, the prince of devils. When Jesus' disciples were unable to cast out one particular devil as described by Matthew in 17:14-21, by Mark in 9:14-29, and by Luke in 9:37-43, the boy's father fell on his knees to Jesus and asked him to cure his son. Jesus again rebuked the devil and he left the child. When the disciples wanted to know why they could not cast him out, Jesus told them it was because of their lack of faith and He went on to say this kind goes out only by prayer and fasting.

On one special occasion, recorded by all four gospel writers, Jesus actually replaced a body part. In Matthew 26:47-56, Mark 14:43-50, Luke 22:47-53, and John 18:1-11 we have the account where Peter had cut off the ear of Malchus, a servant of the high priest when they had come to arrest Christ before His crucifixion. Jesus replaced the ear. In addition to being an important account of a miracle of Jesus, this record also presses home the point concerning the importance of reading all the Bible has to say on a subject. If one only read the account given by Matthew or Mark, much information would not be known. Luke's account said Jesus healed him and John's account gave us the man's name.

Not only did Jesus heal all manner of diseases, cast out devils, and replace body parts, but He also raised the dead. In Luke 7:11-17, Luke told the readers about a young man who died. His mother was a widow. The people were carrying him out in an open coffin and Jesus stopped them and said to the body, "Young man, I say unto thee, Arise." He arose and the people feared and glorified God. It was right after this John's disciples went to Jesus to ask if He was the One for whom they were waiting.

Then as recorded in Matthew 9:18-19, 23-26; Mark 5:21-24, 35-43; and Luke 8:41-42, 49-56, Jesus was called upon by Jairus, a ruler of the synagogue, to come and heal his twelve year old daughter. While Jesus was on the way to Jairus' house, the daughter died. Jesus went in and raised her from the dead. Jesus charged the parents not to tell anyone what He had done.

Possibly the best known raising from the dead by Christ is the account of Lazarus recorded only by John in John 11:1-

46. In this case, Lazarus had been dead four days before Jesus got to his tomb. Jesus was friends with Lazarus and his sisters Mary and Martha. Both Mary and Martha told Jesus if He had been there when Lazarus was sick, he would not have died. On His way to the tomb, in John 11:35, in the shortest verse in the Bible, John recorded, "Jesus wept."

Jesus went to the tomb and told the people to remove the stone at the mouth of the cave. They did and Jesus said: "Lazarus, come forth." Lazarus arose from the dead. According to verses 45-53, there were some who believed on Jesus but there were others who wanted to kill Him. At this time Caiaphas, the high priest prophesied Christ should die for all the people and gather together in one the children of God who were scattered (verses 51-52).

In addition to healing and raising from the dead, Jesus did other types of miracles. Several of these miracles were done on or near the water. In Luke 5:1-11 early in Christ's ministry, Jesus was teaching the people from Peter's ship. He told Peter to cast his net out for a big catch. Peter told Him they had fished all night and taken nothing, but nevertheless, he cast out the net and caught so many fish the net broke. On another occasion recorded in John 21:1-14, Jesus again told Peter to cast out and he did and brought in so many fish they were not able to haul in the net.

Even Jesus' own disciples were amazed at times over the miracles which Jesus did. In Matthew 8:23-27, Mark 4:35-

41, and Luke 8:22-25 is given an account of an occasion when Jesus and His disciples were in a ship and a great wind came up so the ship was overcome with waves. Jesus rebuked the winds and the sea and there was a great calm. The reply of the men in Matthew 8:27 gave us the lyrics of one of our favorite songs: "The winds and the waves shall obey Thy will."

In Matthew 14:22-33, Mark 6:45-52, and John 6:15-21, Jesus again showed His power over the water. Here we have another time when the disciples were in the ship but Jesus was not with them. Again there was a storm on the water, and Jesus came toward the disciples walking on the water. According to Matthew's account, when Peter realized it was Jesus walking on the water, he asked Jesus to bid Peter to come to Him. Jesus did and Peter started out walking on the water, but like so many of us today, he lost faith and began to sink. Jesus reached out and caught him and they both went into the ship.

Finally, one other miracle from the water is recorded in Matthew 17:24-27 where Jesus and His disciples needed to pay the temple tax or tribute money. They did not have any money with which to pay. Jesus told Peter to go and cast a hook in the water and take up the first fish he caught. Jesus said there would be a piece of money in his mouth and for Peter to take that money and pay the tax. This was one of the few recorded miracles where Jesus produced something to be spent or used in some way.

In addition to changing the water to wine, producing the temple tax, and providing two large catches of fish, on two other occasions, the authors recorded accounts of Jesus creating something to be used by man. In Matthew 14:13-21, Mark 6:30-44, Luke 9:10-17, and John 6:1-14 is recorded the miracle of feeding 5000. Jesus had been preaching to the people and when the evening came, the disciples wanted to send the people away to buy themselves food, but Jesus told the disciples to feed them. There was a lad in the group who had five loaves of barley bread and two small fish. So Jesus told the disciples to make the people sit down in groups of fifty. Jesus looked up to heaven and gave thanks for the food and gave it to His disciples who gave it to the people. When everyone had finished eating all they wanted, Jesus told the disciples to gather up the left overs so that nothing was lost. They had twelve baskets of left overs. According to John 6:14, there were those who once they had seen this miracle were convinced this was the prophet who was supposed to come into the world.

In another feeding miracle, there were 4000 fed as recorded in Matthew 15:32-38 and Mark 8:1-9. This time, the disciples had seven loaves of bread and a few small fish with them. Jesus commanded the people to be seated on the ground and once Jesus had given thanks, He gave the bread and meat to the disciples who gave it to the people. Everyone had enough to eat and this time there were seven baskets of food left over. Notice in both feeding accounts, are examples of giving thanks for food before eating and of picking up the leftovers so nothing will be wasted.

The final miracle was a different type of miracle. This one was not done to help someone but apparently to show not only what would happen to Israel, but to show His disciples what they could do with faith. In this case, Jesus approached a fig tree having had no figs. The account is recorded in Matthew 21:18-22 and Mark 11:12-26. Jesus pronounced a curse on the tree in saying to it, "Let no fruit grow on thee henceforward forever" (Matthew 21:19). The tree withered and the next day when the disciples passed by it, the tree was dried up from the roots. In Mark 11:21, Peter brought it to the attention of Jesus and Jesus told him to have faith in God and whatever he desired, when he prayed, he needed to believe he would receive and he would (verse 24).

As noted earlier, the miracles Jesus did served the purpose of fulfilling Old Testament prophecies. In addition, Jesus' miracles got the attention of the people. Sometimes the miracles caused people to believe in Jesus and to listen to His message. At other times, while the people may have believed, they chose to not listen to the message, and as we saw earlier, sometimes they chose to believe the miracles were through the power of the devil. For those who chose to listen, Jesus had a great message as we will see in the next chapter.

Chapter 8
Jesus' Teachings

Just as God chose to give the prophecies of the coming Christ and His kingdom through several men in the Old Testament, He also chose to give the work and words of Jesus through different men in the New Testament. Those same four gospels containing information about the miracles of Jesus, Matthew, Mark, Luke, and John also include His teachings. Some of the teachings of Jesus are recorded by all of these men, some by three of them, some by two, and some by only one of the four. As noted in Chapter 6, it was prophesied Jesus would teach in parables. In the current chapter are many of those parables and a discussion of how they showed the people two of the main themes of Jesus Christ, loving God with all of your heart and loving your neighbor as yourself, and choosing your way carefully. In addition, other teachings of Christ will be examined.

After Jesus began His ministry with miracles of healing and teaching and preaching, He had a following of many people (Matthew 4:25). In Matthew 4, as noted earlier, He was tempted by the devil to cast Himself down because the scriptures said the angels would protect Him even if He dashed His foot against a stone. During this period of temptation, the devil tempted Christ in the three ways we are tempted, by the lust of the flesh, lust of the eyes, and the pride of life which were the same ways mentioned earlier Eve was tempted in the beginning.

Jesus had fasted forty days and nights and was hungry. The devil tempted Him to yield to the lust of the flesh by changing stones to bread. Then came the temptation already mentioned where the devil wanted Him to jump from the pinnacle of the temple which would have been yielding to the pride of life. Finally, the devil took Jesus up in a very high mountain and had Him look at all the glory of the kingdoms of the world. The devil told Jesus if He would fall down and worship him, he would give Jesus all the kingdoms of the world which would have been yielding to the lust of the eyes if Jesus had accepted the offer. Of course, Jesus answered the devil each time with scripture and the devil left Him.

Jesus proceeded to select His twelve apostles from His followers and in choosing, He chose two sets of brothers, Peter and Andrew and James and John, all four of which were fishermen. Others He chose included Philip; Bartholomew; Thomas; Matthew, the tax collector; James, the son of Alphaeus; Lebbaeus, also called Thaddeaus; Simon the Canaanite; and Judas Iscariot, who betrayed Christ (Matthew 10:2-4). Later after Judas committed suicide, the other apostles by lot replaced him with Matthias (Acts 1:26) and Paul was an apostle (1st Corinthians 15:8-9) bringing the total to 14.

Interestingly, it seems when Jesus called at least four of these men, they left everything and followed Him. In Matthew

4:18-22 is the account of the calling of Peter and Andrew and James and John and in both cases, the writer said they straightway or immediately followed Him. In Mark's account in Mark 1:16-20, James and John left their father, Zebedee, in the ship with the hired servants and followed Jesus while Peter and Andrew left their nets and followed Him. Would it not be wonderful today if when people were called to the Lord through His word, they would forsake the world and give their lives totally to Christ?

In Matthew 5-7 is an extensive account of Jesus' teachings often referred to as the *Sermon on the Mount.* The title comes from the fact Jesus had those great multitudes following Him and He had gone up into a mountain. They followed Him and "He opened his mouth, and taught them" (Matthew 5:2). In verses 3-10 is recorded what is commonly called the Beatitudes. These are the blessings Jesus pronounced on people with certain characteristics. They make up ten verses that I encourage all of my Bible students to memorize and try to emulate. The content here shows it is the spiritual which is important and not the physical.

From the King James Version of the Bible in the public domain, the verses making up the Beatitudes from Matthew 5 are: "3. Blessed are the poor in spirit: for theirs is the kingdom of heaven. 4. Blessed are they that mourn: for they shall be comforted. 5. Blessed are the meek: for they shall inherit the earth. 6. Blessed are they which do hunger and thirst after righteousness: for they shall be filled. 7. Blessed are the merciful: for they shall obtain mercy. 8. Blessed are the pure in heart: for they shall see God. 9. Blessed are the peacemakers: for they shall be called the children of God. 10. Blessed are they which are persecuted for righteousness' sake: for theirs is the kingdom of heaven. 11. Blessed are ye, when men shall revile you, and persecute you, and shall say all manner of evil against you falsely, for my sake. 12. Rejoice, and be exceeding glad: for great is your reward in heaven: for so persecuted they the prophets which were before you."

By having these characteristics, we know we will be pleasing to God. Just after the beatitudes, the next four verses are often referred to as the similitudes because in these verses, Jesus compared His followers to the salt of the earth and to the light of the world. Just think for a minute what the world would be like without either salt or light. Salt is used for so many things other than cooking. Just a few things salt can be used for include to: soak your feet, kill bad odors, cure meat, melt ice, help a sore throat, clean grease off skillets, kill unwanted grass, and keep cut flowers fresh.

As a Christian, can you think of ways we are like salt or similar to salt? Think about our interactions in the world and how others can see Christ living in us by our actions. We can ease the pains of life in our discussions with others, we can kill the bad seed of false doctrine through the word, we can melt the hearts of sinners with the love of God, and we can clean the dirty soul through the teachings of God's word. We are like salt.

As the light of the world, we are also showing the world Christ. Imagine a world in which there is no light and all is darkness. Then imagine someone shining a light into that dark world. Think how people would gather to see what the light could show them. As Christians, we are the light and we must let Christ show forth in all we do. Note Jesus told the people in Matthew 5:16 to let their light shine before men so they may see their good works and glorify God. He did not tell them to shine their light so they may be glorified. There is a big difference here and Jesus had more to say about this in Matthew 6 when He taught about almsgiving, prayer, and fasting.

After the beatitudes and similitudes, Jesus told His followers He had not come to destroy the law or the prophets, but He had come to fulfill them. Earlier, we looked at many of the prophecies of the coming Messiah and at the way in which Jesus fulfilled them. According to Matthew 5:18, the law would not pass away until it was fulfilled and Christ was even then fulfilling the law.

In the rest of Matthew Chapter 5, Jesus showed the people how they not only needed to keep the commands they had been taught, but they also needed to do so from their heart and not just with a show of actions. He told them their righteousness had to exceed the righteousness of the scribes and Pharisees in order for them to enter the kingdom of heaven. For example in verses 21-26, He told them they had heard the command not to murder but Jesus was making that command even stronger. Not only were they not supposed to murder, but they were not to even be angry with a brother without a cause. If one brought his gift to the altar and remembered a brother had something against him (not he had something against the brother), he was to go and find the brother and make it right before he offered his gift.

As far as adultery was concerned, Jesus told the people they knew the command not to commit adultery (Matthew 5:27), but He was going even farther with the adultery command too. He told them if a man even looked on a woman to lust after her, he had committed adultery in his heart. Then he went right into divorce and told the people divorce was only allowed in the case of fornication. He said one who put away his wife except for fornication committed adultery and also caused the spouse to commit adultery. Over in Matthew 19:4-9, Jesus told the people from the beginning God had made marriage for life but because of the hardness of their hearts, Moses had allowed them to divorce. He went on to tell them this was not the case and as He stated here in Matthew 5, divorce was only allowed for fornication.

The next topic Jesus covered in the sermon was swearing (Matthew 5:33). He told the people they had heard before they were not to swear falsely, but He was telling them they should not need to swear at all. Instead of swearing, their word should be good and they should not need to say more than a "yes" or "no" in order to be believed.

The topic of love ends Chapter 5 of Matthew and love is spread throughout the gospels. Here in Matthew 5:43-48, Christ again compared what they had heard about loving their neighbors and hating their enemies to the truth of the matter which He said was they had to love their enemies too. He told them they needed to pray for those who persecuted them so they could be the children of God. He reminded them when they chose to keep only the letter of the law, they were no better than the publicans. Later in Matthew 22:36-40, when a lawyer asked Christ what was the greatest commandment of the law, Jesus told him the greatest commandment was to love God with all of your heart, soul, and mind and the second greatest commandment was to love your neighbor as yourself. Jesus said, "On these two commandments hang all the law and the prophets."

Beginning in Matthew 6, Jesus expanded upon the idea from the similitudes of Matthew 5:13-16 of letting your light shine in a discussion concerning giving of alms, prayer, and fasting. In each case, Jesus told the hearers when they did these acts, they needed to do them in secret. He said those who gave alms, prayed, or fasted in order to be seen of men, had their rewards in the praise of men, but those who did these acts in secret would have their reward of God. Think about the difference between one who visits the sick, gives food to the hungry, or provides money for the needy and tells all of her friends about it (shining her light) as compared to one who does these things as a Christian giving God the glory but never saying a word about what she has done to anyone (letting her light shine). When those to whom she has provided assistance talk about what a wonderful thing a Christian has done, God gets the glory, and He blesses the Christian.

In teaching about prayer, Jesus shared a model the people could follow in Matthew 6:9-13. It is obvious the prayer was not for His own benefit as can be seen in the section on forgiveness. First, the prayer was addressed to God. Prayer today should be addressed to God and according to Jesus' instructions in John 16:23 after His death and resurrection, prayer should be addressed to the Father and offered in the name of Christ. We have no authority to pray to Jesus, yet it is common to hear prayers being offered to Jesus instead of to God.

After glorifying God as Father and showing respect to His name in the prayer of Matthew 6:9-13, Jesus prayed for the kingdom to come. According to Mark 9:1, Jesus assured His followers the kingdom would come during the lives of some of those standing there. We know the kingdom on earth was in existence during the life of Paul because in Colossians 1:13 he told the Colossians both he and they had been translated into the kingdom of Christ and it was upon earth during the lifetime of John because in Revelation 1:9, he related himself to his readers as their brother in the kingdom. So if we today pray for the kingdom to come, we must realize we are praying for the rule of God to overcome sin with an enlargement of the kingdom over the world and not for the church to be established. This is an important point because if one hears us pray for the kingdom to come, she may get the idea we believe the church is not the kingdom.

Next in the prayer, Jesus prayed for the Father's will to be done (Matthew 6:10). We too should pray for God's will to be done. Even when Jesus was about to be betrayed by Judas, He prayed as recorded in Luke 22:42 asking God to remove this cup from Him, but He said, "…not my will but thine be done." It is our job to accept God's will as our own and not His job to answer us according to our will.

After praising God, praying for His kingdom, and praying for God's will to take over, Jesus then modeled asking God for physical needs. Recorded in Matthew 6:8, before providing the prayer, Jesus said God already knows what we need before we ask, but in verse 11, Jesus asked for daily bread. Even though God knows what we need, we need to ask Him showing our dependence upon Him. Later in the sermon in Matthew 7:7-11, Jesus told the people to ask and it would be given to them, to seek and they would find, and to knock and the door would be opened to them. He explained to them how they who were evil gave good gifts to their children and God the Father would give even better things to those who asked Him. But when we have food and clothes, according to Paul in 1st Timothy 6:8, we should be content and not asking for more so we can consume it upon our own lusts as noted in James 4:3.

Next in the prayer, Jesus modeled asking God to forgive sins (Matthew 6:12). Here is the part of the prayer which makes it clear Jesus was modeling for the people and not praying for Himself. In both 1st John 3:5 and 1st Peter 2:22 in fulfillment of Isaiah 53:9 it is stated Jesus did not sin. We humans do sin and we do need to pray for forgiveness. According to 1st John 1:8-9, if we say we have no sin, we are liars. But notice in the model prayer, we pray for forgiveness as we forgive others. After the conclusion of the prayer, Jesus went on to explain to the people in Matthew 6:14-15 if they wanted to be forgiven, they had to forgive those who had trespassed against them.

Finally in the end of the prayer, Jesus asked God to keep them from temptation and to deliver them from the evil one. We know from 1st Corinthians 10:13 God will not allow us to be tempted above what we are able to bear. He may allow the temptations just as He did for Job and even for Christ, but He will make a way we can resist them. When Jesus was tempted by the devil in Matthew 4:1-11, each time He responded with scripture. When we make it a point to truly know the word, we too can resist the temptations as they come upon us.

In closing the prayer, Jesus again offered praise to God saying the kingdom, power, and glory belonged to God. Note Jesus did not end the prayer in the name of Jesus. But going back to John 16:26, we know it is proper to ask prayer in the name of Jesus once Jesus had gone back to the Father (John 14:13 and John 16:16).

After teaching the people concerning prayer, in Matthew 6:19-34, Jesus told them how God will take care of His people. He told them not to lay up their treasures on this earth but to lay up treasures in heaven. He explained there are two ways: the way of God and the way of man. He stressed in verse 24 man cannot serve both ways. If man chooses the way of God, then God will bless him above the fowls and the flowers both in this life and more importantly in the next life. In verse 33, Jesus made it very clear man needs to seek the kingdom of God first and foremost.

In the final chapter of the sermon, Matthew 7, Jesus first discussed judging others and then He expanded upon the idea of there being two ways from which man could choose. As for judging others, Jesus told the people how they judged others would be the way they were judged. He said it was wrong to judge another when you, yourself, have greater problems in your life. He said to first get rid of your problems and then you could help your brother. Some people have taken these verses on judging to mean we cannot judge others on any issue, but not so. Remember how all of the verses on a topic must be studied in order to have clear understanding of the subject. In Matthew 7:15-20 Jesus warned the people of false prophets coming to them in sheep's clothing. In verse 16, He said they would know these prophets by their fruits. Using the idea of a tree, He continued in the next verses saying a good tree brought forth good fruit and a bad tree brought forth corrupt fruit. Then in verse 20, He said they would know (that is judging) the prophets by their fruits. This type of judging is approved by God. In John 7:24, John recorded Jesus as saying to judge righteous judgment. Paul told the Corinthians, saints would judge the world and in 1st Corinthians 6:1-5, he gave the instructions concerning judging.

Back now to Matthew 7:12 where there is a summary of what Jesus had been preaching to the people, commonly known as the *Golden Rule*. Whatever we want others to do to us, is what we should do to them. So going backwards in His sermon, how we want others to judge us is how we should judge them. How we want others to love us is how we should love them. How we want others to treat us in getting even, telling the truth, marriage, divorce, adultery, or murder, is how we should treat them. If everyone truly believed this one principle and obeyed it, what a pleasant world we would have. We must teach this principle to our children, neighbors, and friends.

If we followed this rule, we would be humble in the sight of God like the publican in the parable Jesus shared in Luke

18:9-14. In this parable, two men, a Pharisee and a publican went up to the temple to pray. The Pharisee's prayer reminds us of how Jesus said not to pray. He stood up thanking God he was not like others including the publican who was there beside him. He told God what great things he did such as fasting and tithing. Can't you just hear him bragging upon himself in a loud boisterous voice? On the other hand, the publican would not even lift up his eyes to heaven but smote upon his breast asking for God's mercy. Many times this parable is used to show all one has to do to be saved is to call upon the Lord, but keep in mind, both of these men were already Jews living under the old law and were not praying for salvation. The principle here is one of being humble.

But even in our humility, we need to be persistent and expectant in our prayers, yet, we must wait upon God for the answer. In Luke 18:2-8 Jesus gave the parable of the woman and the judge. This judge did not answer to anyone. There was a widow who kept asking him to vindicate her against her adversary. This judge would not do so but when she kept coming back, he decided to give her what she was asking for so she would quit troubling him. Jesus then went on to say if such an unjust judge would provide the relief this woman needed, think of how much more God would do for His own elect.

Jesus acknowledged the type of humility we should have in the parable of the guests at a wedding recorded in Luke

14:7-14. He told the people when they were invited to a wedding they should take the lowest seat and when he who had invited them came, he might have them move up. He went on to tell the people in verses 12-14 when they made a feast, they should invite those who could not repay them.

This humility needs to carry over into our attitudes concerning our work for the Lord. In Luke 17:7-10 Jesus had questioned the apostles concerning how they would behave if they had a servant who had been out working in the field and had just come in. He asked if they would tell him to go and eat of if they would tell him to get their food ready. Of course they would have him get their food ready. He was the servant. So it is with us: We are the servants of God. According to verse 9, we should not expect to be thanked when we have done what has been commanded and our attitude according to verse 10 should be we are unprofitable servants; we have just done our duty.

Finally, continuing with the idea of there being both false and true prophets or a way which is right and a way which is wrong, in Matthew 7:21-22, Jesus told the people just calling on Him as Lord, Lord, would not get them into the kingdom. He told them there would be many who claimed to have done wonderful things in His name in an effort to get into the kingdom, but He would tell them to depart. In Luke 6:46, Luke recorded Jesus as saying, "And why call ye me, Lord, Lord, and do not the things which I say?" Then in closing His sermon on the mount (Matthew 7:24-27 and Luke 6:47-49) Jesus gave the parable of two builders. We know them as the one who built upon the sand and the one who built upon the rock. Jesus was trying to get the people to see if they would listen to Him and do what He said, they would be building upon the rock (see 1st Corinthians 10:4 "and that rock was Christ") but if they chose not to hear or not to do what He said, they would be building their lives upon the sand and their end would be to perish.

In Jesus' sermon recorded in Matthew 5-7, He touched upon so many important topics concerned with how man should live. He first explained He had come to fulfill the law and He showed how His teachings would often be contrary to the sayings the people had heard concerning the Old Testament. He taught about how we should love God and our fellow man. He taught about the attitude of humility we need to have and the way we need to live our lives so others can see Christ in us. He prayed for the kingdom of God and He shared not everyone who called on the Lord would be in the kingdom. Finally, He emphasized the need to choose the right way. Next in this chapter, will be a study of the parables found in Matthew, Mark, and Luke by which Jesus taught these basic principles of loving God and man, and choosing the right way.

In a couple of His early parables, Jesus continued one of the ideas He had started to develop in the sermon on the mountain. In that sermon, several times He told the people they had heard something from the old law, but He was expanding upon what they had heard. He showed the people what He was teaching did not always agree with the way the Jews had kept the old law.

In the parables recorded in Matthew 9:16-17, Mark 2:21-22, and Luke 5:36-38, Jesus had been questioned concerning why His disciples did not fast like the disciples of John. Jesus used the examples of the damage to be done by sewing new cloth into an old garment and putting new wine into old bottles as another way of letting the people know what He was bringing to them was different. In the account in Luke, Jesus went on to say when men had drunk the old and then were given the new, they still preferred the old and said it was better. In Matthew 13:52, Jesus explained when a scholar in the old law was given instruction concerning the kingdom of heaven, it was like a house holder who wanted to keep some of the old and some of the new. Jesus was giving them a clue concerning this new way and new kingdom and showing them it was not a patch up job but a totally new beginning for the people.

Another parable in which Jesus noted the Jews were being given time to accept His teachings is found in Luke 13:6-9 where Jesus told about a man who had a fig tree planted in his vineyard but it had not had any fruit. The owner told the dresser of the vineyard he had looked for fruit on the tree for three years and it had not had any. He told the dresser to cut it down. The dresser asked for one more year to dig about it and fertilize it and then if it did not bear fruit, he would cut it. Of course the fig tree can represent anyone who has heard Jesus' teachings and still refuses to accept them, but at the time Jesus gave the parable, it was most likely the unbelieving Jews to whom He was referring.

One of those areas where Jesus was trying to show the people the difference between the old law and what He was teaching was in loving. Remember in the sermon, He told them they had heard it said they were to love their neighbor and hate their enemy, but He told them to love their enemies which was quite different from what they were used to. In Luke 10:30-37 Jesus used a parable to explain to a lawyer what He meant when He said to love your neighbor as yourself. In this parable which many people know as the parable of the Good Samaritan, Jesus told about a traveler who was going from Jerusalem to Jericho and he fell among thieves. They robbed him and left him as dead. A priest came along and when he saw him, he did not so much as even go over to him but passed by on the other side. A Levite came along and at least looked on him, but he too passed on the other side. Then a Samaritan came along. Remember the Jews and Samaritans did not get along. The Samaritan had compassion on the traveler and he stopped and bound up his wounds and took him to the inn to be cared for. He even paid the bill and told the inn keeper to take care of the man and the next time he came by, he would pay the rest. The lawyer understood who his neighbor was. Jesus told him to go and do likewise.

God likewise loves all of us as we know from John 3:16. God loves us so much when we are His children, He hears our cries for mercy. In Luke 11:5-8 Jesus used an example of someone having company at midnight and needing bread to feed the guest. He asked the audience which of them would refuse to give the friend the requested bread if not for the fact they were friends at least because the friend was in need and was persistent in his request. This is the same occasion where Jesus told the audience to ask, seek, and knock and they would receive the blessings because their heavenly Father would answer.

Part of loving others is sharing in their good fortune. There are a couple of parables which include this point although their primary meaning may be another topic. In the parable of the lost sheep from Matthew 18:12-14 and Luke 15:4-7, Jesus asked the people if one of them had one hundred sheep and lost one, would he not leave the ninety-nine and go find the lost one. Then He shared how the person who had found his sheep would go and call his friends and neighbors to rejoice with him. In Luke 15 verses 8-9, Jesus continued the idea of rejoicing over a found item by asking if a woman who had lost one of her ten pieces of silver and found it would not call her friends and neighbors to rejoice with her. In both cases, Jesus took the parable to a much higher message in telling the people how much more rejoicing there would be in heaven over one sinner who repented. The very next parable in Luke made this point even stronger.

In Luke 15:11-32, Jesus continued the idea of losing and finding, but this time the lost was actually a man's son. This man had two sons. The younger son asked for his inheritance and took it to a far county where he wasted it all. He ended up having to work for a pig farmer which in and of itself would have been a cause for grave concern for a Jew because pigs were considered unclean under the old law. The son decided to return to his father and ask to be a hired servant. On the day he returned, his father saw him coming from a long way off and he ran and met him. The son told his father he had sinned against heaven and in his father's sight and he was not worthy to even be called his son. The father had his servants put the best robe on the son along with a ring and shoes. Then he celebrated with the fatted calf. The father was so happy his son was home.

God is so happy when one of His children who has sinned comes home. We too as part of the family of God should rejoice with the one who has come home, but all too often, we see the returned erring child being treated just like this returning son was treated by his brother. According to verses 25-28, the older son was angry and would have nothing to do with the returned son. In verse 27, the servant told the older brother that his brother had returned but in verse 30, the older son in talking to the father would not even acknowledge the returned as his brother but called him "thy son." With true love in his heart he would have recognized him as "my brother" who had finally made the choice to come home. The father loved his son just as God loves His children and wants us to make the right choice.

In many of Jesus' parables, choices were offered. We have already looked at the sermon on the mountain where in Matthew 7:24-27 and Luke 6:47-49, Jesus shared the choices of building upon the rock or upon the sand. In Luke 12:16-21, another building project was about to take place. In this case, a rich man grew more crops than he could use or store, so instead of making the choice to help others with his surplus, he chose to tear down his barns and build bigger ones. God called him a fool for his unwise choice of laying up treasures for himself instead of being rich toward God and told him he would die that very night. While we may not die the very day we make a bad choice, we must always be mindful of the choices we make and keep the kingdom in mind.

Continuing in Luke, is another parable where choosing to live for Christ was compared to building. This time the subject was deciding to give all to follow Christ. One cannot start to build upon Christ and then when the going gets rough, back off and quit the project. In Luke 14:28-33, Jesus asked the people which of them would even start to build a tower without first sitting down and figuring out the cost to see if he had enough to finish paying for it. In the same setting, He offered another comparison when He asked what king would attempt going to war against another without first counting the cost. Before giving the parable, Jesus had told the people how they had to put Jesus before their family and before themselves and bear their own cross in order to be Jesus' disciple (verses 26-27). After the parable, He told them if they did not forsake all, they could not be His disciple. The key here seems to be making plans to follow Christ and sticking to them.

Several other parables show the importance of choosing to serve Christ over the long term and always being ready for His return. In Luke 12:35-40 just after telling the people in verse 34 where their heart is will be their treasure too, Jesus gave a parable concerning being ready at all times. He said in verse 35 to let your loins be girded about and your lights burning and then He talked about servants whose master had gone to a wedding and was coming home. Their job as servants was to be watching for him at all times and no matter at what hour he returned to be ready to let him in. He went on to tell how if a master of a house knew at what hour a thief was coming, he would certainly be ready for him and would not allow the thief to break up his house, so in verse 40, He told the people they needed to always be ready for the Son of man because He would come when they were not expecting Him.

Mark included a similar parable in his account in Mark 13:35-37 where he recorded Jesus telling the people how they needed to watch because they did not know when the Son of man would return. Here Jesus compared His return to a master who had taken a long journey and had commanded the doorkeeper to watch for his return. He told the people they too needed to watch.

Continuing in Luke 12, after Jesus told the people of the need to be ready at all hours, Peter asked Jesus if the parable was for all of the people or just for the disciples. In verses 42-48 Jesus continued His discussion concerning watching and He told Peter and the others those stewards who watched and were ready when their lord came would be placed in positions of authority, but those who had decided their lord had delayed his coming and chose not to watch would be punished when he did return. In verse 48 Jesus said those who had been given much would be expected to produce much but those who had committed things worthy of stripes unknowingly would be beaten with few stripes.

Matthew recorded a similar account in Matthew 24:45-51 where he wrote about the faithful servants who watched and those who chose not to be on the alert. Those who chose to ignore the fact the master was returning found themselves cut asunder and placed with the hypocrites where there would be weeping and gnashing of teeth.

In another parable concerned with those who should be making wise choices to be ready, Christ used wicked tenants to make His point. This parable is recorded in Matthew 21:33-44, Mark 12:1-11, and Luke 20:9-18. In this parable, the landowner had planted a vineyard and let it out to tenant farmers. At harvest time, he sent his servants to get his share. The tenants beat and killed his servants. The owner sent more servants and they treated them the same way. Finally, he sent his son and when the tenants saw the son, they chose to kill him so they could take his inheritance. Jesus asked the listeners what the owner would do to those wicked men. The listeners said the owner would destroy them. Then Jesus asked them if they had ever read the scripture saying the stone which the builders rejected is become the head of the corner. This was a prophecy about Christ from Psalm 118:22. Jesus went on to tell those listeners the kingdom would be taken from them and given to a nation which would bring forth the fruits. Jesus knew these Jews had chosen to reject the stone instead of having chosen to listen to and heed Jesus' words. In Matthew's account (Matthew 21:45-46), the chief priests and Pharisees knew the parable was for them and they were afraid to lay hands on Jesus because the people took Him as a prophet.

Still trying to impress upon the people the need to choose wisely and be watchful, in Matthew 25:1-12, is recorded another parable concerning ten virgins who took their lamps and went out to meet the coming bridegroom. The bridegroom did not come in the time expected but those virgins who had chosen to take extra oil were well prepared for the wait while those who did not take any extra oil for their lamps ran out of oil. When they ran out, they asked the wise virgins for some of their oil. The wise virgins told the foolish ones they did not have enough for themselves and the foolish virgins too so they needed to go and buy their own. While the five foolish virgins went to buy oil, the bridegroom came and those five wise virgins who were ready went in. When the foolish ones returned with their oil, it was too late and they were not allowed in. Again, Jesus ended the parable with a warning to watch because they did not know the day nor the hour when the Son of man would come.

In another parable concerning a marriage, recorded in Matthew 22:2-14, Jesus told of a king who made a marriage dinner for his son. He sent his servants to call the guests who had previously been invited. The guests were very rude. They refused to come and some of them even took the king's servants and killed them. The king was angry and he sent and killed those who were bidden but did not come and then he sent his servants to the highways to find guests for the dinner.

The servants then went out and gathered as many as they could find both the good and the bad. According to history (Bible History, n.d.), the custom for such feasts was for the host, in this case the king, to provide a wedding garment for each guest and the guest was expected to wear it at this feast just as Jesus provides us with a wedding garment when we obey the gospel (new man). When the king came in to the dinner, he saw one there without the expected wedding garment. This one had no excuse because whatever he needed had been provided but he chose not to put it on. The king said to cast this one into outer darkness where there shall be weeping and gnashing of teeth. Jesus added another piece of information at the end of this parable in verse 14 where He said many are called but few chosen.

In a very similar parable in Luke 14:16-24, Luke recorded a certain man had made a great supper and invited many. When the servants went to tell the invitees the supper was ready, all of them made excuses for not attending. One had bought a piece of land he needed to go look at, one had bought some oxen he needed to go see, and one had married a wife and could not come. The master here was angry too and he told his servant to go out and bring in the poor, crippled, lame, and blind to the feast. When the feast was still not well supplied with guests, the master told the servant to go out and compel the people to come in so his house would be full. Jesus' point at the end was none of those who had previously been invited would be allowed in. Once having been bidden and having rejected the Christ, one cannot expect to enter into His supper.

Some will make the wrong choice in the beginning but then repent and some will make the right choice but then backslide. In the parable of the two sons found in Matthew 21:28-32, Jesus told about a man sending his two sons to work in his vineyard. The one son said he would not go and work, but he repented and did. The other son said he would but did not. Jesus asked the hearers which son did his father's will. Of course they said the first one and Jesus told them the harlots and publicans would go into the kingdom before them because the harlots and publicans had believed John's preaching and these to whom Jesus was speaking refused to repent and believe Him.

Just as the two sons made choices concerning what their father wanted them to do, in another parable three servants had to make choices concerning what to do with the money their master had given them. In this parable recorded in Matthew 25:14-30, the master before going to a place far away gave one servant five talents, a second servant two talents, and a third servant one talent. The first two servants traded and accumulated more talents but the third one with one talent dug a hole and buried the talent. When the master returned after a long time, he called in the servants for them to give an account of their work. The master was pleased with the first two servants and he made them rulers over many things. He was not pleased with the servant who had hidden the talent. He called him a wicked and slothful person. He told him he should have put his money in the bank and at least gotten the interest. The master took the one talent away from the servant and gave it to the one who had gained five talents and then he cast the unprofitable servant into outer darkness with weeping and gnashing of teeth.

The talent parable is very similar to another one Jesus spoke recorded in Luke 19:12-27 where a nobleman went to a place far away, but before he went, he gave ten servants ten pounds, one pound each, and told them to do business with the money until he returned. When the nobleman returned, one servant had gained ten pounds and another had gained five but a third had hidden the pound in a napkin. This servant brought the one pound and gave it back to the nobleman. Again, the nobleman condemned the wicked servant and took his pound and gave it to the one who had ten pounds.

As Jesus continued to warn the people about the choices they made and about being ready, Jesus' disciples were figuring out He was describing something which was coming soon and for which they needed to be prepared. They questioned Him in Matthew 24:3 concerning when these things were going to happen. Jesus then shared a parable of the fig tree. This one is recorded in Matthew 24:32-32, Mark 13:28-29, and Luke 21:29-31. In this parable, Jesus told them to consider the fig tree. When its branch was tender and putting forth leaves they knew summer was nigh so likewise when they saw all of the things He was telling them were going to happen, they would know the time was right. He told them in Matthew 24:34 the generation to whom He was speaking would not pass until what He was prophesying would be fulfilled. The king would come in His kingdom during their lifetime.

Many of the parables including some we have already looked at in this chapter can be considered kingdom parables. These parables clearly indicated for what the followers of Christ needed to be watching. Some were able to accept the teachings and remain in them while others were not.

The parable of the sower and the four types of soil clearly indicated this point. This is one of the few parables Jesus not only told but also fully explained. The parable is recorded in Matthew 13:3-8 and explained in verses 18-23, recorded in Mark 4:3-8 and explained in verses 14-20, and recorded in Luke 8:5-8 and explained in verses 11-15. In this parable, Jesus compared the different types of soil to the different ways people would receive His words. Some people will hear His word but not understand it and then forget all about it. These are the ones He compared to seed sown in the wayside and the birds came and ate it. Some will hear and receive Jesus' teachings with joy but because they do not develop the necessary roots (most likely because they did not engage in diligent study), when things get tough, they will no longer be faithful and they will fall away. These Jesus compared to seed sown in stony places which grew for a while but because the ground was stony and the seed could not develop strong roots, it died. Then there are some who will hear the word and receive it, but when the cares of the world and deceitfulness of riches chokes out the truth, these become unfruitful. He compared these to seed planted among thorns and when the thorns grew, they choked out the good seed. Finally, there were some who received the seed, understood it, and bore fruit even as much as an hundred fold. These Jesus compared to the seed which when sowed in good ground brought forth fruit.

This last group in the parable of the seeds is the group we want to be in. We want to be women who hear the word and understand it through diligent study. Then we want to be the ones who bring forth fruit in our families and in our friends. We do not want to be those who allow the cares of this world to choke out the truth of the gospel and we do not want to be those who do not even take root in the soil.

Staying with the theme of planting, in another parable the Lord explained how the kingdom will be purged. This parable is located in Matthew 13:24-30 and explained in 36-43. Here Jesus told about a man sowing good seed in the field, but while his men slept, his enemy came and sowed tares or weeds among the wheat. When the wheat came up and brought forth fruit, the weeds were there too. The servants wanted to go out and pull the weeds, but the owner told them not to because in doing so, they would root up the good plants too. Instead, he said to let them grow together and in the harvest the reapers would first gather the tares and burn them before they gathered the good wheat. Jesus compared this to the kingdom or church. He said the field was the world and the good seed were the children of the kingdom but the bad seeds were the children of the devil. He said the harvest would be at the end of the world when the Son of man would send forth His angels to gather out of His kingdom those who offend and cast them into a furnace of fire but the righteous would shine forth as the sun in the kingdom of their Father.

Still showing how the kingdom will be purged Jesus used a parable of the fish net in Matthew 13:47-50 where He explained to His disciples the kingdom would have many kinds of people in it just like a fish net cast into the water would gather many kinds of fish. Just as the fishermen would separate the good from the bad fish, so would the angels do in the end by separating the wicked from the just. The wicked would be cast into the furnace of fire.

For those in the kingdom to be forgiven they need to forgive others for in Matthew 18:23-34, Jesus used the parable of a king who forgave debts but when one of those forgiven refused to forgive a fellowman, the king reinstated his debt. In this parable, one of the king's subjects owed the king 10,000 talents. When he could not pay, the king forgave him the debt, but this same subject went out and found one of his fellow servants who owed him one hundred pence. He demanded pay and when his fellow servant could not pay, the first servant had him cast into prison. When the king heard about it, he was mad and had the first subject delivered to the tormenters until he paid his debt. Jesus said God would do the same to those to whom He was talking if they did not forgive everyone his brother their trespasses.

Jesus showed the people how the kingdom would grow and be harvested, in Mark 4:26-29. Then in Mark 4:30-32, He showed how the kingdom would spread as a plant. He said the kingdom of God was like a mustard seed which was smaller than all the other seeds, but once planted it grows up to be very large with branches so strong even the birds could lodge under its shade. This same parable was also recorded in Luke 13:18-19 and in Matthew 13:31-32 where Matthew recorded Christ as saying the mustard seed becomes a tree in which the birds could lodge.

Similar to the mustard seed in growth, the kingdom would spread as yeast in bread. In Matthew 13:33, Jesus said the kingdom was like leaven which a woman took and hid in three measures of meal until the whole amount of meal was leavened. This reminds me of the friendship bread or friendship cake we sometimes make where you keep a starter and when it is added to more flour it provides raising power for the whole batch. This parable is also recorded in Luke 13:20-21. The same can happen as we spread God's word to our children, families, and friends and as they obey, the kingdom grows.

The value of the kingdom was expressed by Jesus in the parable of the hidden treasure in Matthew 13:44. In this parable, a man found a treasure in a field so he hid it, sold all he had, and bought the field. Then in verses 45-46, Jesus compared the kingdom of heaven to one who was seeking goodly pearls. He found one so he sold all he had in order to buy it.

Those entering the kingdom can expect to be blessed but the blessing is up to the master. In Luke 7:36-39, Jesus was eating with a Pharisee in the Pharisee's house. A sinful woman had anointed Jesus' feet and washed them with her tears and dried them with her hair. Jesus presented a parable in which He told Simon, the Pharisee, about two debtors who owed a master. One owed the master five hundred pence and one owed him fifty. The master forgave both of them. Jesus asked Simon which of the debtors would love the master the most. Simon said the one to whom the most was forgiven, and Jesus agreed. Then He went on in verses 44-47 to explain to Simon how this sinful woman had much to be forgiven but how she had given so much more to Jesus than Simon had. At the end, in verse 48, Jesus forgave her of her sins.

Then from Matthew 20:1-16, those who enter the kingdom late can still expect the blessings. In this parable, a man hired workers in his vineyard early in the morning and agreed to pay them a penny. He went out a few hours later and hired others. He went out again, two more times and hired workers. At the end of the day, he chose to pay each of them a penny. When the workers who were hired first realized the others had the same pay, they were not happy. The master explained to them in verses 13-16 that as the master, he had the right to pay as he chose and they had no right to complain. In verse 16 Jesus said many would be called but few chosen. This parable was not giving people an excuse to refuse to obey

God in their youth and wait until they were old, since it seems as soon as the workers were called they went to work. Many times people do not hear the truth until they are older, but as soon as they hear, they should accept and begin working for the Lord.

There will be judgment based upon the works of man. In Matthew 25:31-46 Jesus explained how in the judgment those who had done good would be given life eternal and those who had not done good would be given everlasting punishment. The Lord blessed those who on earth had ministered unto Him and when they questioned Him as to when they had done such ministering, He told them as much as they had done unto His brethren they had done it to Him. When those who were judged as doing evil were told about doing evil to the master, they wanted to know when they had done such. He told them as much as they had done evil to the brethren, they had done evil to Him.

In Luke 16:19-31 is a vivid account of what awaits those who choose to not enter the kingdom and work for God but choose to accumulate their riches and withhold from those in need. Here we have the parable of a rich man who had everything he could want at whose gate laid Lazarus, a poor man full of sores. Both men died and the rich man found himself in torment while Lazarus was in Abraham's bosom. The rich man begged Abraham to send Lazarus back to talk to his brothers so they would change their ways and not go to the awful place. Of course, Abraham told the rich man one was not going back. He even went so far as to say if those left at home would not hear Moses and the prophets, they would not be persuaded though one rose from the dead. We know One who did raise from the dead and He is the reason we want to do our part in converting this world for most of the world will not hear Him.

While Jesus used many parables in His teaching, not all of His teaching was done by parables. He had other lessons to share with those who would listen to Him. Jesus was preparing the people for His coming kingdom. The Jews would have naturally been expecting an earthly kingdom in which things would be like they had been in the past when God fought their battles for them, but Jesus' kingdom was not to be that type of kingdom. In Matthew 11:28-30 Jesus said, "Come unto me, all ye that labour and are heavy laden, and I will give you rest. 29. Take my yoke upon you, and learn of me: for I am meek and lowly in heart: and ye shall find rest unto your souls. 30. For my yoke is easy and my burden is light." He condemned the Pharisees for vain worship in Matthew 15:8-9 when He quoted from Isaiah 29:13. In condemning the Pharisees for their worship, He said what they taught as doctrines were the commandments of men. They were honoring God with their lips but they would not give heed to His Son.

Faith in Christ was one of the principles recorded in several verses of John (John 5:24; John 6:29, 40, 47). In John

8:24 Jesus was recorded as saying, "...if ye believe not that I am He, ye shall die in your sins." But believing in Jesus was not enough according to John 8:31-35 where Jesus was recorded as telling those who believed in Him if they continued in His word they were His disciples indeed and they would know the truth and it would set them free. So they needed the truth to set them free. In Jesus' prayer recorded in John 17:17 Jesus said God's word was truth. In verse 14 Jesus said He had given God's word to His disciples so Jesus' word and God's word were the same. So now it should be clear the word in which Jesus was telling the people they had to abide was the word of God.

In addition, Jesus taught confession of Him before men was necessary. In Luke 12:8-9 and Matthew 10:32-33, Jesus was recorded as telling the people those who confessed Him before men would be confessed by Him before God, but those who denied Him would be denied by Him. One would be wise to deny himself rather than denying Jesus.

Jesus taught the people if they wanted to save their lives, they would have to deny themselves and take up their cross and follow Him (Mark 8:34-38; Matthew 16:24-26; and Luke 9:22-26). John recorded Jesus as telling Nicodemus one could not see the kingdom of God without being born again in John 3:3. Nicodemus who was a teacher of the Jews, was confused by Jesus' statement concerning being born again and wanted more information. Jesus went on in verses 5-8 to explain this being born again. He said in verse 5 unless a man was born of water and of the Spirit, he could not enter into the kingdom of God. He shared with Nicodemus in verse 16 how God had given His only begotten Son so those who would believe on Him could have everlasting life. In verse 18 Jesus explained those who did not believe on Him, were already condemned.

As noted previously in John 6:47, Jesus was recorded as saying one who believed on Jesus had everlasting life. In this passage, Jesus went on to say He was the bread of life, the living bread which had come down from heaven. He said in verse 51 His flesh was this living bread He would give for the life of the world. He said whoever ate His flesh and drank His blood had eternal life (verse 54). When Jesus knew some of His disciples were upset with what He had said, He continued this discussion with His disciples in verse 63 where He explained to them the words He spoke to them were spirit and life. He said it is the spirit that quickens or gives life. By understanding this concept, it becomes clear when Jesus said to Nicodemus one had to be born again of water and the Spirit in order to see the kingdom of heaven, the spiritual part of the new birth that gives us life comes through the words spoken by Jesus. The water part of the new birth, Jesus clarified later in Mark 16:15-16 and Matthew 28:18-20 where He authorized the apostles to go and baptize those who believed His words.

Jesus taught He was the bread of life in John 6:35, 48, and 51. As such, He compared Himself to the manna the Jewish fathers had eaten in the wilderness and died (verse 49). But He said when one ate of Him, he would live forever. He was not talking about eating His physical flesh, but the words He taught.

Jesus said He was the light of the world in John 8:12. Remember back in the Sermon on the Mount, Jesus told His followers they were the light of the world. Here He said He was the light of the world. In John 9:5, Jesus said as long as He was in the world, He was the light of the world. In John 12:35, Jesus told the people the light was with them for a little while. He told them to walk while they had the light and to believe in that light (verse 36).

Jesus said He was the door of the sheep in John 10:7. In verse 9 He said if any man entered by Him as the door, he would be saved. This statement excludes any other way of entering if one wants to be saved. In John 10:1, Jesus had said anyone who entered not by the door was a thief and a robber. In addition to being the door of the sheep, Jesus said He was the good shepherd in John 10:11 and He said the good shepherd gives His life for the sheep. In John 10:14, He said He knew His sheep and was known by them and then in verse 16, He said He had other sheep who were not of that fold but He had to bring them into the same flock so there would be one flock with one shepherd. Jesus was here paving the way for the entrance of the Gentiles into the same flock with the Jews.

In John 11:25, Jesus said He was the resurrection and the life. This was on the occasion of the death of Lazarus and Jesus told Martha whoever believed in Jesus even though he might die physically, he would live again. Then in John 14:6, Jesus said He was the way, the truth, and the life. He went on to say no man comes to God but by Him. Previously in John 14:2, Jesus had told His disciples He was going to go and prepare a place for them in His Father's house. Phillip, one of the apostles, seemed to be having trouble understanding so in verses 9-21, Jesus gave them a short sermon. Here He explained how He and God were one in mind and purpose. He told them He would be going to the Father but He would send a Comforter, the Spirit of truth who would be with them forever. Then when Judas asked Him how He would show Himself to the apostles and not to the world, Jesus told Him if a man loved Him he would keep His words and He and the Father would make abode with that man (verse 23). In verse 26 Jesus promised the apostles God would send them the Comforter or the Holy Ghost and He would bring to their remembrance whatever Jesus had taught them.

Then in John 15:1-5, Jesus explained to the disciples He was the vine and His followers were the branches. He said if a branch bore fruit, it would be pruned so it would bring forth even more fruit, but if it did not bear fruit, it would be taken away. In order to bear fruit, according to verse 4, the vine had to remain in Jesus. In verse 5 Jesus said he who abides in Jesus, and Jesus in that person, the same brings forth much fruit. In verse 7, He showed it is when His words abide in a man He is abiding in the man. In verse 10 He said if one keeps His commandments then he abides in Jesus' love. From all of these verses concerning the vine and the branches, it is clear the way a man abides in Jesus and Jesus abides in a man is by man having the words of Jesus and obeying them.

Jesus wanted everyone to obey His words so all would be of one mind. Just before His arrest Jesus prayed. In this prayer recorded in John 17, are several important points. First, in verse 5 if there is any doubt left, we have Jesus' own words indicating He was with God before the world began. Then in verses 6-19, Jesus prayed for His apostles. He said in verse 8 He had given those disciples the words God had given Him. In verse 11 Jesus asked God to keep those apostles in God's own name so they could be one just as Jesus and God were one. In verse 12 Jesus acknowledged Judas was lost so the scripture would be fulfilled. In verse 18, Jesus said as God had sent Him into the world, He was sending the apostles into the world. Beginning in verse 20, Jesus prayed for the rest of the world. He prayed they would all be one as Jesus and the Father were one. Again in verse 24 Jesus mentioned in His prayer how God had loved Him even before the foundation of the world.

In several places Jesus taught there would be an eternal reward and an eternal punishment. In Mark 10:28-31 when Peter asked Jesus what would be the blessing for those who had left everything to follow Jesus, Mark recorded Jesus telling about the eternal life to come. Back in Mark 9:42-47, Jesus had warned the people concerning hell. Again in Matthew 25:31-46, Matthew recorded Jesus' words concerning the judgment to come where the sheep and goats would be divided. The sheep would inherit the kingdom prepared for them from the foundation of the world and the goats would go into everlasting punishment. In John 5:25-29 Jesus taught concerning the judgment and how those who had done good would be resurrected to life and those who had done evil would be resurrected to damnation. Notice the reward is linked to the life one lived on earth and the deeds performed.

Matthew recorded Jesus as telling the people every plant His heavenly Father had not planted would be rooted up (Matthew 15:13). The only plant to endure was going to be the one He promised to build in Matthew 16:18. He had just asked His disciples in verse 13 who the people were saying He was. The disciples told Him some said He was a prophet, some said He was Elias, some said He was Jeremiah, and some even thought He was John the Baptist. Jesus asked them who they thought He was. Peter spoke up and gave that great and noble confession we must all make (verse 16) "...Thou art the Christ, the Son of the living God."

Jesus blessed Peter upon this confession Christ was the Son of God and in Matthew 16:18 Jesus promised upon that very confession or "upon this rock," He would build His church. He told Peter He would give him the keys to this kingdom of heaven. Here in Matthew 16:19 He told Peter, "…whatsoever thou shalt bind on earth shall be bound in heaven: and whatsoever thou shalt loose on earth shalt be loosed in heaven." In Matthew 18:18 Jesus repeated the promise concerning binding and loosing to the disciples in the context of bringing concerns before the church. Then in John 20:21-23 before Jesus ascended to heaven, on the first day of the week when the disciples were assembled Jesus appeared to them and said in verse 21. "Peace be unto you: as my Father hath sent me, even so send I you." Then according to verse 22, He breathed upon them and said to them: "Receive ye the Holy Ghost: Whose soever sins ye remit they are remitted unto them; and whose soever sins ye retain, they are retained."

Further, both Matthew and Mark recorded that Jesus told the apostles they were to preach the gospel and baptize the believers. Matthew recorded Jesus in Matthew 28:18-20 as saying to the eleven apostles "All power is given unto me in heaven and in earth. Go ye therefore and teach all nations, baptizing them in the name of the Father, and of the Son, and of the Holy Ghost: Teaching them to observe all things whatsoever I have commanded you: and, lo I am with you always, even unto the end of the world." Mark in Mark 16:15-16 recorded Jesus as saying: "Go ye into all the world and preach the gospel to every creature. He that believeth and is baptized shall be saved; but he that believeth not shall be damned."

The question which could be asked concerning how the apostles would be able to remit sins was answered by Jesus when He told them to go and preach and baptize the believers. Later in Acts, when the church had been established and people were being added to it, Luke explained how the sins were forgiven. This forgiveness will be covered in the next chapter which deals with the beginning of the church Christ promised to build.

Chapter 9
Events in the Early Church

In Matthew 16:18 just after Peter's great confession in which he said Christ was the Son of God, Jesus said He would build His church. He said Peter would have the keys to the kingdom. He said in verse 19 whatever Peter bound on earth would be bound in heaven and whatever he loosed on earth would be loosed in heaven. In Matthew 18:18 Jesus told all of the apostles whatever they bound on earth would be bound in heaven and whatever they loosed on earth would be loosed in heaven.

In Luke 24 beginning in verse 47, Jesus was recorded as telling His apostles He would send the promise of His Father upon them. He told them to wait in the city of Jerusalem until they had received this power from on high. Then Luke said Jesus went with the apostles to Bethany and lifted up His hands and blessed them and while He was blessing them, He was parted from them and carried up into heaven. Mark recorded the same event in Mark 16. We know it was the same event, because Mark stated in verse 19 after the Lord had spoken unto them, He was received into heaven. Just like before when studying the parables of Jesus and the miracles of Jesus and even the prophecies about Jesus, one must look at all of the sources to get the full picture. In Mark's account, he wrote that Jesus told the eleven to go and preach the gospel to all and he that believed the gospel and was baptized would be saved.

So when did this preaching begin? According to Mark 16:20 after Jesus was taken up in to heaven, they went forth and preached everywhere. Luke wrote in Luke 24:51-53 Jesus was taken up to heaven and they worshipped Him and returned to Jerusalem and were continually in the temple, praising and blessing God. The writer of Luke was also the author of the book of Acts. In Chapter 1 of Acts, Luke gave a brief history of the last days of Christ on earth. He noted in verse 2 Jesus had through the Holy Ghost given commandments to His apostles. In verse 3 Luke stated Christ had been with the apostles for forty days telling them things pertaining to the kingdom of God. In verse 4, Luke said Christ had told the apostles to stay in Jerusalem and wait for the promise of the Father concerning the baptism of the Holy Ghost which was to take place in their near future. This was in accordance with what Isaiah prophesied would happen in the last days in Isaiah 2:2-3.

Back to Acts 1:8, Luke repeated information concerning Jesus being taken up to heaven and then in verse 12, he said they returned to Jerusalem and went to the upper room where the eleven apostles were dwelling along with other followers. In verses 15-26, Luke gave an account of the selection of one to take Judas' place with that selection falling by lot to Matthias. It is interesting to note the qualifications for filling Judas' place as given in verses 21-22. That person had to have been with the apostles from the time of Jesus' baptism unto the time of His crucifixion and he had to be a witness of the resurrection. We cannot have present day apostles if for no other reason, there are no men today who meet these qualifications.

Luke began Acts 2 telling the readers when the day of Pentecost came, they were all with one accord in one place. After the death and resurrection of Christ, it seems it was a common practice for Christ's disciples to be assembled on the first day of the week. In John 20:19, the day of Jesus' resurrection, the disciples were assembled with the doors shut for fear of the Jews, and Jesus appeared in their midst. This was the assembly where Jesus breathed upon them and they received the Holy Ghost and He told them whosoever sins they remitted would be remitted and those they retained would be retained. According to John 20:26, the next week on the first day of the week, they were again assembled with the doors shut and Jesus appeared. So here in Acts 2, the apostles were once more assembled and it was the first day of the week. According to verses 2-4, they were filled with the Holy Ghost and began to speak what the Spirit directed them to speak. The interesting thing was, they were speaking in different languages.

There were Jews in Jerusalem having come from every nation to observe Pentecost. They were totally confused because they heard the Galilean apostles of Christ in their own individual tongues. Some according to Acts 2:13 accused the twelve apostles of being drunk, but Peter stood up with the eleven (verse 14) and lifted up his voice and told the people the speakers were not drunk but what was happening was in fulfilment of the prophecy of Joel concerning the last days and how those who called on the name of the Lord would be saved. Then beginning in verse 22 Luke recorded the sermon Peter preached that day. Peter told the people how Jesus had come to them and done miracles and wonders but they had delivered Him up to be crucified and slain. He told them God had raised Jesus from the dead and he showed them how this too was in fulfillment of a prophecy by David written in the Psalms. Then Peter told the audience Christ was the promised Son of David who was to rule upon David's throne. In verse 36, Peter told the people this Jesus whom they had crucified had been made both Lord and Christ by God.

When Peter accused the listeners of being the ones guilty of the death of Christ on the cross, they were cut to the heart and wanted to know what they could do. At this moment in the sermon, Peter had the opportunity to use the keys to open the door to the church or the kingdom Christ had promised to build back in Matthew 16 and He purchased with His own blood according to Acts 20:28. Peter used the keys. In Acts 2:38 Peter told the people what they had to do if they wanted to be forgiven. He said, "Repent and be baptized every one of you in the name of Jesus Christ for the remission of sins, and ye shall receive the gift of the Holy Ghost." Peter did not stop there but he went on to use the keys to open the kingdom to all who would follow after. In verse 39 he said: "For the promise is to you, and to your children, and to all that are afar off, even as many as the Lord our God shall call." According to verse 41, those who gladly received the word were baptized and on that day 3,000 souls were added to them. To what were those 3,000 added? In verse 47 is the answer. "...And the Lord added to the church daily such as should be saved."

According to Acts 2:42, those who were baptized on that day continued steadfastly in the teaching of the apostles. They had fellowship with each other, partook of the Lord's Supper (breaking of bread), and prayed together. According to verses 44-46, there were no needs among them because those who had the means of helping others did so. They met with each other daily in the temple for worship and they ate with each other in their houses. The people were praising God according to verse 47.

These people on the day of Pentecost were baptized with a new baptism. According to religious history, there had been other baptisms practiced before the baptism of Christ was begun (The Interactive Bible). In Mark 1:4, even during the time of Christ, John preached the baptism of repentance for the remission of sins. Later in Acts 19:1-5, Luke recorded an account of some who had been baptized with John's baptism. Paul asked them if they had received the Holy Ghost and they told him they had not even heard of the Holy Ghost. Upon hearing these men were not aware of the Holy Ghost, Paul knew they had not been baptized with the baptism of Christ because Christ's baptism involved the Father, Son, and Holy Ghost (Matthew 28:19). Paul then told the men John had baptized with the baptism of repentance telling the people they needed to believe upon the One who would come after John who was Jesus Christ. When the men heard what Paul had to say, they were baptized in the name of the Lord Jesus.

Throughout the book of Acts, Luke recorded several accounts of people obeying the gospel. Before looking at those accounts, it is necessary to establish the term "obeying the gospel." Is this a scriptural term? If it cannot be found to be scriptural, we should not be using it, but if it is scriptural, then we should use this term rather than one such as "joining the church" which is often proposed by man.

In Romans 1:16, Paul said the gospel of Christ was the power of God unto salvation to everyone who believed. In 2nd Thessalonians 1:8, Paul said God would take vengeance on them who do not know God and who do not obey the gospel of Christ. So the gospel has the power to save but it must be obeyed. In 1st Peter 4:17, Peter compared those who are the house of God to those who do not obey the gospel of God. According to Paul in Romans 6:16-18, we are servants of the one we obey. In verse 17 Paul told the Romans they had obeyed from their heart the form of doctrine which was delivered to them and it was upon obedience they were made free from sin and they became servants of righteousness (verse 18). Earlier in Romans 6:2-4, Paul had explained to the Roman Christians how they had obeyed that form of doctrine. He said in verse 3 by being baptized into Jesus Christ they were buried with Him by that baptism into death like Christ was raised up from the dead, so were the Romans raised up to walk in newness of life. So obeying the gospel takes place when one has heard that gospel and fulfilled the commands of Jesus Christ to believe the gospel (Mark 16:16), repents of sins (Acts 2:38), confesses Christ as the Son of God (Romans 10:10, Acts 8:37), and is baptized for the remission of sins (Mark 16:16, Acts 2:38) with the baptism of Christ (Matthew 28:19). At this point one has obeyed the gospel and does not "join" the church but is added to the church by the Lord (Acts 2:47).

In Acts 3, Peter again used the key to open the door to the church. He had another occasion to preach the gospel. In this sermon, he told the people (verses 14-15) they had denied the Holy One and the Just and they had killed the Prince of life. In verse 19, Peter told the people to repent and be converted so their sins would be blotted out. What does this "be converted" mean? This is one of those cases where the reader has to take all available information and allow no contradictions. Some would have us to believe Peter was saying here all one had to do was to repent. By putting this verse, repent and be converted that your sins may be blotted out when the times of refreshing shall come, parallel with Acts

2:38 where Peter said to repent and be baptized for the remission of sins and receive the gift of the Holy Ghost, it is clear that to repent and be baptized is the same as to repent and be converted with the same consequence, remission of sins or having sins blotted out. Of those who heard this sermon, there were about 5,000 who believed according to Acts 4:4.

In Acts 5 we have several important lessons to study diligently so we may share with others. At the end of Chapter 4, Luke recorded how those in the early church who had resources chose to help those who were in need. When Chapter 5 began, Ananias and his wife Sapphira had sold land and brought the money to the apostles. While they only gave the apostles part of the profit, they told the apostles they were giving them all of the money. The response from Peter showed before the land was sold, it fully belonged to Ananias and Sapphira and after it was sold, the money was still theirs. There is nothing in God's word to indicate they had to sell the land nor they had to give all of the money from the sale to the church. The problem was, they lied in saying they were giving it all. The second lesson to be learned is when we lie, we are lying to God. In verse 4 Peter told Ananias he had not lied unto men but unto God. Both Ananias and Sapphira were struck dead for their lie. The third lesson for us is we too will be punished for our evil doings. We may not be struck dead immediately, but God is in control and our punishment will come. Sin is serious and so is the punishment.

Still in Chapter 5 of Acts, Peter and other apostles were put into prison for proclaiming the gospel of Christ. Miraculously, they were released and continued preaching. When those who had put them into prison caught up with them, they again threatened them and told them they were to no longer teach in the name of Jesus. Peter and the other apostles answered in verse 29 saying, "We ought to obey God rather than men." Peter reminded the people how they were the ones who had crucified the Christ. These men were cut to the heart similar to those of Acts 2, but in this case, the reaction was quite different. These men in Acts 5 wanted to kill the apostles (verse 33). Instead of killing the apostles, the authorities beat them and let them go. Peter and the apostles rejoiced (verse 41) because they were able to suffer for the name of Christ and they continued daily teaching and preaching Jesus.

The followers of Jesus were increasing in number and there was a complaint issued in Acts 6 by the Hellenist or Grecian Christians against the Hebrew Christians because their widows were being neglected in the daily food distribution. The apostles called the multitude of disciples together and told them to select seven wise men of honest report who were full of the Holy Ghost to oversee the ministering to these widows and the apostles would still spend their time preaching and praying. Most Christians refer to these seven as the first deacons in the church. Later in 1st Timothy and Titus Paul gave the qualifications for deacons.

One of those who was chosen for this duty of taking care of the needy widows was Stephen. According to Acts 6:8, he was full of faith and power and did great wonders among the people. He also preached and in Chapter 7 of Acts, Luke recorded the sermon Stephen preached in which he took the hearers from Abraham all the way to Christ. At the end of the sermon, he told the people they had killed the Christ. The hearers were extremely mad. They were so mad, they ran upon Stephen, cast him out of the city, and stoned him to death. In his death, he prayed for the Lord not to lay this sin against the people. Stephen is known today as the first Christian martyr.

Standing there while Stephen was being killed was one known as Saul. According to Acts 7:58 through 8:3, Saul was consenting to Stephen's death. The people who were witnesses of the stoning, laid their clothes at Saul's feet. In Acts 8:3, Luke recorded Saul made havoc of the church by dragging men and women disciples off to prison. After a brief account of what was going on in Samaria recorded in Chapter 8 of Acts, Luke returned to Paul in Chapter 9.

At the time of Stephen's death, there was a great persecution of the church and the disciples were scattered everywhere. Philip went down to the city of Samaria to preach. We can infer from the information provided that this Philip was one of the seven chosen to minister to the widows rather than one of the twelve apostles as will become clear later in the account. Philip healed many and cast out evil spirits as he preached. Simon, a sorcerer, was in Samaria. He was one who had practiced magic and astonished the people of the area with his great abilities. But when the people heard Philip and saw the miracles he performed, they believed his teaching and according to Acts 8:12 were baptized. This Simon also saw the miracles and heard the preaching and according to verse 13, he too believed and was baptized. Simon then continued with Philip beholding the miracles and signs that were done.

While Acts 8:14-17 may seem to be just a continuation of the account by Luke, these verses provide the reader with some very important doctrinal information. First, Luke stated when the apostles heard Samaria had received the word of God, they sent unto them Peter and John who when they came prayed for them to receive the Holy Ghost. In verse 18, Simon saw it was through laying on of the apostles' hands that the Holy Ghost was given. Thus we can infer from the provided information laying on of an apostle's hands was necessary in order for one to receive the Holy Ghost (except in the case of Cornelius to be studied later). We can also infer the Philip who was preaching and baptizing here was one of the seven and not one of the apostles because if he had been an apostle, there would have been no need for Peter and John to come and lay on hands. We know Philip had miraculous powers because the passage previous to this one indicated he was performing healings and other miracles. But, he was not able to lay on hands to impart the miraculous powers to others. Thus, the final doctrinal piece we can infer is when the last apostle died, the power to lay on hands to give the Holy Spirit to others so they could perform miracles ceased.

When Simon saw the apostles had this power to lay on hands so others could perform miracles, he wanted the same power. Remember, he had been fooling the people with his sorcery and he knew what the apostles were doing was not a trick. He offered them money so he could have this power. Peter in verse 20 rebuked Simon sharply and told him in verse 22 to repent of his wickedness and pray to God the thought of his heart would be forgiven. Simon did repent and he even asked Peter to pray for him. A special point needs to be noted here. It was Simon who asked Peter to pray for him and not Peter telling Simon he needed to go before the church and ask for prayers because he had sinned. Peter simply told Simon to repent and to pray. Simon was a baptized believer who had sinned and as such, he still had the ability to repent and pray for himself. We do not need a priest or other earthly intercessor to whom we confess our sins and he prays for us; instead, God has given us the privilege to go to Him through Christ on behalf of ourselves. This fact that one can pray for herself does not make it wrong for one to ask the church members to pray when she has failed in her duty as noted in James 5:16 where James said to confess our faults to each other and pray for each other.

Philip was called away by the Lord in Acts 8:26 to go unto Gaza which was a deserted place. There, Philip met up with a eunuch who had charge of the treasure of the queen of Ethiopia. He had been to Jerusalem to worship, so he was already a worshiper of God. He was riding in his chariot and reading from Isaiah when Philip caught up with him. Philip asked him if he understood what he was reading. The eunuch said he did not and he asked Philip to help him. Philip got in the chariot with him and using the scripture in Isaiah 53:7-8 concerned with Jesus being crucified, he preached unto him Jesus (Acts 8:35). Luke did not record what Philip said in that sermon. But, we know from the sermons in Acts 2, 3, and 7 what it means to preach Jesus. Whatever he preached, we can know he preached baptism because in Acts 8:36, they had come to some water and the eunuch asked what hindered him from being baptized. Philip told him if he believed with all of his heart he could be baptized. The eunuch stated what is commonly referred to as the great confession. It is the same confession each person makes before she is baptized. The eunuch said: "I believe that Jesus Christ is the Son of God." With that confession, they stopped the chariot and went down into the water, both Philip and the eunuch, and the eunuch was baptized.

Again, in the passage from Acts 8:38-39 is another important doctrinal matter. They went down into the water and they came up out of the water. Some denominations teach baptism can be sprinkling or pouring of water. If sprinkling or pouring of water would have been sufficient, what was the need for the two of them to go down into the water and come up out of the water? A look at the word baptize in the original language makes it clear the meaning was to dip or plunge, but even without knowing anything about the Greek language, just from this example and Paul's statements in Romans 6:4 and in Colossians 2:12 concerning being buried in baptism, it should be clear to any reader baptism by sprinkling or pouring is not Bible baptism.

Acts 9, along with other accounts of the same event recorded in Acts 22 and 26, contains the conversion of one of the most outspoken persecutors of Christ's church. Remember back in Acts 7-8 the mention of one Saul at whose feet those who killed Stephen laid their clothes. In the beginning of Acts 9, Saul was even fiercer in this persecution. He had letters from the high priest allowing him to go to Damascus and if he found any who were followers of Christ, men or women, he could take them bound to Jerusalem. As he approached Damascus, a light shined around him. He fell to the earth. A voice asked him: "Saul, Saul, why persecutest thou me?" Saul asked, "Who art thou, Lord?" Jesus responded and told him He was Jesus of Nazareth (Acts 22:8) whom Saul was persecuting. Saul trembled and immediately asked what Jesus wanted him to do. Jesus told him to go into the city and he would be told what to do. Notice here the emphasis on "do." Saul asked what Jesus wanted him to "do" and Jesus told him to go to the city and he would be told what to "do." Saul arose but when he opened his eyes he was blind. They led him into Damascus where he was three days without food or drink.

The Lord appeared to Ananias, a disciple at Damascus, and told him to go to the house of Judas and to lay his hands upon Saul that he might receive his sight (Acts 9:11-12). At first Ananias was afraid to go because he knew about Saul and his persecution. The Lord provided reassurance to Ananias by telling him Saul was chosen to bear the Lord's name before Gentiles, Jews, and even kings. Ananias went to Saul, addressed him as "Brother Saul" not in the religious sense but as fellow Jews. In the account given in Acts 9, Ananias put his hands on Saul and told him Jesus had sent him to Saul so Saul might receive his sight and be filled with the Holy Ghost. Then in verse 18 the author stated Saul received his sight and was baptized.

According to Saul's account in Acts 22:13, Ananias went to Saul and told him to receive his sight and in that same hour Saul looked upon Ananias who asked him as recorded in verse 16 what he was waiting for. Ananias told him to arise and be baptized and wash away his sins, calling on the name of the Lord. If one only read the account given in chapter 9, she would not realize why Saul was baptized. Again, it is essential to take all references to any particular topic in order to have the complete account. Saul remained with the disciples at Damascus for a period of time and then the Jews wanted to kill him. Saul escaped over the wall in a basket and went to

Jerusalem. The disciples there were afraid of him but Barnabas took him to the disciples and told them how Saul had seen Jesus in the way and how he had preached boldly at Damascus in the name of Jesus. The disciples accepted Saul and sent him to Tarsus.

Next in Acts, Luke recorded the account of the first Gentile converts. Remember from the Old Testament prophecy in Isaiah 11:10 the Gentiles were going to seek the root of Jesse. Up to this point the gospel seems to have been preached to the Jews but beginning in Chapter 10 of Acts, the Gentiles were admitted to the kingdom. Cornelius was a man who according to Luke's account feared God. He gave charitable gifts to the people and he prayed to God. God sent an angel to him through a vision and told him to send to Joppa and call for Simon who was surnamed Peter and he would come and tell Cornelius what he needed to do. Note the word "do" again. It seems there has always been something to do to please God.

Cornelius sent his men to get Peter and as they were getting close to Joppa, Peter went upon a housetop to pray. While he was praying he became very hungry and he fell into a trance. He saw heaven opened and all kinds of animals let down to him in a sheet. A voice told him to rise, kill, and eat, but Peter, being a Jew who knew there were unclean meats of which he was not allowed to partake, replied nothing common or unclean had ever entered his mouth. The voice spoke to him three times and then the sheet was lifted up to heaven.

Peter came out of the trance and while he was wondering what the meaning of the vision was, the men from Cornelius arrived and asked for Peter. The Spirit appeared to Peter and told him three men were looking for him and he was to go with them. Peter went to the men and they told him why they were there. They said Cornelius had been warned from God by an angel to send for Peter and to hear words of him. The next day Peter went with them and he took six brethren with him (Acts 11:12). When they got to Cornelius' house, he had called in his kin people and friends so they could hear too. Cornelius understood the importance of sharing the gospel with others.

When Peter started to talk to those who were gathered, he told them they knew it was not lawful for a Jew to keep company with one of another nation but God had showed him he should not call any man common or unclean. He asked them for what reason they had called him. Cornelius then told Peter about his vision and how he had been told by the angel to send to Joppa for Peter and when he came he would talk to Cornelius. So Cornelius and his household were there expecting Peter to tell them all things commanded by God.

Peter then preached unto those present concerning Jesus. In Acts 11:15, when Peter was called into question by the disciples in Jerusalem for preaching to the Gentiles, Peter told them it was when he began preaching to the Gentiles the Holy Spirit came upon them as on the apostles in the beginning. It was because of this baptism of the Holy Spirit (11:16), Peter knew God was approving water baptism for the Gentiles (10:47). So after Peter preached to the Gentiles, he commanded them to be baptized in the name of the Lord in water (10:47-48). Thus Peter again opened the door to the kingdom using the key given by Christ, the gospel. These Gentiles had to do the same thing those on the day of Pentecost had to do in order to have their sins forgiven. They heard Peter preach the word. Obviously, they believed what he said as Peter preached repentance and remission of sins to them (10:43). Then Peter commanded them to be baptized in water. So Jew or Gentile, it does not matter, we must all do the same thing to have our sins forgiven. At the end of Acts 11, Luke said the disciples were called Christians first in Antioch (verse 26).

Up through Chapter 12 of Acts, the work of Peter has the most coverage, but beginning in Chapter 13, the work of Saul becomes most prominent. It is also in this chapter where Luke began referring to Saul as Paul. Paul's first recorded sermon is in Acts 13 where he gave an historical account of the Jews from Egypt through David and then he began to preach about Jesus. He covered the death and resurrection and how Jesus was seen of the people after His resurrection. In verse 38, he told the people it was through Jesus he was preaching the forgiveness of sins. The Jews left and the Gentiles begged Paul to preach to them the next Sabbath. He agreed and on that day almost the whole city of Antioch in Pisidia came out to hear his preaching. The Jews were envious and spoke against what Paul and Barnabas were preaching.

In Acts 13:46, Paul told the Jews it was necessary the word of God was preached to them first, but since they had judged themselves unworthy of everlasting life, they were turning to the Gentiles and he quoted Isaiah 42:6 and 49:6 concerning how the Gentiles would be given the light. The Gentiles were happy and those ordained to eternal life believed. The Jews retaliated by stirring up the people and raising a persecution against Paul and Barnabas so they left the city. They continued their journey as documented by Luke in Acts 14. In some places they were well received and in some they were persecuted. On their return trip to Antioch, they stopped by the cities where they had previously preached and ordained elders in every church (14:23).

In Acts 15, Peter came back on the scene in a debate concerning whether or not the Gentiles needed to be circumcised. Some men had gone to Antioch and taught the Gentiles had to be circumcised to be saved. Paul and Barnabas and some others went to Jerusalem to the apostles and elders there to discuss the issue. After some discussion, Peter spoke in favor of not requiring the Gentiles to be circumcised. Paul and Barnabas then spoke concerning the wonders God had worked through the Gentiles. James then spoke and quoted from the Old Testament prophets and gave his judgment in agreement with Peter saying the Gentiles did not need to be circumcised while they did need to abstain from idols, fornication, and eating of blood. Their decision was made through the Holy Ghost as evidenced from verse 28.

Paul picked up another disciple, Timothy, in Chapter 16 of Acts. Timothy's mother was a believing Jew but his father was a Greek. Some would question why Paul had Timothy circumcised since previously it was Paul who carried the message that non-Jewish disciples did not need to be circumcised. The answer was clearly stated in verse 3. Paul had him circumcised because of the Jews. According to Coffman (n.d.), Paul knew the Jews would give Paul trouble because they knew Timothy's father was a Greek. So Paul did not have Timothy circumcised for any religious purpose.

According to Acts 16:5, the churches were increasing daily in number. In Chapter 16 is given the account of the conversion of Lydia, a seller of purple. She was a worshipper of God who when she heard Paul's preaching was baptized along with others in her house.

Also in Chapter 16 Luke gave the account of the conversion of a jailor in Philippi. Paul and Silas had been put in prison after they cast a spirit out of a woman thus causing her masters to lose a lot of money because they had used her in fortune telling. While in prison, Paul and Silas were praying and singing. Here is a lesson for all of us for when we are having troubles. Sing and pray to God. In the case of Paul and Silas there was an earthquake so the prison shook and the doors came open and everyone's bands opened up. The jailor thought everyone had fled and knowing he would be killed for not keeping the prisoners bound, he drew his own sword to kill himself. Paul called out to him to not harm himself because everyone was still there. The jailor was trembling and he fell before Paul and Silas and asked them: "Sirs, what must I do to be saved?" They told him to believe on the Lord Jesus Christ and he would be saved and his house. He obviously believed what they told him for he took them that same hour of the night and was baptized along with those in his house.

Paul and Silas should not have even been put into the prison as it violated their legal rights. When day came, the magistrates sent word to let them go, but Paul appealed to his legal rights and in Acts 16:37 Luke recorded Paul as sending the authorities back word they could come themselves and get them out of prison. When the authorities realized Paul and Silas were Romans they were afraid because they had illegally bound them. The authorities went to the prison and released them. Paul and Silas continued on a journey of preaching and teaching as recorded in Acts 17.

While in Athens, Paul saw an altar to the unknown god. The philosophers of the area around Athens wanted to hear what Paul had to say, so he took the opportunity to preach them a sermon in which he shared with them the Lord God. He told them at one time God overlooked the ignorance of the people (Acts 17:30), but now He commands all men everywhere to repent because He has appointed a day when He will judge the world by Christ (verses 30-31). When the philosophers heard the words "resurrection of the dead," some of them mocked but others wanted to hear more. Paul left the area and went on to Corinth.

In Corinth, Paul found Aquila and Priscilla who were tentmakers as was Paul, so he stayed with them and continued to teach in the synagogue every Sabbath. When the Jews would not hear him, he moved on to the house of Justus where Crispus the chief ruler of the synagogue heard him and believed on the Lord. According to Acts 18:8, many of the Corinthians heard, believed, and were baptized. In the meantime, the husband and wife team of Aquila and Priscilla heard one named Apollos in the synagogue diligently teaching the things of the Lord, but he only knew about the baptism of John. When they heard him, they took him unto themselves and taught him the way of God more perfectly.

God allowed Paul to do many miracles as noted in Acts 19:11. Then in Chapter 20 while Paul was preaching for a long time, one fell out of a window and was taken up dead. Paul was allowed to restore his life. On this occasion, Paul was meeting with the disciples of that region who upon the first day of the week had met to partake of the Lord's Supper (Acts 20:7). Here is another of those passages that can be used to help present day Christians know when the early church met and part of their purpose.

Paul insisted he had not failed to declare the whole counsel of God to those who had heard him preach, but in Acts 20:28-30, he warned the elders of the church in Ephesus (20:17) there would be grievous wolves entering the flock and drawing away disciples after themselves. He told them the wolves would even be from their own group. He told them to watch and to remember he had warned them it would happen. And happen it did. Religious history accounts show it was not very long before the church was falling away and going after strange doctrines just like the Jews of the Old Testament did.

Paul continued to preach from city to city and he continued to be arrested. He spoke before captains, before centurions, before the Sanhedrin, before Governor Felix, before Governor Festus, and even before King Agrippa and his wife Bernice. In Acts 26:28, King Agrippa told Paul he almost persuaded him to be a Christian. Almost but lost is in one of the songs the church sings. How many of our friends and family are almost but lost? What more can we say to persuade them to diligently study the law of the Lord?

This chapter has been concerned with events in the early church recorded in Acts. In the next chapter will be more information concerning the early church and factors in salvation as recorded by Peter, Paul, James, and Jude.

Chapter 10

Salvation in the Letters

Luke in the book of Acts gave the reader an understanding of how the promise Jesus made to build His church was fulfilled and how Peter used the keys to the door of the kingdom in preaching to both the Jews and the Gentiles. Just like God chose to give the prophecies of Christ and His kingdom and the works and words of Christ through different men, He also chose to give His words concerning salvation, through several writers. In this chapter, the emphasis will be on salvation in Christ and His church as explained by the writers of the epistles Romans through Jude. Many readers will already know Romans, 1st and 2nd Corinthians, Galatians, Ephesians, Philippians, Colossians, and 1st and 2nd Thessalonians were written by Paul to the churches, and 1st and 2nd Timothy, Titus, and Philemon were written by him to individuals. The author of Hebrews was not specifically stated in that book, but due to the content and writing style, many believe it to have been written by Paul. James was written by James; 1st and 2nd Peter by Peter; 1st, 2nd, and 3rd John by John (the writer of the Gospel of John and Revelation); and Jude by Jude.

Most of the above mentioned books have something to say about salvation and the church. Again, it is essential the readers of the Bible put together everything written concerning a subject so the right choices are made concerning what is believed. As noted in the previous chapter of this book in both the account of Saul's conversion and the account of the conversion of the household of Cornelius, if one did not read all of the verses pertaining to the conversions then the whole story would not be known.

The book of Romans has a reputation for being one of those books where if a person used only one or two verses taken out of context, she could most likely establish multiple ways to answer the question: "What must I do to be saved?" Below are some scriptures with possible answers if one was to use only the cited scripture for the answer.

Paul said in Romans 1:16 the gospel is the power of God unto salvation to everyone who believes, so all you need to do is believe the gospel. In Romans 2:6 he said God will render to every man according to his deeds, so you just have to do good deeds to be saved. According to Romans 3:24 we are freely justified by God's grace, so we really do not have to do anything to be saved. In Romans 4:5, Paul said our faith is counted as righteousness and 5:1 we are justified by faith, so faith is all we need to be counted righteous and justified. Again in Romans 5:9, we are justified by His blood and saved from wrath through Him, so there is nothing for us to do. This salvation is a free gift according to Romans 5:18 and it is for all men. Then in Romans 6:3-4, Paul said when we were baptized into Jesus we were raised to a new life, so all one needs is to be baptized and she has the new life. In Romans 6:17, Paul mentioned obeying from the heart that form of doctrine so maybe that is what it takes. But then in verse 23 he again said eternal life is a gift of God. Maybe all one needs is hope, for in Roman 8:24 Paul said we are saved by hope. Wait a minute, according to Romans 8:30, none of this matters for we are predestinated (chosen beforehand with nothing we can do either way). Then in Romans 10:9 Paul said if one confesses with the mouth and believes in the heart God has raised Jesus, he will be saved. Dropping down to verse 13, Paul continued with whoever calls upon the name of the Lord will be saved. But then in verse 16 he mentioned something about those who have not "obeyed the gospel." Then in verse 17, he said faith comes by hearing the word of God.

Admittedly, this salvation thing looks very confusing. Every answer proposed above could be a proper answer but none of the answers taken alone provides the full answer to the salvation question. For those of us who are grounded in the faith, imagine for a minute truly not knowing what you know and being given the above paragraph. Which of the ways to salvation would you choose? This may be the predicament of some of those friends you are trying to convert. We must be able to sort out the plan that fits with all of these verses and the many others in the New Testament. With diligent study one should be able to see God's plan keeping in mind two very important verses. First Paul wrote to Timothy in 2nd Timothy 2:15, "Study to show thyself approved unto God, a workman that needed not to be ashamed, rightly dividing the word of truth." Second, Paul wrote to Timothy in 2nd Timothy 3:16, "All scripture is given by inspiration of God, and is profitable for doctrine, for reproof, for correction, for instruction in righteousness: That the man of God may be perfect, thoroughly furnished unto all good works." So we are going to have to study and we are going to have to study all of the scripture. That is why this book began with a review of the Old Testament and led up to this all important topic of salvation.

There are many good people in our land who have not learned to search the scriptures and to study them diligently. They are somewhat like those of the Old Testament who instead of reading for themselves, they listened to someone else read the word. Today, in many cases the ones listened to only read part of the scriptures pertaining to salvation simply because that is all they have been taught. While many of those in the Old Testament times had no choice concerning the readings, we do. We can read the word for ourselves.

Somewhere along the line, just like in the Old Testament, people forgot their responsibility to diligently study and teach the full word of God. They forgot to share those words with the children in the morning and in the night. They forgot to impress upon their children the importance of serving God and not idols (worldly activities). In some cases as noted by Paul in Acts 20:29-30, this lack of attention to spreading the true word may have been intentional. In either case, when the children of those parents and the following generations grew up, they were not prepared to continue the ongoing process of teaching others, so now the work is greater, but we women who know the truth have a responsibility to share it with others and those who do not have the whole truth have a responsibility to learn what they are missing. Keeping these thoughts in mind, this study becomes an essential endeavor.

The hope is when the reader has finished this chapter she will be able to put together many of those verses mentioned above concerning salvation along with others found in the letters to have a plan in agreement with what Jesus and the apostles taught in the gospels and Acts. Remember when Jesus was about to be taken into heaven, He told His apostles to go into all the world and preach the gospel to every creature (Mark 16:15-16) and to baptize the believers in the name of the Father, Son, and Holy Ghost (Matthew 29:18-20), for he that believes and is baptized will be saved (Mark 16:15-16). Then when the apostles preached the first gospel sermon in Acts 2, Peter told the people to repent and be baptized in the name of Jesus Christ for the remission of sins (Acts 2:38) and then the saved were added to the church (Acts 2:47). As one reads the epistles, this plan is actually the same plan taught in the letters.

Having already looked at several verses in Romans concerned with salvation, it may be helpful to look at some of the other letters of Paul to see what he said in them concerning salvation and the church. But first, back in Romans 12:4-5, Paul set the background for this study when he said in verse 4 we have many members in one body and then again in verse 5, these many members are one body in Christ. In 1st Corinthians 1:10, Paul exhorted the brethren of the church to all speak the same thing and not to have divisions among themselves. He went on to show how Christ was not divided and neither should His teachers be in what they proclaimed. In Chapter 6, after describing several unrighteous characteristics of those who will not inherit the kingdom of God, Paul told the Corinthians in 1st Corinthians 6:11 some of them had in the past had those characteristics but now they were washed, sanctified, and justified in the name of Jesus. In 2nd Corinthians 5:17 he told the brethren if any man is in Christ, he is a new creature and old things are passed away.

      Along the same line, Paul told the brethren in the Galatian church as recorded in Galatians 3:26-27 they were in Christ by being baptized into Him. He went on in verse 28 to say they were one in Christ which is what he said needed to happen in 1st Corinthians 1 where he pled for unity in the body. Of particular importance Paul said in Galatians 3:29 if they were in Christ (through baptism), they were Abraham's seed and heirs according to the promise. This verse should clarify how the promise to Abraham of a seed which would save all nations was fulfilled. In Galatians 4 Paul continued this discussion concerning Abraham and his seed. In verse 28, he told them they were the children of promise.

At the very beginning of Ephesians, Paul made it clear how predestination was part of the plan. He said in Ephesians 1:4 God had chosen them before the foundation of the world and in verse 5, he said they were predestinated unto the adoption of children by Jesus Christ. In other words, before the foundation of the world, God knew the Jews would disobey and fall from being the chosen people. He knew the Gentiles would be given the opportunity to be adopted into the family of God. It was God's plan, thus it was predestined to happen. It was not predestined who would and who would not accept the grace of God and obey His gospel. That was left totally up to each person's choice.

Paul continued in Ephesians 1 to explain Christ had been placed at the right hand of God and then in verses 21-22, he gave the Ephesians a picture of the kingdom over which Christ was prophesied to rule. This kingdom over which Christ was to rule was the church. Note in verse 22 Christ was made the head over all things to the church. In verse 23, Paul said the church was the body of Christ and the fullness of Him that fills all in all.

In Ephesians 2:12-22, Paul explained to the Ephesians how they had been able to come into the kingdom of Christ. He told them in the past as Gentiles, they were called Uncircumcision by those who were called Circumcision and at that time, they were without Christ being aliens from the commonwealth of Israel and strangers from the covenant of promise. In verse 13, he showed them how it was in Christ they had the opportunity to be part of that covenant of promise. In verse 14, Paul said Christ had made both Jew and Gentile one and broken down the wall which was between them in the past.

In Ephesians 2:15, Paul made it clear it was in Christ's death He took away the law of commandments and again by uniting the Jew and Gentile, He made them to be one. Jesus had prayed in John 17 for all to be one in Him and He in the Father. Finally in Ephesians 2:20-22, Paul compared the people to stones of a building and he said they were built upon the foundation of the apostles and prophets with Jesus Christ being the chief corner stone. Remember in the prophecy from the Old Testament (Psalm 118:22) the stone the builders set aside had become the chief corner stone.

Moving on over to Ephesians 4:4, Paul again mentioned the fact there is one body. Remember back in Ephesians 1:23, he had said the body was the church; thus, there is but one church and according to Ephesians 4, we must all come into the unity of the faith (verse 13), not allowing ourselves to be carried about by false doctrine (verse 14), but grow up into Christ who is the head (verse 15), from whom the whole body (church) is joined together and growing (verse 16).

In Ephesians 5, Paul continued describing this church over which Christ was the head. In verse 23, he said the husband is the head of the wife even as Christ is the head of the church and savior of the body. In verse 24, he said just like the church is subject to Christ, so wives should be to their own husbands. Then in verses 25-26 Paul showed how Christ loved the church and gave Himself for it to sanctify it and cleanse it with washing of water by the word.

Before leaving Ephesians and going to Philippians, back in Ephesians 2:8, between the sections concerning the church, Paul again stated it is by grace through faith people are saved. He went on to say salvation did not come from humans but was given as a gift of God. In verse 9, he said salvation was not of works, yet in verse 10, he noted we are to walk in good works.

In the letter to the Philippians, Paul again encouraged a congregation to be of one mind. In Philippians 1:27, he told them to let their conduct be worthy of the gospel of Christ and then he told them to stand fast in one spirit with one mind striving together for the faith of the gospel. Paul told them in 2:9-11 how God had highly exalted Christ and had given Him a name above every name. In verse 10, Paul stated at the name of Jesus every knee should bow and in verse 11 he said every tongue should confess Jesus Christ is Lord.

More was stressed about the church being the body in Colossians. Here in Colossians 1 Paul used the terms church and kingdom interchangeably. In 1:13, he said God had delivered them from the power of darkness and translated them into the kingdom of His dear Son. It is through this Son, they had redemption and forgiveness of sins (verse 14) and He is the head of the body, the church (verse 18). So it follows if the

Colossians had been translated into the kingdom of the Son they were in the church of His dear Son which was why Paul addressed them in 1:2 as the saints and faithful brethren in Christ which are at Colosse. In 2:12, Paul noted how those at Colosse had been buried with Christ in baptism and risen with Him through the faith of the operation of God and in verse 13 he said they had their trespasses forgiven.

Those in Thessalonica had become followers of the "churches of God which in Judaea are in Christ Jesus" (1st Thessalonians 2:14). In 2nd Thessalonians 2:14, Paul said the Thessalonians had been called to the obtaining of the glory of Jesus, and here is the passage where he clearly stated how they were called. Often those whom we are teaching about Christ will say one has to be called before she can be saved. According to this passage, one is called by the gospel. Remember in Romans 1:16, Paul said the gospel was the power of God unto salvation.

In Acts 16, Paul had met with Timothy and formed a bond. Two of Paul's letters were written to Timothy. Paul began the first letter by calling Timothy his "own son in the faith." You can imagine how Paul felt about Timothy especially if you have someone to whom you have taught the word and helped to make that person a stronger Christian. Paul told Timothy in 1st Timothy 1:4 not to listen to fables and endless genealogies but rather to deal with godly edifying. He told Timothy how as Paul said would happen back in Acts 20, some had left the Lord and were desiring to teach what they did not even understand (1st Timothy 1:6-7). Paul said he was writing to Timothy so if Paul did not see him for a while, Timothy would know how to behave himself in the church of the living God, the pillar and ground of the truth (3:14-15). Then in 1st Timothy 4:1-3, Paul stressed his earlier point to the elders in Acts where he reminded them there would be those who would depart from the faith. He even told Timothy some of the activities in which they would engage included forbidding to marry and commanding to abstain from meats.

Paul shared with Timothy in 2nd Timothy 2:2, the need to continue committing God's word to those who are able to teach others. Paul reminded Timothy in 1st Timothy 3:14-15 from a child he had known the Holy Scriptures which were able to make him wise unto salvation through faith in Christ Jesus. Just like Timothy could by knowing the Holy Scriptures (which in his case had to be the writings of the Old Testament) be wise unto salvation through Christ, so then can we be wise by knowing and rightly dividing all scripture. According to verse 17, we can be completely provided by them with all we need to be perfect or complete. We do not need any creeds of men but only the word of God.

The possibility of people falling and failing to serve God must have been so strong on Paul's mind as he again in 2nd Timothy 4 reminded Timothy it was going to happen. He said in verse 3 the time would come when people would not listen to sound doctrine but would gather themselves teachers who would teach what the people wanted to hear. It continues to happen today and we must be ready to fight it just as Paul exhorted Timothy to be ready.

Another of Paul's sons in the faith was Titus as shown in Titus 1:4. In 2nd Corinthians 8:23, Paul had told the Corinthian church Titus was his partner and fellow helper. In his letter to Titus in Chapter 3 Paul said in verse 3 they had at one time been living in a sinful manner but the love of God had appeared (verse 4) and by God's own mercy, He had saved them by the washing of regeneration and renewing of the Holy Ghost (verse 5). He said in verse 7 they had been justified by grace to be made heirs to the hope of eternal life.

The little letter to Philemon was not written for the purpose of sharing the plan of salvation, but Paul did mention the church and its members. In this letter of one chapter, Paul was asking Philemon to allow him to have the use of one of Philemon's slaves, Onesimus, while Paul was in prison. It seems Onesimus had ran away from Philemon and Paul had converted Onesimus while in prison (verse 10). The reader can glean there were churches in the houses of the people because in verse 2, Paul indicated he was writing not only to Philemon but to the "church in thy house." It is also indicated the term saints is a good one to apply to the brethren (and sisters) of the household of God (verses 5, 7) as is brother (verses 16, 20).

As noted earlier, the writer of the book of Hebrews did not choose to identify himself, but many Bible scholars believe the writer was Paul. No matter the writer, the book is filled with ways in which the way of Christ is superior to the Judaic or Old Testament way. The writer began the book by saying in the old times, God spoke to the fathers by the prophets, but in the last days He had spoken by His Son who had purged the people from their sins and then sat down on the right hand of God. The writer then went on to show how Christ was superior in His deity because He was God (1:4-13), in His humanity because He was man (2:5-16), in His work because He built the house (3:1-6), and in His position because He was the high priest (4:14-16). The writer summed everything up in Chapters 8-10 where he explained there was a new covenant brought in by Jesus.

In Hebrews 11, the author provided the readers with a brilliant example of the meaning of faith. First he gave a definition for faith as "the substance of things hoped for, the evidence of things not seen" (verse 1) but then he gave at least twenty examples of this faith. In almost all of them, the faith was a working faith such as we must have to please God. According to verse 6, without faith it is impossible to please God because for anyone to come to God, he has to first believe in Him and believe He is a rewarder of those who diligently seek Him. There is our word again. It is only those who diligently seek God who are pleasing to Him and they do it by the type of faith described in this chapter.

The many accounted as faithful in Hebrews 11 included: Abel who offered (verse 4); Enoch who pleased (verse 5); Noah who prepared an ark (verse 7); Abraham who obeyed (verse 8), sojourned (verse 9), and offered up Isaac (verse 17); Isaac who blessed (verse 20); Jacob who blessed and worshipped (verse 21); Joseph who gave commandment (verse 22); Moses' parents who hid Moses (verse 23); Moses who refused and chose (verses 24-25), forsook Egypt (verse 27), and kept the Passover (verse 28); Israelites who passed through (verse 29); Joshua who marched (verse 30); Rahab who received spies (verse 31); and others who subdued kingdoms, wrought righteousness, obtained promises, stopped mouth of lions, quenched violence of fire, escaped sword, and waxed valiant, (verses 32-38). Note in each of these cases, the people had faith, but they had to do something which is a theme covered in the book of James.

In Hebrews 12:18-29, the writer made one final comparison between the old and the new. He told the people to whom he was writing they had not come unto the mount that burned with fire from the Old Testament period, nor had they come to the sound of trumpets but they had come to Mount Sion and the city of the living God and to the general assembly and church of the firstborn and to Jesus the mediator of the new covenant. He warned them in verses 25-26 not to refuse the voice of the One who spoke, whose voice in the past shook the earth. In verse 28 he told them they had received a kingdom which could not be moved. Remember Jesus said in Matthew 16:18 He was going to build His church and the gates of hell would not prevail against it and in Joel 2:28 the prophet said the deliverance would come in Jerusalem and Mount Zion. When you put these passages together, it should be very clear that the church is the fulfillment of this prophecy.

Going from Hebrews right into James with the idea of faith on one's mind will lead one to better understand this faith required by God. In James 1:6, James said if anyone lacked wisdom let him ask of God in faith. Then in verse 22 he said to be doers of the word and not hearers only. If anyone is just a hearer of the word and does nothing about it, then James compared him to one who looked at himself in the mirror and then went away not remembering what he looked like.

In James 2:14, James asked what profit there was in faith without works. He asked if faith could save anyone. Then he gave an example of faith without works in which one told a brother or sister who was in need to depart and be warmed or filled but did not give them anything to warm or fill them. He said in verse 17 faith without works was dead. He continued in verse 19 to say to those who claimed faith without works that even the devils believe and tremble. He again stated in verse 20 faith without works is dead and then he used some of the same examples from Hebrews concerning Abraham and Rahab and how they showed their faith. In verses 24 and 26 James insisted a man was justified by works along with faith. In verse 24 is the only place in the Bible where one will find "faith only" and in this context, James said justification was not by faith only. Never let anyone convince us faith alone can save!

In James 5:16, James told the readers what one who had faults needed to do. He said to confess your faults to each other and pray for each other. In verses 19-20, he said when one was able to convert a sinner from the error of his ways, he was saving a soul from death and hiding a multitude of sins.

The books of 1st and 2nd Peter were written by the apostle to whom Christ gave the keys to the kingdom. Peter in 1st Peter 1:13 clearly stated how the grace of God was brought unto man. He said it was brought unto them at the revelation of Jesus Christ. Thus Jesus Christ was God's grace by which they were saved. He was the free gift through which mankind was offered salvation. Peter told the readers in 1st Peter 1:18-20 they had not been redeemed with corruptible things but with the blood of Christ which had been foreordained before the foundation of the world. Then he told these Christians how they had purified their own souls in verse 22-23. He said they had obeyed the truth, being born again by the word of God. Recall in John 3 Jesus told Nicodemus in order for one to enter the kingdom, he had to be born of water and of spirit. This new birth, according to Peter is not of corruptible seed but of the incorruptible word of God known as the gospel (verse 25).

In 1st Peter 2, Peter told the people they were a chosen generation, a royal priesthood, a holy nation, and a peculiar people. In verse 10 he told them they were the people of God. He showed them in chapter 3 how just like eight souls were saved by water in the ark, so even does baptism also now save them (verse 21). Peter said baptism was not to get rid of the filth of the flesh but was the answer of a good conscience toward God. He said this baptism saved them by the resurrection of Jesus Christ. Without Christ having risen, the baptism would have been of no effect. Then in verse 22, Peter made it very clear Christ was then reigning in heaven with authorities, powers, and angels being made subject to Him.

Peter told his readers in 1st Peter 4:16 if they were called upon to suffer as a Christian they should not be ashamed. Instead of being ashamed they should glorify God because they were counted worthy to suffer for His name. Then in verse 17, Peter mentioned obeying the gospel of God. He asked if judgment must begin at the house of God what would be the end of those who did not obey the gospel of God. The contrast between those who obey and those who do not is the same contrast between the righteous and the sinner in verse 18.

Finally, in Chapter 5 of 1st Peter, he himself gave an indication he was a married man because he said he was an elder. Later in this book will be covered the qualifications for an elder in the church, but one of those was to be the husband of one wife.

In 2nd Peter 2, Peter also reminded the readers of those false teachers who would actually be among them. He said they would bring in heresies and even deny Christ. Then later in the chapter, Peter described a fallen Christian as one like a dog eating his own vomit or a pig that had a bath going back out into the mud (verse 22). This is a situation in which no one should allow herself to be found.

John's three epistles are very short. In 1st John, he described God as light, love, and life. In 2nd John, he encouraged the elect lady and her children to walk in truth, and in 3rd John, he encouraged the church to have fellowship among Christian brethren.

In 1st John 1, John told the readers for one to say he had no sin, he was lying, but if one confessed his sins, Jesus was faithful and just to forgive those sins. In 1st John 2:1, John told the readers they had an advocate with the Father and if they sinned, Jesus Christ was their propitiation. But for one to say he knew Christ and did not keep his commands, then he was again a liar. We know John was writing to Christians in 1st John, because in Chapter 2 verse 12 he said he was writing unto them because their sins were forgiven.

Interestingly, John also warned the readers concerning those who were going to go out from them and be teaching a false doctrine. He told them in 1st John 2:18 there were already many antichrists and they could know they were living in the last time because of this fact. These antichrists were in the church. In verse 24, John showed the readers how when they are in Christ, they are also in the Father. In 1st John 3:1-2, John showed the readers how they were the sons of God. In verses 8-10, he explained how those who commit sin are of the devil, but those who are born of God do not stay in a state of sin.

In 1st John 4, John stressed the importance of not believing everything one hears religiously but trying the spirits to see if they are of God. He said those spirits who do not confess Christ as having come in the flesh are of the spirit of antichrist which was already in the world at the time of John's writing. He went on to write concerning the importance of confessing Jesus as the Son of God (verse 15). In chapter 5 of 1st John, he wrote in verse 1 of the importance of believing in Jesus as the Christ. In verse 6, John noted Christ came by water and blood. Then in verses 7-8 John noted there are three that bear record in heaven, the Father, the Word, and the Holy Ghost and these three he said are one. On earth there are three that bear witness, the Spirit, the water, and the blood and these three agree in one.

In 2nd John addressed to the elect lady, John again made mention of deceivers who had entered the world and did not confess Christ had come in the flesh. He said in verse 9 whoever did not abide in the doctrine of Christ did not have God. He also said if any came in unto the people and did not bring the doctrine of Christ, they should not receive that one into their house nor bid him God speed.

Finally in 3rd John, an account was given of one of those who must have been a wolf among the flock. John said when he had written to the church this one, Diotrephes, who loved to have the preeminence would not receive him. John cautioned Gaius in verse 11 to follow what was good and not that which was evil because those who did good were of God.

The last of the letters, written by Jude and addressed to those who were sanctified by God the Father and preserved in Jesus Christ and called, once more addressed certain men who had slipped in unexpectedly and were turning the grace of God into sin and denying Christ. Jude reminded the brethren how God having saved the people out of Egypt, when they refused to believe Him, He destroyed them. Jude reminded the brethren how God even cast out the angels who chose not to obey Him. Then he reminded them of Sodom and Gomorrha and how they were also examples for the faithful.

Jude encouraged the brethren in verses 20-23 to be built up and to help build up the other followers of Christ. The words Jude had for those who were sanctified by God in the first century are words good for us today. We must be workers who help to save others pulling them from the fire (verse 23). That is what we are doing when we are fulfilling our responsibility to teach others, having first diligently studied for ourselves.

Having now completed a very brief look at the words written by Peter, Paul, James, and Jude in the epistles concerning salvation and the church, and having already looked at what Jesus taught in Matthew through John and what the early preachers taught in the book of Acts, one should be able to put together all of the information into a complete and concise plan for salvation. This plan must include all of what was taught without creating any strife or contradictions between and among the teachings. Following, will be such a plan the reader can teach to her family and friends knowing it is completely scriptural.

From the Old Testament prophecies, it was clear God promised to provide a way of salvation for man through the seed of Eve, Abraham, Isaac, Jacob, and David. Many prophecies concerning the life and death of this One were provided in the Old Testament. According to the Gospels, this One was Jesus and the many prophecies concerning Him were fulfilled in His life, death, and resurrection. He was born of a virgin, lived among mankind, performed miracles, taught the people using parables, chose His apostles, was betrayed by one of them, died on the cross, was buried in the rich man's tomb, rose from the dead the third day, taught His disciples for another forty days and was then taken up to heaven where He currently reigns over His kingdom the church.

It was by God's grace (Ephesians 2:8) or free gift that Jesus was sent to earth to die for the sins of the world and all have sinned (Romans 3:23). The wages of sin is death but the gift of God is eternal life through Jesus Christ (Romans 6:23). God has given humans a choice to accept or reject the free gift.

If one chooses to accept the free gift, then one must obey Christ, for He asked the people why they called Him Lord but did not do what He commanded (Luke 6:46). Christ sent His apostles into all the world to preach the gospel. He said those who believed the gospel and were baptized would be saved (Mark 16:16). When believed, this gospel, which is the power of God unto salvation, will prick one's spiritual heart and cause one to repent of sins (Acts 2:38), confess faith in Christ as the Son of God (Acts 8:37), and be baptized for the remission or forgiveness of sins (Acts 2:38) thus following the pattern of Christ in that He died, was buried, and arose. We too will die to sin, be buried in water, and arise to walk in newness of life (Colossians 2:12-13, Romans 6:1-6). While baptism is only one of the essentials in salvation, it is in this baptism when it follows faith, repentance, and confession that one: puts on Christ (Galatians 3:27), washes away sins (Acts 22:16), has sins forgiven (Colossians 2:12-13), is born again (John 3:5), is saved (1st Peter 3:21), and is added to the church (Acts 2:38, 41, and 47). Once added to the church it is necessary to continue living a faithful life as will be covered in Chapter 12 of this book.

As we go about telling others the plan of salvation, we will find many very good people who have been baptized and believe they are saved. The problem is these fine folks are just like those in Acts 19:1-5 who had been baptized but needed to be baptized again because they did not have the right baptism.

The right baptism is not one performed when the person is an infant; it is not one performed by sprinkling or pouring; and it is not one performed after one is saved by faith, or by grace, or by a sinner's prayer (nowhere found in the Bible). It is the baptism authorized by Jesus in Matthew 28:19 and performed after one who has heard God's word realizes her lost condition, believes in and confesses Christ as the Son of God, and repents of sins. Once a person has obeyed this way of salvation, remaining faithful is essential (Revelation 2:10). We must diligently teach the way of salvation to our children so they are prepared when the false doctrine tries to enter the church.

In addition to teaching the way of salvation to others, we must also be prepared to teach the scriptural organization, worship, and work of the church to which the saved are added. This too is another area requiring diligent study for those who were in the first century church desiring to spread false teachings have continued through the ages and have done a great job in teaching a perverted gospel (2nd Peter 2:1-2). In the next chapter, the concern will be with the organization, worship, and work of the church Christ built and to which all Christians have been added.

Chapter 11
The Church's Organization, Worship, and Work

In Chapter 10, many verses concerning salvation and the establishment of the church were considered. In this chapter, the church is still the central idea, but now the content will be concerned with the organization of the church, its worship, and its work. Many would have the church to be a social club or organization catering to all of the needs of the people including physical, social, recreational, mental, and spiritual. Some would have several churches overseen by a group of officials, with an earthly headquarters, and creeds written by humans. Some would have great social programs with gymnasiums for play and cafeterias for serving both the members and the needy from the streets. Some would offer day care and schools for the children and teens and homes for the widows and orphans. While none of these activities may be wrong, unless there is Biblical authority for them, none of them can be right when the church is responsible for them.

The only way to know what is authorized for the church is to once more go through the Bible to see what has been provided to the reader concerning the organization, worship, and work of the church. In some cases the writers have been very clear in giving commands or examples and in other cases the reader must look at commands and examples and make inferences concerning what is lawful and what is not. Jesus made it clear He was going to build the church in Matthew

16:18. In John 17:21, He prayed to God desiring His followers to be one. In Acts 2:47, the saved were added to the church. In Colossians 1:18 Paul declared Christ to be the head of the body or the church and in Ephesians 4:4, he said there was one body.

In addition to the term "body," (Ephesians 1:22-23), this church has been identified by several terms. Some of those include: flock (Acts 20:28), house of God (1st Timothy 3:15), household of faith (Galatians 6:10), kingdom (Colossians 1:13, Matthew 16:18-19), church of God (1st Timothy 3:5, 1st Corinthians 1:2), church of the Thessalonians which is in God the Father and in the Lord Jesus Christ (1st Thessalonians 1:1), churches of Christ (Romans 16:16), and church of the firstborn (Hebrews 12:23). According to 1st Peter 2:5, 9, Christians are a royal priesthood, a chosen generation, a holy nation, a peculiar people, and a spiritual house.

Interestingly, nowhere in scripture is Christ's church referred to by some man's name. Actually, in 1st Corinthians 1:10-15, Paul reprimanded the church at Corinth for the contentions among them in which some were calling themselves by the name of a man. In verse 12, Paul said the people were saying they were of Paul, Apollos, Cephas, and Christ. He asked them in verse 13 if Christ was divided or if Paul was crucified for them or if they were baptized in the name of Paul. Paul was glad he had only baptized a few of them simply because he did not want them calling themselves by his name (verse 14-15). But in today's religious world, it is common to hear of churches or congregations being called by some man's name or being referred to by some term that cannot be found in the scripture. These things should not be happening but just like John noted in 3rd John verse 9, there are those who want the preeminence in the church. These people will not allow Christ the preeminence even over His own church in allowing it to be called by His own name.

According to Acts 14:23, elders were appointed in each congregation. In Titus 1:5 Paul said he had left Titus in Crete to appoint elders in each of the cities. The qualifications for these elders is given in both in Titus 1:5-9 and 1st Timothy 3:1-7. Of great importance is the idea these leaders were always males. They were to be the husband of one wife and have faithful children. They were to be blameless and not self-willed. They could not be easily angered. They were not to drink, be violent, or be greedy for money. They had to be ones who showed hospitality to others and be just, holy, and have self-control. They had to be able to teach and they had to have a good report from those who were not part of the church.

These men were to be the leaders of the flock and were called by several names. In 1st Timothy 4:14, Paul referred to them as presbyters; in Philippians 1:1 and 1st Timothy 3:1-2 they were called bishops; in Acts 20:28 the term overseer was used; in Ephesians 4:11-12 they were called pastor; and in 1st Peter 5:1-4 they were called shepherds.

The job these shepherds were charged with was having the oversight of the congregation. As noted earlier, each congregation was to have its own elders which has led to the idea congregations of Christ's church are autonomous or self-governing using only the word of God as their guide. In Acts 20:28, Luke wrote concerning Paul telling the elders in Ephesus to feed the church of God which He had purchased with His own blood. Paul told them it was the Holy Ghost who had made them overseers of the flock. In 1st Timothy 5:17, Paul told Timothy the elders who rule well were worthy of double honor; thus, a duty of the elders is to rule. In 1st Peter 5:1-3, Peter who as noted earlier was an elder himself, wrote to the elders to feed the flock of God willingly and not as being lords over them but to be examples to the flock. The writer of Hebrews told the audience in Hebrews 13:7 to remember the ones who had the rule over them and in verse 17, the writer said to obey them which have the rule over you. These are the ones who watch for the souls of the congregation.

Because of the job God has given the elders to do, we need to be willing followers of their lead. Because of the need for qualified elders in the congregations, we need to diligently study and teach the passages concerning the qualifications of elders to our children so our males will begin early to develop those characteristics and will be prepared to serve when they are mature in the faith and meet the requirements. We need to instill in them the desire to serve by leading.

Deacons were in the early church. Their qualifications are also given in 1st Timothy 3:8-13. A deacon was to be the husband of one wife ruling his children well. He was to be reverent, not a drinker, and not greedy of money. He too was to be blameless. Interestingly, in the qualifications for a deacon, Paul included information concerning their wives. The wife of a deacon was to be reverent, not a slanderer, temperate, and faithful in all things.

The term translated deacon in the King James Version of the Bible was the Greek word "diakonos" which according to the New Testament Greek Lexicon meant servant. The person who was a deacon was one who served or cared for others. Due to the definition of the word, it is believed those chosen in in Acts 6:1-6 were deacons. Their responsibility in that case was to minister to the Grecian widows.

Serving others was a theme of Jesus all during His ministry. In Mark 10 when two of Jesus' disciples wanted to be given the opportunity to sit one on each side of Jesus in His glory, Jesus told them as recorded by Mark in Mark 10:42-44 the importance of serving others. In verse 45 Jesus said even the Son of man came not to be ministered to, but to minister to others. Similarly in Matthew 23:11 Jesus said the greatest among the disciples would be the servant. In Galatians 5:13, Paul told the readers to serve one another humbly in love. Here again it is so important we teach our children the necessity of serving one another and we teach the males to work diligently in this area so when they are mature Christians, they will be ready to fill this great need for deacons in the congregation.

There were teachers and preachers in the churches. In the very beginning of the church, Jesus commanded His disciples to go and teach and to teach those they baptized to observe all Jesus had commanded. This would mean those who were baptized also needed to go and teach. It is by this continual teaching of the gospel that souls are saved and the church grows. When the first recorded gospel sermon was preached in Acts 2, there were 3,000 who responded positively. Throughout the book of Acts, preachers and teachers continued to preach and people continued to obey. The work of preachers and teachers is great for according to Romans 10:14, it was through the preacher the lost would hear the word and obey.

What may be a surprise is nowhere in scripture were these teachers or preachers called reverend or father or Rabbi or master. Actually, Jesus spoke against calling men by these titles. In Matthew 23:8-10 Jesus told the people they should not be called Rabbi because Christ was their Master. He said in verse 8 they were brethren. In verse 9, Jesus told them not to call any man on earth their father because they had one Father in heaven. Then in verse 10, He told them not to even be called master because Christ was their Master. The only time the word "reverend" appeared in scripture was in Psalm 111:9 where it was applied to God as "Holy and reverend is His name." We must never allow ourselves to place men on the same level or higher than God and Christ. Preachers were not called pastor either as that was a term used for elders. Some preachers incuding Philip (Acts 21:8) and Timothy (2nd Timothy 4:5) were called evangelist. Thus, we need to be sure we are using God approved terms when we speak of the preachers and teachers.

Members of the churches were called by different terms too. As just noted above, in Matthew 23:8, Jesus told His followers they were brethren. Paul used the term brethren in Galatians 1:2 when he addressed the church at Galatia sending them greetings from himself and the brethren with him. He used the term sister in Romans 16:1 concerning Phebe who was a servant of the church at Cenchrea. James in James 2:15 used both terms brother and sister referring to those of their group who could be naked or destitute of food. Several terms were used in Acts in identifying the followers of Christ. They were called saints in Acts 9:13, and believers in Acts 5:14. In Acts 11:26 the disciples were called Christians first in Antioch. The term Christian was used two more places to identify the members. In Acts 26:28, King Agrippa told Paul he had almost persuaded him to be a Christian and then in 1st Peter 4:16, Peter said if anyone suffered as a Christian, he should not be ashamed. According to 1st Corinthians 12:20 we are members of the body.

Again, it might come as a surprise that nowhere do we find these members called by titles to associate them with some person other than the term Christian associating them with Christ. Actually, as noted earlier, Paul spoke strongly against such names in 1st Corinthians 1:12-13 where he condemned calling themselves after a man's name. The term Christian should say it all: a follower of Christ.

Members included both male and female but to become a member, the person had to be able to believe the gospel, repent of sins, confess Jesus Christ as the Son of God, and be baptized for the remission of sins. When one knows what it took to become a member of the church, it is obvious babies were not members of the church and were not baptized. Babies could not "obey from the heart" and since they did not inherit the sin of Adam as some teach, they had no need to become members until they reached the time they were able to commit sin. The members met with each other to worship God.

The worship of the church was simple when compared to the Old Testament worship. In Hebrews 9, the writer described the Old Testament worship. He mentioned the tabernacle, with the candlestick, table, and shewbread in the sanctuary. Then behind the veil the Holiest of all with the golden censer and Ark of the Covenant overlaid with gold and containing Aaron's rod, the golden pot with manna, and the tables of the Ten Commandments. Over the ark were the cherubims of glory (verses 2-5). But note the author in Hebrews

9:1 said the first covenant had these ordinances of divine service and a worldly sanctuary. In verse 11, he said things had changed now with Christ having become the high priest. Then in verse 15, he said this Christ was the mediator of the new testament. It is from this New Testament then we today must find the worship of the church.

From the very beginning of the church, as recorded in Acts 2:42 and mentioned earlier in this book, the church joined in fellowship, in breaking of bread or participating in the Lord's Supper, and in prayer. They met in the temple (Acts 2:46) where the apostles preached (Acts 3, 4). Some preached in the synagogue (Acts 6:9, 13:15, 14:1, 17:1, 18:4, and 19:8). Paul preached by the riverside (Acts 16:13-15). Paul preached from his own hired house (Acts 28:30-31).

Jesus had prepared the disciples for partaking of the Lord's Supper before His death. As recorded in Matthew 26:26-29, Mark 14:22-25, and Luke 22:19-20, and reviewed by Paul in 1st Corinthians 11:23-36, Jesus shared with the apostles the manner in which this memorial was to be observed. Combining the information in all of the accounts gives the following picture.

Jesus took the bread and gave thanks and broke the bread and gave it to the disciples telling them to take and eat of this His body which was broken for them. He said to do so in remembrance of Him. Then after the same manner, He took the cup and gave thanks and gave it to the disciples to drink. Jesus said the cup was His blood of the new testament which was shed for many for the remission of sins. Jesus told the apostles He would not drink of the fruit of the vine until the day when He drank it new with them in His Father's kingdom. He told them as often as they ate the bread and drank the cup they proclaimed the Lord's death.

In this establishment of the memorial, Christ did not tell the disciples when they would be expected to eat the bread and drink the fruit of the vine, so as has been stressed before for all Bible topics, the reader must look for other passages that share that information. In 1st Corinthians 11:17-34, the Corinthian church was not observing the Lord's Supper in the right manner and Paul was providing correction for them. It appears here they were coming together for a common meal, and then partaking of the Supper as part of that meal. Paul asked them in verse 22 if they did not have houses in which to eat. Then he reviewed for them how Jesus established the practice of the Lord's Supper and in the final verse of the chapter, Paul told them if they were hungry to eat at home. But we still do not have a particular day upon which to observe the Lord's Supper.

According to Acts 20:7, the early Christians met upon the first day of the week to break bread. (Acts 20:7). Some have asked upon which first day. Here is where it is helpful to know the Old Testament so we can use it as a school master to guide our thinking. Recall back in Exodus 31 when God commanded the Jews to keep the Sabbath (verse 14), He did not say which Sabbath, but the Jews knew it was every

Sabbath, and when in Numbers 15:32-35 one was found picking up sticks on a Sabbath, he was stoned.

In Hebrews 9, the writer stressed the comparisons between the old and the new and showed how the new was superior to the old in all aspects. In verse 15, the writer said Christ was the mediator of the New Testament. Then he showed Christ was the better sacrifice. In Chapter 10, he stated in verse 9 Christ came to do God's will and He had taken away the first so He might establish the second. In verse 20, the writer said this was a new and living way and then he went on to exhort the brethren to hold fast the profession of their faith (verse 23), provoking each other to love and good works (verse 24). Then he told them how to do this in verse 25. He said, "Not forsaking the assembling of ourselves together, as the manner of some is, but exhorting one another: and so much the more, as ye see the day approaching." Obviously there was to be an assembling of themselves together. In this assembling there were some things they were to do including partaking of the Lord's Supper.

From Acts 20:7, one can already see the example of those disciples meeting upon the first day of the week to break bread, which should be sufficient in establishing the first day of the week as the Lord's day, but just in case it was not, Paul in 1st Corinthians 16:1-2 made it very clear upon which day the disciples were to meet. In this case, he was writing to them about the collection, but he said, "Upon the first day of the week let every one of you lay by him in store..." Having the understanding concerning the frequency of the Old Testament Sabbath (weekly) which was taken out of the way, and the verses concerned with partaking of the Lord's Supper, a reader can infer if the disciples met on the first day of the week to break bread, they met on each first day.

Actually, after Christ's resurrection, two accounts of such a meeting were recorded in Luke 24:1, 15, 29-36; and John 20:19-26 where the disciples were meeting on the first day of the week and Christ met with them. So must present day disciples who wish to continue the practice of the early church continue to meet each first day of the week and in that meeting partake of the Lord's Supper.

In this passage in 1st Corinthians 16:1-2, Paul brought up another act of worship in which the church engaged, that of giving back to God as God had prospered each one. In Acts 20:35 when Paul spoke to those elders he had told them it was more blessed to give than to receive. In 2nd Corinthians 9:6 when Paul was writing to the Corinthians concerning ministering to the saints, he said those who sowed sparingly would reap sparingly and those who sowed bountifully would reap bountifully. Then in verse 7 he said for every man to give as he purposed in his heart but not grudgingly because God loves a cheerful giver. In the Old Testament, people were required to give a tenth or to tithe. This command is not found in the New Testament, but today Christians are to give as they have prospered.

Just like people ask when to partake of the Lord's Supper, some may question when we are to give to this collection. Some churches take up an offering every time they assemble. But, there is no scripture to authorize this collection. The only scripture provided concerning the day to give is the one in 1st Corinthians 16:2 which was upon the first day of the week. In addition, this is the only method of supporting the work of the church authorized by the scripture. There are not any examples of bake sales, begging letters, or any other means of providing for the work of the church other than the collection of the saints upon the first day of the week.

Prayer was common in the early church. As has been noted already from Acts 2:42, the new Christians continued in prayers. In Acts 4:23 after Peter and John were released from prison, they went to their brethren and in verse 24, they prayed to God. In Acts 13:2-3 when the church in Antioch sent out missionaries, they prayed before sending them. When Paul and Barnabas had ordained elders in every church they prayed with them in Acts 14:23. In Ephesians 6:18, Paul told the Ephesians to pray always. He told the Thessalonians to pray without ceasing in 1st Thessalonians 5:17. In 1st Timothy 2:1-8 Paul told Timothy some of the things for which we should pray. He included praying for kings, those in authority, and even for all men. He said to pray for a quiet and peaceable life. In

Colossians 4:3-4 Paul asked the brethren at Colosse to pray for him that God would open doors for him to preach.

In Acts 16:25 Paul and Silas had been put in prison. Earlier in Matthew 18:20, just after telling the disciples how to discipline an unruly brother and whatever they bound on earth would be bound in heaven and whatever they loosed on earth would be loosed in heaven, Jesus had said where two or three were gathered in His name, He would be in their midst. Here in Acts 16 in prison, Paul and Silas were praying and singing unto God.

Again in Acts 20:17-35, Paul had called for the elders of the church in Ephesus so he could give them a farewell. During this assembly, he had shared a sermon in which he told the elders their duty to feed the church of God which He purchased with His own blood. He told the elders the Holy Ghost had made them, the elders, overseers of the flock. When Paul left the assembly he prayed with them.

Prayers were offered to God through Christ. As mentioned earlier, Jesus told His disciples they should pray to God (John 16:23). In the model prayer, Jesus prayed, "Our Father which art in heaven" (Matthew 6:9). Prayers were to be offered in the name of or by the authority of Christ as found in Colossians 3:17. Jesus is the mediator according to 1st Timothy 2:5 and the advocate according to 1st John 2:1-2.

Finally, the early church engaged in singing. In addition to the passage in Acts 16 where Paul and Silas were praying and singing, when Christ instituted the Lord's Supper, the records in Matthew 26:30 and Mark 14:26 both noted afterwards they sang an hymn. The command to sing was given by Paul in Colossians 3:16 where he said to teach and admonish each other in psalms, hymns, and spiritual songs. He told the brethren there to sing with grace in their hearts to the Lord. In Ephesians 5:19, Paul told the brethren to speak to themselves in psalms, hymns, and spiritual songs, singing and making melody in their heart to the Lord. James said in James 5:13 for anyone who was merry to sing. Paul quoted in Romans 15:9 from the Old Testament prophecy of Psalm 18:49, "...I will confess to thee among the Gentiles, and sing unto thy name."

In 1st Corinthians 14:15, in discussing tongues, Paul said he would sing with the spirit and with the understanding. In singing with the spirit, we put our whole being into our singing just as we do our praying. In singing with the understanding, as mentioned earlier in this book, we need to be sure we understand what we are singing and that it is scriptural. When one finds unscriptural verses in a song, she needs to bring it to the attention of the elders or men who oversee the congregation so they can take the appropriate actions. In some cases it may be as simple as substituting other words but in some cases, the song may no longer be one the congregation can sing. The writer of Hebrews attributed a passage in Psalm 22:22 as coming from the Lord. Hebrews 2:12 "I WILL DECLARE THY NAME UNTO MY BRETHREN, IN THE MIDST OF THE CHURCH WILL I SING PRAISE UNTO THEE."

One with a good Old Testament knowledge would be quick to see a difference between the above passages and some of those in the Old Testament concerning music in praise to God. Many passages particularly in the Psalms mention instruments of music, but nowhere under the new covenant did mechanical instruments of music appear. Instead as recorded in Hebrews 13:15 "...let us offer the sacrifice of praise to God continually, that is the fruit of our lips giving thanks to His name."

From the aforementioned scriptures one can use the examples, commands, and inferences, to create a picture of the simple worship service in which a first century Christian would have engaged. While the assembly could have taken place on any day of the week, since the disciples met daily, there was a special assembly that happened weekly upon the first day of the week. In this assembly, the Christians came together to break bread in the Lord's Supper and they gave of their prosperity for the work of the Lord. In addition they prayed to God, sang praises to His name, and listened to preaching. There are no scriptures to indicate in what order the acts of worship took place, but we can know for sure what those acts were.

Having established the organization and worship of the church, one should also know the work of the church. What was the church authorized to do as a church? Again, one must look at all of the scriptures concerning what the church did in order to answer the question.

The command by Jesus to the apostles was to go and preach the gospel or to go and teach all nations and once the people had obeyed, to teach those people to go and teach others. All throughout the book of Acts, followers were going elsewhere to preach. In Acts 8 just after Stephen was killed for what he preached, the church scattered abroad and went everywhere preaching the word (Acts 8:1, 4, 11:19). Paul and his fellow companions were sent out by the churches to go and spread the word (Acts 13:1-3). Paul himself sent out brethren to carry the gospel (Acts 19:21-22). Paul told Timothy in 2nd Timothy 2:2 to commit what he had heard to faithful men who would be able to teach others the same.

While the whole membership of the church was to be spreading the word, there were some as noted earlier called preachers for whom the church had authority to support as they spread the word. Jesus gave the principle upon which the practice of paying the preacher has been established. In Luke 10:7 when He sent out the seventy on the limited commission, He told them not to take provisions because the laborer is worthy of his hire. Those to whom they preached were responsible for supporting them.

In Matthew 10:9-10 when Jesus sent out just the twelve apostles, He told them not to take provisions because the laborer was worthy of his hire. This was a principle from the Old

Testament where the tribe of Levi from which the priests came was to be supported by the other tribes (Numbers 18:21).

Paul in his letter to Timothy quoted Jesus in 1st Timothy 5:18. He said elders who also labored in the word should be counted worthy of double honor (verse 17) and then he gave two reasons. First he gave the quote from the Old Testament concerning how they were not supposed to muzzle the mouth of the ox as he worked in the corn but let him eat as he wanted and then he quoted Jesus' words concerning the laborer being worthy of his hire.

Paul also told the Corinthians they had an obligation to pay the preacher. In 1st Corinthians 9, he used examples of those in the Old Testament who ministered about the holy things of the temple and those who waited at the altar (verse 13) and then he said in verse 14 the Lord had ordained those who preached the gospel should live of the gospel or in other words should be allowed to reap materially (verse 11). This preaching and teaching of God's word is often divided into two type of preaching: edification of the saints (2nd Corinthians 12:19) and evangelism or converting sinners to Christ (Matthew 28:19). In either case, preaching and teaching are taking place and have the support and authority of scripture. In either case, there is also authority for the preacher to be paid.

In addition to continuing to spread the word, members had other obligations. From the very beginning of the church, members were helping each other. In Acts 2:44-45 those who had possessions sold them and gave to those who were in need. In Acts 4, beginning in verse 32, Luke recorded none of the believers had any needs because those who had took care of those who did not have.

Members gave of their means not only to help those in the local congregation, but to help saints in other places. Paul told the church at Corinth how the churches of Macedonia had so liberally given to help in the ministering to others, but of particular importance is the verse at 2nd Corinthians 8:4 where Paul specifically said the money was for the saints. Back in Romans 15:25, Paul said he was going to minister to the saints at Jerusalem because those of Macedonia and Achaia had made a contribution for the poor saints at Jerusalem. Again, the contribution was for the poor saints. Nowhere can we find the authority to use the Lord's money to help non-Christians, but as individual Christians, we have other duties one of which is to help anyone in need and will be covered in the next chapter.

Another duty of the church was to keep itself pure. This obligation though mentioned several times is one that causes churches and families a lot of problems. According to Paul in Romans 16:17, those who cause divisions in the church and who do not walk according to the doctrine they have been taught are to be marked and avoided. In 1st Corinthians 5 after Paul reprimanded the church for allowing a fornicator to remain in their company, he went on to say in verses 9-13 when one who was a brother in the church was a fornicator, a covetous person, an idolater, a railer, a drunkard, or an extortioner the church was to not keep any company with him to the point the members would not even eat with such an one.

In 2nd Thessalonians 3:6 Paul told the brethren there they were to withdraw themselves from every brother that walked disorderly and not after the traditions which he had received. I know of several families who have had members withdrawn from by the church and the families did what was required. I know of other families who have chosen not to adhere to the withdrawing but to continue fellowship. We need to teach this principle diligently to our children so they understand the dangers of falling away from the Lord. They need to know while Christians love each other dearly, if anyone falls away from the Lord, even if that one is a family member, we must follow Christ's teachings in Matthew 10:37 which says we cannot love father, mother, son, or daughter more than we love Christ.

The church needs to keep the unity of the faith. Paul told the church at Ephesus they needed to keep the unity of the Spirit in the bond of peace in Ephesians 4:3. But this unity cannot come at the price of accepting false doctrine. In Philippians 1:27 Paul told the members of the church to conduct themselves in a manner becoming of the gospel of Christ and to have one mind, striving together in the gospel. He wanted them to work together and get along.

In Colossians 3:17 Paul told the church at Colosse all they did needed to be by the authority or in the name of Jesus. In 1st Corinthians 1:10, Paul begged the brethren in Corinth to all speak the same thing and have no division among themselves but to be perfectly joined together in the same mind and judgment.

James encouraged Christians to get along without envying and strife but he noted in James 3:17 we need wisdom that is first pure and then peaceable and gentle so we must be careful we do not get along with others just for the sake of getting along. If someone wants to bring in some doctrine different from what we know to be the truth, there is no purity there and we must fight it.

Finally, going back to John 17 where Jesus prayed before His arrest, Jesus prayed to God in verse 21 for all of His followers to be one. While Christians must work together as a church to keep this unity in the body of Christ, there is also work we must do as individual Christians. This work will be looked at in the next chapter.

Chapter 12
Christian Living

As has been discussed in the previous chapter, Christ's body of believers or His church has been given much work to do as the body and guidelines for doing that work. In addition, individual Christians have work to do for themselves, for other Christians, and for the world. In some cases the combined work of the individuals makes up the work of the church. In some cases it is hard to distinguish between individual and group work, but in other cases, it is very clear what work is meant for the individual. Knowing the difference is very important because when the church takes on duties given to individual Christians and not to the church as a whole, then the work of the church is no longer scriptural.

When reading the New Testament and looking specifically for the work of the church, the church was involved in preaching and teaching the lost, edifying the saved, caring for the needy saints, and keeping the church pure. Nowhere in scripture can be found examples of or commands for the church concerning supporting social events and activities for the families, creating and maintaining nursing homes or orphanages, establishing schools or colleges for teaching secular subjects, or caring for non-Christians other than spiritually. While there are no scriptures to indicate these as being sinful activities, there are no scriptures to allow the church as the body of Christ to provide the support for such;

thus, for a congregation to engage in these activities is not scriptural. Christ said He had all power or authority in heaven and on earth in Matthew 28:18, so for His church to go beyond what He has commanded would be to add to His word and we have already established adding to the word as being wrong. Yet, as individual Christians, we do have responsibilities not given to the church as a whole. In this chapter, are some of those responsibilities.

One of the clearest individual responsibilities is found in 1st Timothy 5:4-8 where Paul was telling Timothy how widows needed to be treated. Recall back in Acts 6 when the church appointed men to take care of the widows that it was a church obligation. Here in 1st Timothy, Paul explained the meaning of a widow and he said if a widow had relatives, specifically nephews which is also translated grandchildren, those relatives were to provide the care. In verse 16 Paul specifically said if any man or woman that believed had widows, then they needed to take care of the widows so the church was not charged with the responsibility.

Paul gave a pretty clear command to individual Christians to take care of widows in her family, but in 1st Timothy 5:8 Paul went farther when he said if any provide not for his own and especially for the ones in his own household, he has denied the faith and is worse than an infidel. In 2nd Thessalonians 3:10 Paul said if one did not work, he should not eat thus establishing a principle that says, we each need to be working so we can take care of our own. In addition, in Ephesians 4:28, Paul said anyone who used to steal needed to quit doing so and labor with his hands so he would have something to give to him that needed it. Commands such as this take us back to Jesus' teachings in Matthew 5:42 where He said to give to him that asks and in Luke 6:34, He said not to even expect anything in return.

As we saw earlier, the church has authority to help needy saints. But, we as individuals are allowed and even instructed to help both saints and non-saints. In Galatians while Paul was writing collectively to the churches in Galatia, several of the principles he stated were to individuals. In chapter 6, verse 3, he said "if a man" then in verse 4, he said "let every man." Beginning in verse 6, Paul was still talking to individuals and in that section, he told each person to share with the one who is teaching. In verse 7, he said a man would reap what he sowed. In this context of individual responsibility, Paul said in verse 10 to do good unto all especially unto those who were of the household of faith. So he told the Galatian Christians, individually, each person who has the opportunity should help anyone in need, Christian or not.

While Paul was writing in the context of monetary provisions in Galatians 6, there are additional ways other than by financial means we as individuals can help others. Of course, we can individually teach others as we have already seen in many passages and which is one of the main reasons for this book. The more we learn, the better we can help others know the truth. In addition, we are to love others.

As noted earlier, the second great commandment is to love our neighbor as ourselves. How can we show this love? In Romans 13 beginning in verse 8, Paul instructed the Romans to love one another and then in verse 9, he quoted five of the Ten Commandments including: thou shalt not commit adultery, kill, steal, bear false witness, and covet. He then said if there was any other commandment it could be summarized as "thou shalt love thy neighbor as thyself." In Romans 13:10, Paul showed how all five of the commandments he had included were observed when one loves the neighbor because when we love someone, we will not do that person wrong.

First Corinthians 13, often referred to as the love chapter of the Bible, provides many ways to show love. Beginning in verse 4, Paul said charity or love suffers long and is kind. It does not envy. Love does not brag on itself. It is not puffed up or arrogant. It does not behave itself rudely. Love does not keep account of evils. Love does not seek her own good and is not easily provoked. It does not think evil nor rejoice in iniquity but rejoices in the truth. Love puts up with a lot and endures a lot. Paul said at the end of Chapter 13 there were three abiding qualities, faith, hope, and love, but the greatest of all these was love. When we have this kind of love, we will want to grow in our faith and help others grow but we must be sure this love is in the right place for in 1st John 2:15, John clearly said we are not to love the world nor the things in the world. Our love must be toward God and His creation.

Growing in the faith is one of the next obligations of the individual Christian. In 2nd Peter 1:5-7, Peter provided the readers with seven graces to add to their faith. He included virtue, knowledge, temperance, patience, godliness, brotherly kindness, and love. He said in verse 8 if these characteristics are in a person and abounding, then that person will not be barren or unfruitful in the knowledge of Jesus Christ but one who lacks these characteristics is blind and has forgotten he was cleansed from his old sins.

To not be barren or unfruitful means one is fruitful. Jesus wanted His followers to be fruitful. In John 15:2, Jesus said God takes away every branch in Jesus that does not bear fruit but those bearing fruit He trims so they will bear even more. If we abide in Jesus, we should bear the fruit of the Spirit. In Galatians 5:22-24, Paul showed the readers how the fruit of the Spirit was different from the works of the flesh. Back in verses 19-21, he had warned the Galatians of the works of the flesh. He named them as adultery, fornication, uncleanness, lasciviousness, idolatry, witchcraft, hatred, variance, emulations, wrath, strife, seditions, heresies, envyings, murders, drunkenness, revellings, and such like. He said those who engaged in such would not inherit the kingdom of God. But here in verses 22-23, Paul encouraged the Galatians to engage in the fruit of the Spirit which included love, joy, peace, longsuffering, gentleness, goodness, faith, meekness, and temperance.

Similarly, in Colossians 3, Paul told the saints there to put to death the old ways of fornication, uncleanness, inordinate affection, evil concupiscence, and idolatry. He said these were things done by the children of disobedience. He also told them to put off anger, wrath, malice, blasphemy, filthy communication, and lying. Then in verses 12-14, he told them to put on tender mercies, kindness, humbleness, meekness, longsuffering, and love. He told them to bear with each other and forgive each other.

Forgiving others can be hard at times, but we are commanded to do so. Remember in the model prayer in Matthew 6, Jesus taught the disciples to pray asking God to forgive them as they forgave others. Paul told the Ephesians in Ephesians 4:32 to forgive each other just as God for Christ's sake had forgiven them. When we consider how much God has forgiven us, it should be easy for us to forgive those who sin against us.

We need to remember others have problems too and according to Romans 15:1 and Galatians 6:1 we are responsible for helping others bear their burdens. If one has been overtaken in a fault, Paul told the Galatian brethren to restore that one in a spirit of meekness. In Romans 15:1 he said the strong needed to bear the weak. In doing so, according to Paul in Romans 12:15, we will weep with those who weep and rejoice with those who rejoice.

Sometimes, we have to bring ourselves under control before we are able to help others. Jesus taught in Matthew 7:3-5 about trying to cast the mote out of a brother's eye before taking care of the beam in our own eye. One of the beams we may have in our own eye is concerned with how we use our tongues. Just as Jesus taught in Matthew 12:36-37 we need to watch our tongues because we will be justified or condemned by our words. James taught in James 3:1-12 there are many dangers associated with the tongue. James said man cannot tame the tongue. Yet, we must try to tame our tongues and keep our mouths from evils such as those Paul wrote to the Corinthians about in 2nd Corinthians 12:20 including debate, wrath, strife, backbiting, and whispering or like those things Paul said younger widows might resort to in 1st Timothy 5:13 including tattling and speaking things they should not speak.

Another beam we may have is our attitude toward those in authority. Many people complain about the government, but according to Romans 13:1-7, one of the duties of a Christian is to be subject to those who are over us in the government. God is in control of everything and even those in power on earth are subject to Him (verse 4). Peter wrote in 1st Peter 2:13-15 we need to submit ourselves to those in authority, but always remember if the government goes against God's word, we as Christians are bound to obey God's law as Peter told the officials in Acts 4:19-20 when they told him and John not to speak any more in the name of Jesus. Again in Acts 5:29 Peter clearly stated: "We ought to obey God rather than men."

We as Christians really have no fight with the government as long as we obey the laws and the laws allow us to be obedient to God. Instead, our fight is of a different nature. Our battle is a spiritual one (Ephesians 6:12) and in order to fight it, we must have the right weapons. According to Ephesians 6:10-18, our weapons have already been prepared for us and all we need to do is use them. Paul told the Ephesian Christians to put on the whole armor of God so they could stand against the devil. That armor includes the truth and righteousness (verse 14), the gospel of peace (verse 15), the shield of faith (verse 16), and the helmet of salvation and sword of the Spirit which is the word of God (verse 17). In addition, according to verse 18, we need prayer. If we so equip ourselves with this armor we will be as Paul said in verse 10 strong in the Lord and in the power of His might. He is our strength and through Him we will persevere.

There are some specific commands and examples for Christian women that we must look at or our study would be incomplete. Some of these we have touched upon in previous chapters but having them here in one place may be helpful. First, as noted earlier, there were specific requirements for the wives of deacons. In 1st Timothy 3:11, Paul told Timothy the wives of deacons needed to be reverent, temperate, not slanderers, and faithful in all things.

Earlier in this book, mention was made of how widows were to be supported. In that same passage in 1st Timothy 5:3-14, Paul told Timothy the attributes of a widow indeed. She was to be one who trusted in God, and continued in supplications and prayers night and day. She was to be at least 60 years old and well reported for good works. She needed to have brought up children, been the wife of one husband, lodged strangers, washed the saints' feet, relieved the afflicted, and diligently followed every good work. In comparison Paul showed what younger widows might be found doing if they were not pleasing to God. These attributes included growing wanton against Christ, being idle, wandering about from house to house as tattlers and busybodies, speaking things they did not need to be speaking. In verse 14, Paul actually encouraged the younger women to marry, bear children and guide the house so the adversary would have nothing about which to speak poorly concerning these women.

Continuing on the idea of marriage, in 1st Corinthians 7:1-16, Paul gave commandments concerning married women. In verse 2 he said in order to avoid fornication to let every man have his wife and every woman her own husband. Then in verse 3 he cautioned both the husband and wife to give to each other the affections due because of the husband and wife bond. He noted in verse 4 the husband has power over the wife's body just as the wife does over the husband and in verse 5 he said neither should deprive the other of the pleasure allowed only in marriage so Satan did not get the opportunity to tempt either the husband or the wife due to them not engaging in the marriage act.

Paul seemed to be speaking about a different situation in 1st Corinthians 7:8 when compared to what he told Timothy in 1st Timothy 5 concerning widows. Here in 1st Corinthians, he said to the unmarried and the widows, in his opinion, it was good for them to remain unmarried and then in verse 9, he said if they could not exercise the necessary self-control, they should go ahead and marry.

Beginning in 1st Corinthians 7:10, Paul shared the woman should not leave her husband but he said in verse 11 if she did leave, she needed to either remain unmarried or be reconciled to her husband. He also said for the husband not to put away the wife. This goes right along with what Jesus taught in Matthew 5:31-32 concerning divorce.

Beginning in 1st Corinthians 7:12, some things Paul said could be easily misunderstood but always remember all scripture was given by the inspiration of God so when it seems there is a contradiction, we must reconcile the accounts. Paul said in verses 12-15 he was giving an opinion of his own. He said if a brother or sister (Christian) had a spouse that was not a believer but the unbelieving spouse was willing to remain with the Christian, then the Christian should not leave the non-

Christian. In verse 15 he said if the unbelieving one chose to depart then the Christian was not under bondage. The question has been often asked if the unbelieving departs does the Christian have the right to remarry. Based upon Christ's words in Matthew and Paul's words in verses 10-11, the safe route is to remain unmarried or be reconciled.

According to Titus 2:3-5, Paul said the older women should have a holy behavior. They should not be false accusers. They should not be enslaved to much wine. They should teach good things. It is important to know what the older women should teach, because in knowing what they should teach, we have an even better idea of what all women should do. They should teach the younger women to be sober minded, to love their husbands, to love their children, to be discreet, chaste, keepers at home, good, and obedient to their husbands. Paul in Ephesians 5:22-24 told the wives at Ephesus to submit to their own husbands just like the church was to submit to Christ. Peter also said in 1st Peter 3:1-2 the wives were to be in subjection to their own husbands so if a husband was not a Christian, he might see the behavior of the wife and be won to the Lord.

Peter went on in 1st Peter 3 to comment concerning the dress of the female. He said in verses 3-4 the adorning of the woman should not be outward adorning of plaiting the hair and wearing of gold and fine apparel, but it should be the hidden man of the heart having a meek and quiet spirit. Paul, on the other hand did talk about the actual physical apparel in 1st Timothy 2:9-10 where he said women should adorn themselves in modest apparel with propriety and moderation, not with braided hair, gold, pearls, and costly array. He too then discussed the spiritual dress by saying instead of having a concern about the physical appearance, the woman needed to be adorned with good works professing godliness (verse 10).

Paul had one other command for the women in Corinth concerning their appearance as recorded in 1st Corinthians 11:1-16 where he provided them with several reasons for being covered during prayer. Among those reasons Paul included: the head of the woman is the man, every woman praying or prophesying with her head uncovered, dishonors her head, because of the angels, comeliness, and nature. Many today teach this was only a custom for that time and for those women, while others teach as long as the reasons given for the covering still exist, so does the need for the covering whether it was a custom of that day or not. In verse 16, Paul said if any man seemed to be contentious, we have no such custom, neither the churches of God. This verse too has been explained in several ways. One explanation is if anyone was inclined to be contentious and cause problems concerning the covering, the church did not have such a practice as being contentious. Another explanation given is Paul was saying if anyone wanted to be contentious over the matter of the covering, the church had no other practice than males being uncovered and females covered in prayer. A final explanation given is Paul was saying this covering concerning which he wrote several lines was just an unnecessary custom. This is a definite area for diligent study and soul searching.

While some have found Paul to be against women due to the two times he mentioned the fact women were to keep silent in the church, it is obvious he was not against women when one looks at the references Paul made to women in the church. In Romans 16:1-2 Paul commended "Phebe our sister." He called her a servant of the church at Cenchrea. He told the Romans to receive Phebe in the Lord and to assist her in whatever business she had need because she had been a helper of many including Paul. Then in verse 3, Paul greeted Priscilla and her husband, Aquila, who we met earlier when they were together teaching Apollos in Acts 18:24-26. In verse Romans 16:6, he greeted Mary who he said had bestowed much labor on him. In Philippians 4:3, Paul again told the church at Philippi to help the women who had labored with him in the gospel. We have already looked at the good work Timothy's mother and grandmother did for Timothy in teaching him the scriptures. All of these are included here so we as women can see there is much we can do in the church.

What we do in this life is so important. We have looked at many areas from the New Testament where we can be involved as women. We have looked at areas clear in meaning and some you may want to dig deeper in to develop your own understanding. How we love and help each other will help to determine our own judgment. According to Galatians 6:7-8, there will be a reaping time and if we have sowed to the flesh, of the flesh, we will reap corruption but if we have sowed to the Spirit we will reap everlasting life for which we are now preparing. In the final chapter of this book, are hopefully thought provoking passages concerning the certainty of an eternal abode.

Chapter 13
There Will Be a Judgment

Jesus often talked about the judgment. In many of His parables He ended by indicating where the righteous or unrighteous would be in the judgment. There are so many reasons for serving God and teaching His word to others, but one of the very best is the fact when one dies, it is not the end but the beginning. In order to be ready for such a beginning, one must have finished the course and ran the race well as Paul told Timothy he had done in 2nd Timothy 4:6-8 where he said he was ready for his departure. Paul said he had fought a good fight and finished his course having kept the faith. Because of his fight and his keeping the faith, he was able to say in verse 8 there was laid up for him a crown of righteousness which the Lord, the righteous judge, would give not only to Paul but to all those that love the Lord's appearing. One wonders if Paul was thinking back to what Jesus said in John 14:2, when He told His disciples in His Father's house were many mansions and He was going to prepare a place for them. In verse 3, Jesus said if He went and prepared a place for them, He would come again and receive them unto Himself. In Matthew 6:19, Jesus had told His followers to lay up their treasures in heaven and not on the earth because where their treasures were so would their heart be also.

As early as Matthew 5, Jesus mentioned the judgment in verse 22 when He said one who was angry with his brother without a cause would be in danger of the judgment. In Matthew 10 when Jesus sent out the twelve apostles to preach, He told them in verse 15 in the Day of Judgment it would be worse for those cities who would not hear the apostles than it would be for Sodom and Gomorrah. Then in Matthew 11:22 when the people where Jesus had done miracles refused to repent, He rebuked them and told them it would be more tolerable for Tyre and Sidon at the day of judgment than it would be for them.

In Matthew 12:36, Jesus told the people they would give account in the Day of Judgment for every idle word they had spoken. Paul continued this idea of giving account in 2nd Corinthians 5:10 where he said everyone would appear before the judgment seat of Christ to receive according to what they have done whether good or bad. In Romans 2:6 Paul quoted from Psalm 62:12 and Proverbs 24:12 in telling the Romans God would render to every man according to his deeds. For those who did well, there would be eternal life (verse 7) and for those who did not obey the truth there would be tribulation and anguish (verse 8) and he stressed in verse 9 these rewards would apply to both the Jews and Gentiles. Then beginning in verse 11 and going through verse 16, Paul showed God had no respect to persons but each person would receive according to what he or she had done. In verse 16, he said this would happen in the day when God would judge the secrets of men by Jesus Christ.

It is for this judgment we want to be ready. We do not know when it is coming, but we can rest assured just as all of God's other promises came true, so will this one. In 2nd Peter 3:8-10, Peter was reminding his readers concerning the coming of the Lord. He told them in verse 9 the Lord was longsuffering and did not want any to perish but in verse 10, he assured them the day of the Lord would come when it was not expected. Jesus told His followers in Matthew 24:36 not even the angels of heaven knew the time of the return of the Son of man, but only God. In verse 44, He told them to be ready for in such an hour they did not expect His coming, it would happen.

Paul told the Thessalonian brethren in 1st Thessalonians 4:13 he did not want them to be ignorant concerning the outcome of those who had already died. He said Jesus would descend from heaven with a shout and with the trump of God and the dead in Christ would be raised first and then those Christians who were still alive on earth would be caught up together with them in the clouds to meet the Lord in the air and to then always be with Him. Note Paul did not say anything about Christ setting foot on earth for a 1000 year reign as so many teach is going to happen. Actually, no writer in the New Testament mentioned a 1000 year reign of Christ on earth. Instead, Christ is currently reigning over His kingdom, the church. That reign is shared with Christians as John stated in Revelation 1:6, and 5:9-10. When the end comes, Jesus will give that reign back to God according to 1st Corinthians 15:24-28.

When that end comes, we will all be called for our judgment. According to Matthew 25:32, all nations will be gathered together to be judged. The King will separate the people as sheep and goats with the sheep on the right hand and the goats on the left. The sheep will be those who will be blessed with the kingdom (verse 34) based upon their life while upon earth (verses 35-40) and the goats will be those who are sent into everlasting fire prepared for the devil and his angels (verse 41) also based upon their lives while on earth (verses 42-46). The everlasting punishment lasts as long as the eternal life (verse 46).

Just as the individual judgment will be based upon each person's life on earth, there will be a standard against which those actions in life will be judged. According to John 12:48, the standard will be the words Jesus spoke. In verse 49, Jesus said that word was from the Father who had given Jesus what He was to say. John was able to see a glimpse of the final judgment and he recorded his vision in Revelation 20:11-15. Here he said the dead stood before God and the books were opened and the dead were judged based upon what was written in those books according to their works. Those who were not found written in the book of life were cast into the lake of fire.

Ladies, we must have our names in the book of life and we must spread the gospel to our families and friends so they too have their names in the book of life. For in 1st Corinthians 15:19 Paul made it very clear if our only hope is in this life, we are most miserable, but he went on to show how through the life of Christ we have a great hope. We have the hope of being in the kingdom when it is delivered to God by Christ at the end (verse 24). We will persevere and we will make it!

Everything in this book has been leading to this day of judgment. This is the day for which we ladies must complete our responsibility in teaching our children, families, and friends the whole of God's word from Genesis through Revelation using the opportunities God gives us in the manner in which He has authorized us to share His word. Once we have done all we can do, then we too can say with Paul, "I have finished my course, I have kept the faith," and we can join with Timothy's mother and grandmother in knowing we have diligently shared our faith so our children and their children for generations to come may do the same.

References

Bible History Online. (n.d.) Ancient marriage. Retrieved from http://www.bible-history.com/biblestudy/marriage.html March 17, 2017.

CBN. (n.d.). Biblical prophecies fulfilled by Jesus. Retrieved from http://www1.cbn.com/biblestudy/biblical-prophecies-fulfilled-by-jesus February 27, 2017.

Coffman, J. B. (n.d.). Commentary on Acts. Retrieved from http://www.studylight.org/commentaries/bcc/acts-16.html February 27, 2017.

Coffman, J. B. (n.d.). Commentary on Joel. Retrieved from http://www.studylight.org/commentaries/bcc/joel-3.html February 27, 2017.

Coffman, J. B. (n.d.). Commentary on Nehemiah. Retrieved from https://www.studylight.org/commentaries/bcc/nehemiah-8.html February 27, 2017.

Fairchild, M. (2016). Prophecies of Jesus fulfilled. Retrieved from http://christianity.about.com/od/biblefactsandlists/a/Prophecies-Jesus.htm February 27, 2017.

Global Population Past and Present (n.d.) Retrieved from http://www.creationconcepts.org/resources/POPULATE.pdf

Hamilton, J. W. (n.d.). A study of Ezekiel. Retrieved from http://lavistachurchofchrist.org/LVstudies/Ezekiel/Ezekiel.htm February 27, 2017.

Hodge, B. (2010). Was the dispersion at Babel a real event? Retrieved from https://answersingenesis.org/tower-of-babel/was-the-dispersion-at-babel-a-real-event/

LaVista Church of Christ. (n.d.). Answer concerning alcohol. Retrieved from http://lavistachurchofchrist.org/LVanswers/2008/04-10b.html February 27, 2017.

Lyons, E. (2003). Did Saul know David prior to Goliath's death? Retrieved from http://apologeticspress.org/apcontent.aspx?category=6&article=807

Lyons, E. (2008). When did Job live? Retrieved from http://apologeticspress.org/APPubPage.aspx?cid=2516 February 27, 2017.

Miller, D. (2003). How old was Isaac when Abraham was told to offer him? Retrieved February 27, 2017 from https://www.apologeticspress.org/apcontent.aspx?category=11&article=1272

New Testament Christians. (n.d.). 351 Old Testament prophecies fulfilled in Jesus Christ. Retrieved from http://www.newtestamentchristians.com/bible-study-resources/351-old-testament-prophecies-fulfilled-in-jesus-christ/ February 27, 2017.

New Testament Greek Lexicon. (n.d). Definition of diakonos. Retrieved from http://www.biblestudytools.com/lexicons/greek/kjv/diakonos.html February 27, 2017.

Padfield, D. (n.d.). The destruction of Nineveh. Retrieved from http://www.padfield.com/1996/nineveh.html January 14, 2017.

Palmer, K. (n.d.). Life of Christ. Retrieved from http://www.lifeofchrist.com/life/lifeofchrist.pd February 27, 2017.

Pelletier, W.T. (2014). Population growth-How many people died in Noah's flood? Retrieved from https://bibliescienceguy.wordpress.com/2014/06/18/4-population-growth-how-many-died-in-noahs-flood/

Robinson, R. (2015). Jews for Jesus. Retrieved from https://jewsforjesus.org/answers/prophecy/top-40-most-helpful-messianic-prophecies/ February 27, 2017.

The Interactive Bible. (n.d.). Baptism: A pre-Christian history. Retrieved from www.bible.ca/ef/topical-baptism-a-prechristian-history.htm February 27, 2017.

The Interactive Bible. (n.d.). The book of Ruth. Retrieved from http://www.bible.ca/archeology/bible-archeology-timeline-date-chronology-of-ruth-1300bc.htm February 27 2017.

Wood, B.G. (2008). The discovery of the sin cities of Sodom and Gomorrah. Retrieved February 27, 2017 from http://www.biblearchaeology.org/post/2008/04/The-Discovery-of-the-Sin-Cities-of-Sodom-and-Gomorrah.aspx#Article

About the Author

Sarah Lee Brown has been a member of the church of Christ for over 50 years. She has taught Bible class for children and young adults where she attends worship and has held Bible classes for ladies in her home.

Retired from the public school system where she was a teacher, principal, and director of curriculum for pre-k through adult education, Sarah currently teaches online for a university. Her education includes a Bachelor of Science Degree in Elementary Education, Master of Arts Degree in Educational Administration, Master's Degree in Religious Studies, and a Doctorate in Educational Leadership.

Sarah and her husband Roger, who preaches and teaches Bible class, live on a farm in southern WV. They enjoy nature, studying the Bible, playing together, and sharing God's word with all who will listen.

Special thanks from Sarah to her husband, Roger, for his guidance and comments on the book, to her sister Reva Kay Holder for her editorial services, and to the many sisters in Christ including especially Dianna Adkins, Decretia Cales, and Cara Belknap who proofread the manuscript and made great suggestions for improvements.

www.ingramcontent.com/pod-product-compliance
Lightning Source LLC
LaVergne TN
LVHW051541070426
835507LV00021B/2351